LAMAR
LAMAR

the Butterfly Effect

the Butterfly Effect

How Kendrick Lamar Ignited
the Soul of Black America

Marcus J. Moore

ATRIA BOOKS

New York   London   Toronto   Sydney   New Delhi

ATRIA
BOOKS

An Imprint of Simon & Schuster, Inc.
1230 Avenue of the Americas
New York, NY 10020

First Atria Books hardcover edition October 2020

Endpaper photo credits: Kendrick-Lamar-2013-Sweetlife-02.jpg
(Photo by Kyle Gustafson/For The Washington Post)
Kendrick-Lamar-Sweetlife-8.jpg
(Photo by Kyle Gustafson/For The Washington Post)
Kendrick-Lamar-Kennedy-Center-DC-11.jpg
(Photo by Kyle Gustafson/For The Washington Post)
Angelo-Merendino-Kendrick-Lamar.jpg
(Angelo Merendino Photography, LLC)
Kendrick_Grammy.jpeg
(Robert Deutsch - USA Today Network)

ATRIA BOOKS and colophon are trademarks of Simon & Schuster, Inc.

For information about special discounts for bulk purchases, please contact Simon &
Schuster Special Sales at 1-866-506-1949 or business@simonandschuster.com.

The Simon & Schuster Speakers Bureau can bring authors to your live event. For
more information or to book an event, contact the Simon & Schuster Speakers
Bureau at 1-866-248-3049 or visit our website at www.simonspeakers.com.

Interior design by Alexis Minieri

Manufactured in the United States of America

1 3 5 7 9 10 8 6 4 2

Library of Congress Cataloging-in-Publication Data is available.

ISBN 978-1-9821-0758-1
ISBN 978-1-9821-0760-4 (ebook)

To God and the spirits: Ida Hart, Raymond Hart, Eric Hart,
Loumanda Moore, and Troy Perryman.

To Landover and Prince George's County, Maryland.

To Breonna Taylor, Ahmaud Arbery, George Floyd, and the countless
souls we've lost to state-sanctioned violence against Black people.

Contents

1

How "You Got Robbed"

There are musicians, and then there's Kendrick Lamar Duckworth. A welterweight, and just five feet, five inches tall, he looks more like a Baptist youth minister than the greatest rapper of his generation. But he is the greatest rapper, and he worked damn hard to make it so. Kendrick wasn't some sort of prodigy; he didn't descend from his bassinet with a microphone and a composition book. Instead, he simply found something he loved and stuck with it. Through creative writing, he could say things on paper that he couldn't say out loud. He was shy, an only child until the age of seven. He grew up in Compton, California, in the early to mid-1990s, not even a decade after the city's police brutality and gang culture were immortalized by the rap group N.W.A in 1988. Young black and brown children had to navigate that land before they could fully comprehend street politics. They had to learn the differences between the Piru and

Crips gangs on the fly, in a city where wrong decisions could mean the difference between life and death. Kendrick spent time alone, cultivating his art in hopes of becoming great. For a naturally quiet being like Kendrick, writing poetry gave him the space to reveal his innermost thoughts without judgment from others. Prowess came in silence.

Kendrick ascended to the top of the music industry by being himself and staying true to what drove him artistically. He's been called esoteric and downright weird, but really he's just an old soul with a profound reverence for hip-hop, R&B, and funk—*black* music—and he moves throughout life with Compton in his mind and heart. Maybe that's why he's so beloved, because he stresses the importance of home no matter where he goes.

Yet at the beginning of the 2010s, Kendrick was just another up-start lyricist trying to find his place in music. In July 2011, Kendrick released his first official album, the kaleidoscopic *Section.80*, to an unknowing public just a month before hip-hop megastars Jay-Z and Kanye West dropped their long-awaited joint record, *Watch the Throne*, to widespread acclaim. Where that album unpacked the pleasures of hedonism and the glory of black decadence, Kendrick's record was something different. It had everything: brassy jazz, mid-tempo soul, and headbanging street anthems. In it, one could hear Kendrick's love of J Dilla—the experimental hip-hop producer from Detroit, whose mix of hard drums and unique sampling techniques made him an icon in alternative rap—as well as Pusha T, the resilient Virginia Beach rapper whose explicit lyrics cut straight to the heart. Kendrick was the cerebral introvert with theatrical flair, the quiet kid who patiently absorbed the fullness of his environment and spun what he saw into heartfelt streams of pain, struggle, and perseverance. *Section.80* was deemed an achievement in an era of hip-hop in which lyricists could build sizable followings online without having to come up through local open mic circuits. And while it wasn't Kendrick's first project (he had released five mixtapes before then—2004's *Hub City Threat: Minor of the Year*, 2005's *Training Day*, 2007's *No Sleep Til NYC* with rapper Jay Rock, 2009's *C4*, and 2010's *Overly Dedicated*), *Section.80* put the music industry on notice: they'd never seen a creative flair like Kendrick's, and there was no doubt now he was here to stay.

Section.80's acclaim set the stage for Kendrick's next achievement, 2012's *good kid, m.A.A.d city*, an instant classic that catapulted him to heights for which he wasn't fully prepared. Powered by the singles "Backseat Freestyle," "Swimming Pools (Drank)," and "Bitch, Don't Kill My Vibe," Kendrick's second studio album proved a massive hit, and almost overnight he went from enigmatic upstart to full-fledged superstar. Just two years later, in 2014, Kendrick was supposed to enjoy a grand coronation, at the 56th Annual Grammy Awards, but destiny had a different timeline.

The twenty-six-year-old had pushed his way to the Staples Center, having dropped a steady stream of music that garnered universal acclaim and brightened his star to its most brilliant point. With guest appearances from hip-hop superstar Drake, and gangsta-rap-pioneer-turned-headphone-mogul Dr. Dre, *good kid, m.A.A.d city* debuted at number two on *Billboard*'s Top R&B/Hip-Hop Albums chart and sold more than 240,000 copies in its first week out. Kendrick had been dubbed L.A.'s next great lyricist, another in a decades-long list of local rappers gone big. But Kendrick wasn't

Dre. He wasn't Ice-T, Ice Cube, or Snoop Dogg. Those men had been synonymous with gangsta rap, a reality-based strain of hip-hop that documented L.A.'s turbulent gang culture and systemic racism in searing detail. On *good kid, m.A.A.d city*, Kendrick presented himself as the conflicted soul with one foot on solid ground and the other in the streets. He'd survived the stress of L.A. gang culture to finally *arrive* at music's biggest night in downtown L.A.—some fourteen miles from his childhood home at West 137th Street.

There'd been a palpable buzz leading up to this point, yet Kendrick didn't seem fazed by the moment. Despite all the pageantry that usually comes with the Grammys, there was a remarkable sense of calm on his face. It was like he'd been there before, like he belonged in this environment. It was the gaze of a man who'd already won, whether or not he collected hardware on that stage. He'd soon have the public's full attention, and the awards, well, that'd be icing on the cake. (He was never one to get hopped up on accolades, anyway.) There was also a hint of resignation in his eyes; the Recording Academy hadn't rewarded artists like Kendrick, at least not right away. They usually had to *come around* to people like him, eschewing his blend of intellectual street rap for palatable, pop-oriented work. Year after year, the industry rewarded safety, not the groundbreaking art of wise young poets.

But there he was anyway, dressed to the nines in a bespoke electric-blue tuxedo with his longtime girlfriend, Whitney Alford, at his side. Earlier that night, Kendrick had ignited the crowd with a brilliant performance of his track "m.A.A.d city," with the high-profile rock group Imagine Dragons as the backing band. On a night of scintillating performances, Kendrick's set was perhaps the strongest, foreshadowing what would become a regular run of iconic sets from the Compton rapper on the music industry's grandest stage. In the crowd, Taylor Swift, the industry-minted country artist turned pop star with a penchant for lovelorn breakup songs, swayed joyously on camera. Minutes later, with the music in full swing, Queen Latifah, the Afrocentric rap pioneer turned star actress, gazed delightfully at the stage—her face teeming with pride, bewilderment, and pure excitement. This was arguably Kendrick's crossover moment, the culmination of three years of steadily increased momentum.

Compton kids aren't supposed to make it past the city limits—Willowbrook to the northwest or Paramount to the east. If you let the media tell it, those kids are not even supposed to make it out alive. Though the town wasn't the epicenter of violent crime it had once been in the 1980s and '90s, it was still fertile ground for gang activity, and by 2015, it would receive federal aid to help prevent gang violence and human trafficking while addressing the prevalence of narcotics and gun possession. Kendrick had Compton and a large swath of hip-hop culture on his side—the gangbangers, the college kids, and the aging B-boys. He was the perfect combination of old- and new-school rap who could spit incisive rhymes in underground ciphers and beside the biggest pop stars. "He's the king," says Otis "Madlib" Jackson Jr., an acclaimed hip-hop producer from Oxnard with a sizable cult following. "I knew he was the king when I first heard *Section.80*. He's the new king of the West Coast. And he's spiritual. That's rare for West Coast artists." In the modern era of glossy pop hybrids driven by multimillion-dollar budgets, he was a throwback to rap's "golden era" of the early to mid-1990s, when the complexity of one's lyrics was more important than the instrumentals underscoring them. Kendrick embodied that nostalgia, and for those who grew up listening to Dre, Cube, and Snoop, his music struck the right balance of past and present, navigating both worlds with incredible ease and fluidity. This wasn't just rap; Kendrick spoke to black and brown people on the grind, those who fought to make a way for themselves and their families against overwhelming odds. He was the voice of his community, even if the audience was much smaller.

Still, it was somewhat surprising to hear other names deemed award winners throughout the evening. Jay-Z and Justin Timberlake? Sure. They were all bona fide stars in rap and pop music, both of whom had sold millions of records throughout the years. Rihanna? Absolutely. The pop star had a golden ear for catchy hooks and massive dance tracks that lingered inside your head.

Then there was Macklemore, a rapper from Seattle who was a relative newcomer to those beyond his hometown. The lyricist had been releasing music since 2000, and over the years, he'd proved his ability to spit rapid-fire verses that delved into his own struggles with drug addiction and depression. Self-released projects like *Open Your Eyes* (released under the name Professor Macklemore), *The Language of My World*, and *The Unplanned Mixtape* had found him wrestling with his own identity as a white man in a black genre. Then in 2012 and 2013, respectively, he and producer Ryan Lewis scored two chart-topping hits: "Thrift Shop," which eschewed monetary excess for a life of limited spending, and "Can't Hold Us," a foot-stomping party anthem about persevering through overwhelming odds. "Thrift Shop" dispelled the notion of decadence; to Macklemore and Lewis, it was unnecessary to spend so much money on cars, clothes, and jewelry. While the message resonated during the economic downturn, it also seemed to mock the very genre from which Macklemore earned his living. Hip-hop was black music, and for Macklemore to release such a song felt like a slight to the art form and to the minorities for whom Kendrick Lamar spoke. Macklemore seemed to appropriate not just a genre but black culture itself, using its music to peddle safe messages to a mostly white audience.

Yet in 2005, the lyricist had released a song called "White Privilege," in which he openly questioned his own existence in hip-hop. In a world that justly excoriated whites for not acknowledging black plight, one could respect Macklemore's effort to hold himself accountable.

However, Kendrick represented more substantively those who'd been harassed by police or denied opportunities because of their hue. Hip-hop was a way to document the trauma of racism and celebrate the unparalleled fortitude of blackness. It allowed a group like N.W.A to denounce law enforcement, and for a man like the Notorious B.I.G. to walk us through the grittiest sections of 1990s Brooklyn without stepping foot on the C train. Through hip-hop, black people were able to synthesize hardship into radiant poetry, and for Kendrick, the culture allowed room to wrestle with the yin and yang of life as a young black man in modern America. In a country still largely uncomfortable with people of color, hip-hop was a community that needed to be protected.

So Macklemore wasn't supposed to defeat Kendrick—not on this day, not ever. But he did, walking away with the Grammys for Best New Artist, Best Rap Performance, Best Rap Song, and Best Rap Album for his 2012 project, *The Heist*. Compared with the confessional *good kid, m.A.A.d city*, *The Heist* was destined for mainstream acceptance, its broad synthesis of pop and 1980s rap tailored for wider appeal. People of color were still fighting to be seen beyond hip-hop culture, and Macklemore's skin tone allowed him to navigate black music while giving older white listeners the freedom to enjoy rap in the open. Macklemore was considered safe, discussing topics of which they could relate; by and large, those same people couldn't fathom a young black male driving his mom's Dodge Caravan across town to have sex, only to rob a house with his friends and witness a friend get murdered. Despite that, many fans—including Macklemore—believed Kendrick should've won at least one Grammy. So much so that Macklemore texted Kendrick and posted a screenshot of the private interaction on Instagram. "You got robbed. I wanted you to win. You should have," Macklemore wrote. "It's weird and sucks that I robbed you. I was gonna say that during the speech. Then the music started playing during my speech and I froze. Anyway, you know what it is. Congrats on this year and your music. Appreciate you as an artist and as a friend." Macklemore wrote in the Instagram post's caption that Kendrick deserved to win the Grammy for Best Rap Album, and that he was "blown away to win anything much less 4 Grammys."

The rap community reacted sharply: in the days and weeks following the Grammys and that now-infamous screenshot, Macklemore was roundly criticized. It was one thing to text Kendrick privately, but letting the world know about it felt disingenuous. "I think it was uncalled for," Kendrick told New York radio station Hot 97 in November 2014. "When he sent it to me, I was like, 'Okay.' I could see him feeling that type of way because he's a good dude, but I think for confirmation from the world, he probably felt like he had to put it out there, which he didn't need to do." Drake felt the same way, telling *Rolling Stone* that Macklemore's text was "wack as fuck." "It felt cheap. It didn't feel genuine. . . . He made a brand of music that appealed to more people than me, Hov [Jay-Z], Kanye [West] and Kendrick. Whether people wanna say it's racial, or whether it's just the fact that he tapped into something we can't tap into. That's just how the cards fall. Own your shit." Macklemore had gone to Hot 97 before the Grammys and predicted he'd probably win the award for Best Rap Album, even though he didn't think he deserved it. "Then he came back on afterwards and said the same thing again," cohost Ebro Darden told Kendrick at the time. "I think everybody knows the politics of it, where it's kinda like, 'Here's this white kid who had Top 40 success,' so he was . . . on the radar of all these old people who vote in the Grammy academy." In his own Hot 97 interview following the 56th Annual Grammy Awards show, Macklemore said racism was to blame for his receiving the statue. He also chastised the voting process, which supposedly allowed members to elect potential winners even if they weren't familiar with the music at all. "Knowing how the Grammys usually go, I knew that there would be a great chance that we'd win that award and in essence rob Kendrick," Macklemore said. "I think we made a great album, I think Kendrick made a better rap album. In terms of people who are voting on those ballots that are filling out those bubbles, we have an unfair advantage due to race, due to the fact that we had huge radio success." In subsequent interviews, Macklemore took it a step further, admitting that he could have worded his text differently. "The language that I used was a bad call," he told Hot 97 in December 2014. "White people have been robbing black people for a long time—of culture, of music, of freedom, of their lives."

But while the Kendrick-Macklemore exchange was the most dramatic example of a good deed gone wrong at the Grammys, it certainly wasn't the last time something like that would happen. In 2017, UK singer Adele won Album of the Year for her record *25*, beating Beyoncé's *Lemonade* in the process. Powered by "Hello," a soaring piano ballad steeped in romantic heartbreak, *25* had shot quickly up the charts, selling more than 10 million albums to mark Adele's grand return after five years away from the music industry. In her speech, a tearful, almost frantic Adele gave Beyoncé all the praise, even saying she couldn't accept it. "My artist of my life is Beyoncé and the *Lemonade* album was just so monumental," she proclaimed, her voice audibly shaken. "We all got to see another side to you that you don't always let us see, and we appreciate that. And all us artists here, we fucking adore you. You are our light. . . . The way that you make my black friends feel is empowering and you make them stand up for themselves." Some criticized Adele—a white artist—for using the term "black friends," and the Recording Academy for once again shunning a black artist for the Grammys' top honor. Beyoncé was the biggest pop star in the world and this was her third time being denied. In a *New York Times* article published shortly after the awards show, critics predicted that black musicians would soon start boycotting the ceremony altogether. "They absolutely, positively got it wrong," said popular radio personality Charlamagne Tha God, according to the *Times*. "The Grammy committee should all feel foolish this morning, because even Adele acknowledged that she should not have won album of the year." Frank Ocean, one of music's most popular singer-songwriters, said he hadn't submitted music for the 2017 Grammy Awards because there was a cultural bias within the Recording Academy that blindly awarded white artists year after year. "Believe the people," he wrote in a blog post. "Believe the ones who'd rather watch select performances from your program on YouTube the day after because your show puts them to sleep. Use the old Gramophone to actually listen."

There was a precedent for this. In 1989, rap duo DJ Jazzy Jeff & the Fresh Prince, nominated for Best Rap Performance for their crossover hit "Parents Just Don't Understand," boycotted the Grammys after the academy decided not to televise the award presentation. Though the duo won the award, they, Public Enemy, and Slick Rick did not attend the ceremony.

According to the Recording Academy, album submissions are reviewed by more than 350 experts throughout the music industry, all of whom work to make sure the records are sorted into their appropriate categories. Once the submissions are filed into rap, jazz, classical, and so on, first-round ballots are sent to members in good dues standing, and they're asked to vote only in their areas of expertise. Both the first-round ballots and final ballots are tabulated by an independent accounting firm, and the winner is announced.

Despite that process, some have criticized the academy for seeming out of touch with what's really popular in modern music. They say voters don't choose based on artistic merit, that they mark the same familiar names year after year. Still, that doesn't explain why reggae icon Bob Marley and guitar god Jimi Hendrix never won Grammys at all, and why someone like Jay-Z has gone home without a trophy from time to time. In 2018, for instance, the rap mogul's thirteenth studio album, *4:44*, earned eight Grammy nominations, but he lost in every single category, including Album of the Year, Best Rap Album, and Record of the Year for "The Story of O.J." The academy, he told *Billboard*, is "human like we are, and they are voting on things that they like. We can pretend we don't care, but we do. We really care because we are seeing the most incredible artists stand on that stage, and we aspire to be that." In an essay posted to Complex, music journalist Rob Kenner—a voting member of the academy—scrutinized the process, calling it disorganized. "Along with the official guidelines," Kenner wrote, "I soon learned another unwritten rule during private conversations with other committee members: be careful about green-lighting an album by someone who was really famous if you don't want to see that album win a Grammy. Because famous people tend to get more votes from clueless Academy members, regardless of the quality of their work."

The Recording Academy established a private committee to scrutinize voter submissions after Lionel Richie's *Can't Slow Down* won Album of the Year over Bruce Springsteen's *Born in the U.S.A.* and Prince's *Purple Rain* in 1985. As cultural website Vox points out, "Richie was far from the best choice that year, and his win helped create the public perception that the Grammys were cut off from what 'good music' meant." In Kenner's essay, published before the 56th Annual Grammy Awards, he speculated about the likelihood of

Macklemore and Ryan Lewis winning Best Rap Album over more deserving records like Kendrick's *good kid, m.A.A.d city*. "Because of their tremendous commercial success and media exposure there's a good chance they will win, despite the fact that most hip-hop aficionados would prefer to see the award go to pretty much anybody else— be it Kanye West, Jay-Z, Kendrick Lamar, or Drake," he wrote.

In September 2018, in an attempt to resolve its long-standing struggles with diversity, the Recording Academy invited nine hundred music creators to join its ranks as voting members. The request, part of a recommendation earlier that year from the academy's Task Force on Diversity and Inclusion, went out to producers, songwriters, instrumentalists, and vocalists who were women or people of color under the age of thirty-nine. The academy also diversified the composition of its nomination review committees, which determine the final Grammy nominations across categories. "We need a culture change overall," task force chair Tina Tchen told *Billboard*. "We're living through a moment where we're seeing a national culture change on these issues. The music industry and Recording Academy are not immune to that."

In the years since the 56th Annual Grammy Awards, the careers of Kendrick and Macklemore have gone in separate directions. In 2016, Macklemore released a song called "White Privilege II," which, much like "White Privilege" in 2005, found the rapper addressing what other white people with similar platforms have largely failed to do: the fact that his skin color afforded him opportunities and safety that black people simply didn't have. The song arrived at a time of heightened tension between blacks and whites: in the United States, unarmed minorities were being killed by mostly white police officers at an alarming rate, and anyone with a smartphone could see bullets penetrate black bodies on endless loop. It seemed Macklemore wanted to help the cause, to stand in solidarity with those who had lost loved ones and those who were tired of seeing their neighbors murdered without recourse. Yet as the song unfolded, "White Privilege II" became more about Macklemore's own identity struggles and less about the people he wanted to support. In one moment, he wanted to march with those fighting the injustices; the next he was off to the side, wondering if he should have been there in the first place. Ultimately, the song raised questions about Macklemore's authenticity and whether or not he should be inserting his voice into black issues. His perspective threatened to overshadow that of the activists on the ground doing the real work. Such was the dilemma of analyzing Macklemore: while he should have been commended for at least trying to address topics that other white celebrities wouldn't touch, he ended up doing too much to show that he was down for the cause. It was not enough to be a good dude privately; he needed to show the world just how cool he was.

Then there was his subsequent album, 2016's *This Unruly Mess I've Made*, with producer Ryan Lewis once again riding shotgun. Featuring rap pioneers Melle Mel, Kool Moe Dee, and Grandmaster Caz, as well as up-and-coming stars like singers Anderson .Paak, Jamila Woods, and Leon Bridges, *Unruly Mess* was an aptly titled collection of half-baked wokeness meant to show listeners that Macklemore really *did* belong in hip-hop culture. Compared with *The Heist*, which sold millions of records and pushed him to meteoric heights, *Unruly Mess* was a critical and commercial failure, and—without explanation—Macklemore and Lewis didn't submit it for Grammy consideration. A year later, Macklemore quietly released another album, *Gemini*, this time without Lewis as his producer. That album was far less political than anything he'd released. "I think it's mostly the music that I wanted to hear," the rapper told *Rolling Stone*. "I believe that music can be a form of resistance without having to hit the nail on the head in terms of subject matter. It can be something that uplifts, that makes you dance, that makes you cry, that makes you think." Nowadays, Macklemore still tours, playing to thousands of fans in packed arenas, even if his star has dissipated in the States.

Meanwhile, following the 2014 Grammys, Kendrick traveled to South Africa to play a series of shows. The perspective he'd gain from the Motherland would prove invaluable for himself, the rap community, and the world at large.

For eighteen years, Nelson Mandela sat on a remote island in the middle of the sea. It was here—Robben Island in South Africa's Table Bay—where the activist pounded rocks into gravel and wrote letters to his wife, close confidants, and children.

From afar, the island looked inviting, a secluded peninsula surrounded by crisp blue water. "It's a very poignant place to be, because you can see South Africa, but you really can't get there," says Teresa Ann Barnes, an African studies professor at the University of Illinois who lived in South Africa when Mandela was freed from prison. Walking the land was something different: the struggle was baked into it; the souls of political prisoners loomed heavily above the threatening brick walls and looping barbwire. Robben Island was, in a word, hell, but Mandela—the South African philanthropist who was arrested and sentenced to life in prison in 1964—used peace as a weapon against daily hardship. He was a fighter who battled injustice of all sorts, whether it was the inhumane system of apartheid, or the censorship of his fellow inmates on the island. Mandela was a leader with incredible resolve, and though he spent twenty-seven years in prison, his thoughts remained with the oppressed people back on the mainland. The resistance sustained his spirit and kept him mentally sharp in his loneliest moments. He was the ultimate commander and parent, however tough it was to be those things from the isolation of a tiny cell. "Fight on!" Mandela once wrote in a statement made public by the African National Congress in 1980. "Between the anvil of united mass action and the hammer of the armed struggle we shall crush apartheid!" Apartheid would not be abolished until 1994, but anecdotes like these explain how Mandela became *Mandela*: he was just a man, but he cared most about the challenges beyond his immediate gaze. His aim was to unify communities, whether blacks and whites in South Africa or inmates and overseers in prison. He wanted to build a resonant voice that would influence equally resonant voices in the future. Nowadays, Robben Island is preserved as a monument to the friction endured by its prisoners, but it's also a testament to the resolve of a person who'd rise from the shackles of oppression to mend a country wading through the uncertainty of life after apartheid.

Kendrick visited Robben Island in the winter of 2014, not long after the now-infamous Grammy Awards ceremony. He was in

South Africa to play a trio of shows in Durban, Cape Town, and Johannesburg, and needed time away from the music industry machine to recharge and gain a new perspective. The trip was significant for Kendrick; he'd never been to Africa and wanted to absorb the culture for himself and his friends back home in Compton—roughly 9,960 miles away. "This is a place that we, in urban communities, never dream of," Kendrick told comedian Dave Chappelle in a 2017 discussion for *Interview*. "We never dream of Africa. You feel it as soon as you touch down."

Chappelle knew this pilgrimage: In 2005, he had left his highly popular *Chappelle's Show* while filming episodes for its third season and traveled to Durban to visit his friend Salim. He, too, had needed to replenish his spirit: the false rumors claimed he was on crack cocaine, had a meltdown, and checked himself into a mental health facility. It was also said that Chappelle, a black man from the Washington, D.C., suburbs, didn't like the *way* that white people laughed at his particular brand of comedy, which used sharp race-centered parody to mock cultural stereotypes. It was like they were laughing *at* him, not *with* him, and thus the heart of his show had lost its beat. Couple that with the trappings of newfound fame; Chappelle had inked a $50 million deal ahead of the season's production, and—as he told *Time* two weeks after walking away from the show—certain people within his inner circle had begun to change. "If you don't have the right people around you and you're moving at a million miles an hour you can lose yourself," he told the magazine. By the time he got to South Africa, he was stressed and needed new creative energy.

The same went for Kendrick; by the time he got to South Africa in early 2014, his fame was still relatively new. In the U.S., *good kid, m.A.A.d city* had sold more than one million copies—an actual platinum record. Toward the end of 2013, Kendrick had opened for Kanye West for a number of dates on his national Yeezus Tour. West was a dignitary at the time, and to open for him meant even greater exposure. Though Kendrick had spent the previous ten years releasing a number of mixtapes and independent albums— first on Konkrete Jungle Muzik, and then most notably on Top Dawg Entertainment (TDE) —he was, in the eyes of the public, still thought of as an overnight sensation. He wasn't used to all this; he had always preferred to keep to himself in the background.

But now he was out front, and whether he liked it or not, success meant greater visibility, nonstop touring, and less time for himself. The album *good kid* wasn't the only reason he was a star; a certain verse had something to do with that. In August 2013, Kendrick appeared on a track called "Control" with rapper Big Sean and spit a potent rhyme that called out nearly every MC who was popular at the time: J. Cole, Jay Electronica, Drake, Pusha T, and Meek Mill, among others. It was a bold move at a time when hip-hop wasn't so bold; the diss resembled an action from the genre's history, back when hip-hop was still finding its way, when Ice Cube tongue-lashed N.W.A, and KRS-One battled MC Shan about the best borough in New York City. The verse set off a firestorm: some felt attacked by Kendrick's words; others applauded the tactic. "KEN-DRICK!!!!! Ohhhh Shiiitttttt," Diddy tweeted. "I don't feel like @kendricklamar dissed anybody," rapper Trinidad James tweeted. "He just has moved up to another level."

On the road, Kendrick would write rhymes on his phone and

record music on a tour bus equipped with a mobile studio. These were less-than-ideal circumstances for his meticulous creative process, but for almost three years—including his own touring schedule before connecting with West—he had made the most of his time, pulling inspiration from the road. In December 2013, during a tour stop in Atlanta, Georgia, he found himself weighed down by his newfound prosperity. By then, he'd been on the road for four consecutive months, performing almost every night, aside from a few dates when Busta Rhymes, A Tribe Called Quest, and Pusha T opened for West instead. He was homesick and somewhat disillusioned by the massive universal impact of his music. Sure, listeners around the world connected with it, but did it have the same resonance in his hometown? Kendrick felt guilty for making it out when his friends—some of whom were talented musicians in their own right—were either in prison or gunned down. Three of his closest companions had been murdered between 2013 and 2014. He felt he needed to be home with his family and the loved ones of those who were lost.

Kendrick didn't just want to be a voice of reason; he needed that voice to assuage this bout of survivor's guilt. The shooting death of Chad Keaton—his friend's little brother—hit him the hardest. On the evening of July 12, 2013, Keaton was walking down the road when a white sedan darted past him at the corner of Comstock Street and Parmelee Avenue. Shots rang out and wounded Keaton, who never recovered from his injuries. He died in the hospital thirty-one days later. Kendrick was close with Chad's older brother, who was incarcerated and had asked Kendrick to make sure the younger sibling stayed on the right path. Chad was a good kid who had ended up in the wrong place at the wrong time. Ravaged by all the despair back home, Kendrick started screaming in his hotel room; later, he'd use the incident as the basis of a poem woven throughout his 2015 album, *To Pimp a Butterfly*. "It was something that just accumulated," Kendrick told the *Guardian* at the time. "I was able to bottle that moment and put it on record."

Despite his ascension, he rapped about depression and an inferiority complex. Compton—and Los Angeles as a whole—was chock-full of great lyricists with something viable to say, so what made Kendrick the one to rise above it all? It was a question with which he openly wrestled. "I find myself to be quite confident as a person," he continued, "but you're going to have that piece of doubt in the back of your head because we're human." Kendrick faced a great deal of pressure to top *good kid, m.A.A.d city*, a widely heralded classic that forced some to dub the young rapper the King of West Coast Rap. Mind you, Kendrick likely wasn't thinking about that, or if he was, he wouldn't say so publicly. For him, the art was first and foremost, and as long as his music came from an honest place, the accolades were a plus.

South Africa gave Kendrick a chance to reset and be one with his own thoughts. He went to the blighted neighborhoods away from the tourist-centric parts of Cape Town, Johannesburg, and Durban. He spent time with the children who actually *lived* there, using the trip as an opportunity to learn about the plight of their communities. His time on the continent set the foundation for *Butterfly*, a record that was as much about South Africa as it was about his own fight to deal with burgeoning fame. "I felt like I belonged in Africa," Kendrick later told the Recording Academy.

"I saw all the things that I wasn't taught. Probably one of the hardest things to do is put [together] a concept on how beautiful a place can be, and tell a person this while they're still in the ghettos of Compton. I wanted to put that experience in the music." Throughout the album, one can hear subtle nods to both the beauty and conflict seen throughout South Africa. On "Complexion (A Zulu Love)," Kendrick wanted to celebrate the various shades of black women. In the States, some black people were trained to value lighter skin over darker skin, but in South Africa, he saw different shades of people all united by language.

Then on "Mortal Man," *Butterfly*'s tremendous closing track, Kendrick—over a jazz-inflected blend of mid-tempo drums and muffled orchestration—ponders his legacy in relation to Mandela's, wondering if he'll be remembered as a hero or cast as a villain. Here, Kendrick raps: "How many leaders you said you needed then left 'em for dead? / Is it Moses, is it Huey Newton or Detroit Red?" Mandela himself had seen the euphoria of his release and presidential run dissipate by the mid-1990s. While he brought equal voting rights to South Africa (a huge political shift for the country), life didn't change dramatically for black citizens after that. Some chastised him for being too nice to the same white people who, historically, had made life insufferable for black people there. He was charming and deeply charismatic, but also economically conservative. "Mandela, and the things that he stood for, aren't necessarily lauded by young South Africans," Professor Barnes recalls. "They saw the compromises that he made have not led enough people to feel like their lives have improved."

"Mortal Man" delves into the kind of survivor's guilt that Kendrick experienced at the time. On one end, he was beginning to realize his worth, but he couldn't help but question the authenticity of the love being received. Perhaps he hadn't done enough work to warrant this widespread adoration. Kendrick did everything with Compton in mind, and toward the end of the track, he concludes his album-long poem by making direct ties between L.A. gang culture and systemic racism in South Africa: "While my loved ones [were] fighting a continuous war back in the city, I was entering a new one, a war that was based on Apartheid and discrimination. Made me want to go back to the city and tell the homies what I learned." For him, the fight between red and blue was no longer important; black was the most essential color.

He made that message explicitly clear on "The Blacker the Berry," an aggressive album cut near *Butterfly*'s end. The South African dissension he referenced, between Zulu and Xhosa tribes, reminded him of "Compton Crip gangs that live next door / Beefin' with Pirus, only death settle the score." While these young men killed each other over property they didn't own, there was a common enemy on the horizon that was perceived to be an even bigger threat than it had been in years past. South African citizens had been known to take bold steps toward their collective freedom; he thought it was time for black men in Compton to do the same.

Yugen Blakrok, a South African rapper who—in 2018—was chosen by Kendrick to appear on the soundtrack of the block-buster film *Black Panther*, remembers the palpable buzz surrounding Kendrick's visit to the Motherland in 2014. Where other U.S. musicians typically visited Africa and took from its culture, using its sound and fashion to line their own pockets, Kendrick actually gave back to the community—praising it in interviews and on his music. He didn't whisper the wonders of South Africa; he shouted them loudly. "You started noticing things," Blakrok recalls, "like when he started growing his hair out. . . . Black people, we're not the minority out here, we're the majority. It's just different how we wear our hair and our clothes. It's different from what I think is going down in the States." South Africa gave Kendrick the freedom to be himself, to be untethered to the nuanced cultural restrictions of America. According to Mark "Sounwave" Spears, a longtime Kendrick collaborator, something clicked for Kendrick when he went to South Africa, and once he returned home, the rapper scrapped two to three albums' worth of material to create the expansive sonic opus that is *Butterfly*.

In South Africa, Kendrick saw black faces—joyous and resilient black faces—all fighting to navigate their own circumstances. The country was just twenty years removed from the end of apartheid and still segregated, with much of its black African population living in urban townships outside Johannesburg, Kempton Park, Durban, and Germiston. Still, Blakrok says, there's comfort in knowing that black people outnumber other races. "There's a different type of power, a *physical* power," she asserts. "They know they can't fuck with us physically." Blakrok likens Kendrick's visit to that of a humanitarian, and his presence in the region lit a fire beneath some of the rappers there. He was, and still is, a lyricist first and foremost, and for an MC with that level of technical prowess to thrive meant like-minded artists could succeed the same way. "It just showed there was a more open acceptance of that kind of hip-hop, whereas before, it was always pushed to the underground,"

Blakrok says. "It established a trend of listening to rap that's a little more left of center." "He was the amazing artist with a Dr. Dre budget," says the rapper Reason, who opened for Kendrick at Johannesburg Stadium in February 2014. "You could feel it. This guy's not just big, he's not just famous, he can actually *rap*. People were moved when he came through."

Reason recalls the business savvy that Kendrick brought with him. He remembers the so-called "ego walk"—or the long runway that extends from the stage into the crowd—that allowed musicians to perform closer to the audience. It was a way to better connect with the people, thus offering a more intimate show. "Nobody could use the ego walk except for Kendrick," Reason asserts, "and if anybody used it, they were not going to perform." Some resented Kendrick for that. "Others were arguing, 'Why is this guy gonna build a big ego walk, and he's the only one who's allowed to use it? You know this is our country, why can't we use it as well?'" Turns out the answer was simple: "It was always spun around to say, 'You didn't ask for it. He did.'"

The disagreement encouraged local musicians to take those minor details seriously, and to pay stricter attention to the contracts they signed. "It kinda upped the game," Reason says. "It was an interesting experience to go through, but it did have a nice, positive impact, because there was a big change after that." As Sabelo Mkhabela, a noted South African hip-hop journalist, points out, Kendrick performed in the country just as local artists started to rethink those sorts of opportunities. "A lot of South African artists were beginning to refuse to be opening acts for American superstars," Mkhabela declares. "We get treated like shit backstage." Despite the initial hard feelings between Kendrick and local performers, all was forgiven once the headliner hit the stage. "He would just perform and perform, then stand still," Reason recollects. At the Johannesburg show, in particular, Kendrick—dressed in a green hooded jacket, tan shorts, and a gray T-shirt—made great use of silence, using a long break between songs to strengthen the room's energy. The fans started chanting his name, and like Reason said, he was literally just standing there on the ego walk, letting the anticipation climb to frenetic heights. "The crowd would *roar*. They'd make so much noise and it wouldn't stop until he said something. That makes you appreciate how planned that is."

The genesis of modern South African hip-hop can be traced back to kwaito, a style of house music that emanated from the township of Soweto in the mid-1990s, just as the structures of apartheid were being dissolved and Mandela took office as the first democratically elected president of South Africa. Blending elements of mbaqanga, kwela, eighties bubblegum pop, and traditional praise music, kwaito was different from the straightforward rap of South Africa in the 1980s. Groups like Prophets of Da City (P.O.C.) and Black Noise pioneered hip-hop in Cape Town and Johannesburg, and have been credited with ushering in a new wave of black consciousness. P.O.C. was the first rap group in the country to record and release an album; the crew was able to build a fan base overseas and even performed at Mandela's inauguration in 1994. Black Noise signed a deal with Tusk Music—a subsidiary of Warner-Elektra-Atlantic—and released its own album in 1992. That group, led by rapper Emile YX?, harkened back to the foundation of U.S. hip-hop, when break dancing and graffiti were equally essential to the rhymes being said over the music. Kwaito became the voice of disenfranchised youth who had grown tired of white minority rule and wanted apartheid to be abolished once and for all. Rap groups like P.O.C. and Black Noise were chastised for emulating the sound of hip-hop coming from the States.

Conversely, kwaito was celebrated as an authentic sound for South Africa. In 1995, Arthur Mafokate scored kwaito's first commercial hit with "Kaffir," a brash tune with pointed lyrics about white oppressors in South Africa. The song title refers to a derogatory term used in the country against black people, and on the track, Mafokate demands that his boss (or "baas") not call him by it. The song draws immediate comparisons to Sly and the Family Stone's 1969 track "Don't Call Me Nigger, Whitey" for its reclaiming of a word meant to insult a race of people. (To that end, Kendrick would do the same toward the end of *To Pimp a Butterfly*, on a song called "i," in which he subbed the derogatory N-word with the Ethiopian word meaning "king.") The song "Kaffir" passed muster with the youth, some of whom were influenced by Mafokate's music and went on to create their own resonant art. Mafokate was dubbed the King of Kwaito, and from there the music thrived as a bold alternative to the political—albeit, more palpable—songs of yesteryear. In 1998, kwaito group Boom Shaka caught flack for a house music version of the South African national anthem that it created and performed. It was thought by some to be a commercial subversion of the original hymn; the group, in defending its version, said their version was meant to attract younger listeners.

South African hip-hop is still fairly corporate, and rappers who aren't tied to major sponsors have a tough time sustaining themselves in the country. That leaves little to no room for MCs who prioritize the art of making music over the demands of making money. "Black artists here aren't really afforded that luxury of making art for art's sake," Blakrok says. In recent years, members of the African National Congress have used hip-hop to secure votes while trying to rebuild confidence in their mission. As a result, a big-name rapper like Kiernan "AKA" Forbes has been criticized for not speaking truth to power, much as his predecessors would've done decades ago. "The people are questioning him," says journalist Mkhabela. "They're like, 'You, as a young person, how are you campaigning for a party that is failing a lot of young black people?'" Above all, Kendrick served as motivation to traditional lyricists in South Africa who identified with groups like P.O.C. and Black Noise, and who longed for a time when thoughtful lyricism took precedence over glossy, pop-focused hybrids. He represented the roots of hip-hop and all the spoken-word poetry, 1970s funk, and R&B that preceded it. Kendrick was allowed to create authentic music without conforming to what was hot on the radio, and in South Africa, he was a guiding light for unheralded MCs who wanted to succeed on their own terms. In him, they had an example of someone who could have fun without sacrificing content, who could discuss serious issues—like his family's history of alcoholism— over booming bass drums that resonate in nightclubs. By and large, rappers haven't been able to do both, yet Kendrick was breaking the mold for his generation.

Four years after he visited the country, Kendrick would once again cast his eye to South Africa by selecting four of its rappers to appear on *Black Panther: The Album*. Not only was it a soundtrack to a major film, but it was meant to depict Kendrick's broad musical vision of the Motherland. He could've chosen big-name acts from South Africa, but he went deeper into the scene to spotlight artists who were still on the rise. Along with Blakrok, the rapper chose dance music artist Babes Wodumo, rapper Saudi, and singer Sjava to share space alongside noted American rappers ScHoolboy Q, 2 Chainz, and Vince Staples. Blakrok was on tour when she was contacted by Kendrick's label, Top Dawg Entertainment, to appear on the project. Kendrick and the label had been listening to a lot of South African music, and Blakrok—a smoky-voiced lyricist with elaborate wordplay—fit the album's concept. After her inclusion on *Black Panther*, Blakrok found an audience in the United States and Europe, where her style of hip-hop was better appreciated. And because of the Kendrick nod, she suddenly had greater pull. "The fact that I wasn't a mainstream artist with a major label, it really put a lot of attention on me," says Blakrok, who released a critically acclaimed album, *Anima Mysterium*, in 2019. "If you're not on TV, it's almost like you don't exist, so to be included was huge. It opened up a lot of doors for me. It was a cosign and it did wonders."

Ultimately, South Africa played a significant role in Kendrick's career, and in many ways, the time he spent there helped redirect the course of mainstream black music. If he hadn't taken that trip, or opened his eyes to the country's grand splendor, there'd be no *To Pimp a Butterfly*. Free and avant-garde jazz might still struggle to attract bigger groups of fans, and sonically challenging art might still be relegated to smaller venues. South Africa set the stage for Kendrick's greater act. It also allowed him to return to where it all started, this time with a clear head and a full heart.

2

"California Love"

Before Kendrick Lamar was a world-renowned rapper, he was an introverted kid trying to navigate Los Angeles. Ask around and you'll get the same story: the Kendrick we see today is the same mild-mannered child from 1990s Compton who, as a preteen, pedaled his bicycle through the neighborhood, ate Now and Later candy, and played basketball and tackle football with his friends. Kendrick was quick on the court, with nice dribbling skills and a reliable jump shot (though in later songs, he'd admit that it wasn't quite good enough to take him to the NBA). He had dreams of going pro, much like other young black boys in economically challenged communities. In a place like Compton, with its prevalent gang culture, there's a myth that black and Latino children are destined only for the streets, or that they can make it out only by creating music or playing sports at a high level. Some join gangs or sell drugs, but to spotlight that narrative alone is to ignore the support system in towns like this—the mothers, fathers, activists, and local leaders who project positive images to which the youth can aspire.

Compton wasn't always *Compton*: Before World War II, the city was majority white, with racist policies that prohibited black families from moving there. In 1948, the U.S. Supreme Court overturned those laws, and by the early 1950s, black families started buying houses, much to the dismay of the whites already living in the suburban enclave. White people fled the city, fearing that their property values would plummet due to integration. The black population in Compton rose to 40 percent by 1960; a decade later, the neighborhood was 65 percent black. Crime began to rise due to growing unemployment, and in 1971, a gang called the Crips formed. The crew was founded by high school students Raymond Washington and Stanley "Tookie" Williams after they decided to unite their respective gangs to battle South L.A. gangs that were bothering them. The Crips soon became the biggest street gang in the city. In 1972, the Bloods were formed by Sylvester Scott and Vincent Owens along Piru Street in Compton, and were quickly established as a rival gang to the Crips. Members of other local crews had been assaulted by the Crips and were eager to join the ranks of the Bloods for revenge. By the early 1970s, middle- and upper-class black families started moving to nearby towns like Carson, Inglewood, and Windsor Hills. As a result, Compton became the epicenter for violent crime and gang activity in Southern California.

Alonzo Williams, a DJ and nightclub owner who created the World Class Wreckin' Cru (of which Dr. Dre was a member before he became a face of gangsta rap), remembers a different time in Compton. He grew up in the town and used to walk through what are now considered dangerous parts without any issues at all. This was in the 1970s, before crack cocaine hit the streets, back when gangs existed but to interact with them wasn't so dire. You could live near them, not be gang affiliated, and still feel safe. "Compton was like any other city, man. It was *cool*," Williams remembers. "We always had gangbangers, you went to the dances and they'd be there, but you'd walk right past them. Most of the guys you'd play baseball with or you went to school with, and there was a code of the streets that the gangbangers wouldn't mess with the civilians. Gangbangers only fought with the gangbangers. They weren't the ones looking to start no shit, but you don't *fuck* with them."

Crack cocaine changed everything. Gang activity grew out of control, and money was the new motivator. Williams also saw the dynamic shift in his nightclub. In 1979, when he opened the famed Eve's After Dark banquet hall, a small number of his patrons were gang affiliated; by 1990, when crack was in full swing, much of his crowd was gang affiliated. "I had to change my personal attitude and dress code; everybody wanted to be a thug, everybody wanted to sell dope," Williams says. "Everybody wanted to be hard. As soon as somebody got pissed off, they claimed a set. That was how you got people off your ass. It became fashionable to be a gangsta. You just did it because of where you lived, you could claim it." That mentality still exists, Williams says: "Today, a lot of these kids are claiming hoods just because they've been told, 'You live over here, that's where you're from.' A lot of them are not really with the gang life, they've just found themselves attracted to it because it's still fashionable in 2019 to claim a set. Back in the day, you knew why you were with a certain set. Now a lot of guys are doing stuff off the strength that it seems like the hot thing to do."

Kendrick was raised in a working-class environment, first in an apartment building along East Alondra Boulevard, then in a small blue house along West 137th Street with his mother, Paula Oliver, and his father, Kenny Duckworth. Kendrick's parents had moved to Compton from Chicago's South Side in 1984, three years before he was born. Kenny had lived in the notorious Robert Taylor Homes in Chicago and run with a street gang called the Gangster Disciples. Afraid that Kenny could end up dead or in prison, Paula put her foot down: He'd have to quit the crew or their relationship was over. "She said, 'I can't fuck with you if you ain't trying to better yourself,'" Kendrick told *Rolling Stone* in 2015. "We can't be in the streets forever."

Kenny and Paula packed their bags and traveled to California with just $500. They were headed farther east, to San Bernardino, but settled in Compton after Kendrick's aunt Tina put them in a hotel until they could make ends meet. To sustain themselves, Paula did hair and got a job at McDonald's while Kenny worked at Kentucky Fried Chicken and hustled on the side. Times were tough, but they eventually saved enough money for a more stable lifestyle. Then Kendrick was born—on June 17, 1987. As a child, he was a thoughtful wanderer who quietly observed his surroundings. That's not to say he wasn't fully present, but he found inspiration in the nuance of everyday existence. Kendrick, by his own admission, would sit in the corner and carefully watch what happened, taking mental notes on the scenes that unfolded. Even from a young age, he had the makings of a great scribe, yet he wouldn't pursue creative writing until he reached middle school. He was a perfectionist, and one can hear that approach in the poetry he wrote about his youth. Neighborhoods are described with pinpoint accuracy, down to the local landmarks and everyday voices that used to soundtrack his block. On *good kid, m.A.A.d city*, for instance, we hear actual characters from the community—the friends, the devoted church lady, even Kendrick's parents—coming together to contextualize the rapper's life story. On this work and others, he gives ample weight to the good and the bad in equal measure. By connecting lyrically with the Crips, Pirus, and everyday residents, Kendrick envisions a united Compton in which they all live harmoniously.

Kendrick was born just as gangsta rap began to gain traction with listeners beyond Southern California. The year he arrived, rapper Ice-T released a song called "6 in the Mornin'" that detailed the life span of a hustler selling crack cocaine. Through its vivid, lyrical imagery, the track opened a window into the perilous nature of life as a young black man in President Ronald Reagan's America, where a so-called "War on Drugs" implicitly targeted and jailed inner-city minorities. Following Ice-T's lead, in 1988, Compton quintet N.W.A (Niggaz Wit Attitudes) released its debut album, *Straight Outta Compton*, which cast a vicious light on civic despair and the police department's rampant abuse of power. The pioneering L.A. group introduced a wave of rap that went deeper than the materialistic flash that emanated from New York at the time. Sure, the crew flaunted a little on *Straight Outta Compton*, but N.W.A wanted to address real issues in the harshest language possible. It was crude, raw, brutally honest, and shocking, but it also became a massive global phenomenon and set a benchmark for what gangsta rap would be compared with for years to come. "It's the world before N.W.A, and it's the world after N.W.A," group member Ice Cube once told Kendrick in an interview for *Billboard*.

Artists like Ice-T and N.W.A documented the city in which Kendrick grew up, and the music would have a profound impact on him and L.A. as a whole. In 1995, at the age of eight, Kendrick went with his father to the Compton Swap Meet and saw rappers Tupac Shakur and Dr. Dre—the latter also a member of N.W.A—filming the video for "California Love," the lead single from Tupac's 1996 double album, *All Eyez on Me*. That was the first time Kendrick saw Dre in person and the last time he'd see Pac alive (he died in September 1996 of gunshot wounds after an altercation in Las Vegas, Nevada). Though Kendrick didn't start writing rhymes straightaway, he didn't forget the moment. Maybe it was the sense of community that swayed him: Tupac and Dre were superstars, yet there they were in a shiny black Bentley, offering a lasting experience to everyday people. It showed Kendrick that local love was stronger than global fame, and no matter how big he got, in whatever profession he chose, it didn't mean anything if he couldn't celebrate his victory at home.

Twenty years later, Kendrick walked in Pac's and Dre's footsteps, returning to the place where his interest in pursuing rap began. In the 2015 video for "King Kunta," the third single from *To Pimp a Butterfly*, Kendrick danced on the roof of the swap meet as a throng of Compton residents bounced cheerfully underneath. It was a full circle moment for a young man who'd spent his life buying CDs, cassette tapes, and Nike sneakers there.

Kendrick was quite playful when he wanted to be. As a young boy, he'd sometimes peel off his shirt and sneak out of his room into his parents' house parties. He'd dance in the middle of the room to the nostalgic soul and gangsta rap they played. Other times, he and his cousins pedaled their Big Wheels inside and got in trouble. He acted older than his age, so much so that relatives nicknamed him "Man Man."

His family was on and off welfare, but they didn't let their circumstances keep them from putting food on the table and gifts under the tree on Christmas Day. At times they were impoverished and ran out of food, but those were the moments when family meant the most: Kendrick, Paula, and Kenny loved one another, and that sustained them. They wouldn't have been as close without those moments. In 1992, when Kendrick was just four years old, he witnessed the smoke billowing from the streets of L.A. following the massive riot that ensued after the acquittal of four police officers who assaulted an unarmed black motorist named Rodney King. As Kendrick told *Rolling Stone*, he and his father were riding down Bullis Road in Compton where he saw people "just *running*. . . . We stop, and my pops goes into the Auto-Zone and comes out rolling four tires. I know he didn't buy them. . . . Then we get to the house, and him and my uncles are like, 'We fixing to get this, we fixing to get that. We fixing to get *all* this shit!' I'm thinking they're robbing. . . . Then, as time progresses, I'm watching the news, hearing about Rodney King and all this. I said to my mom, 'So the police beat up a black man, and now everybody's mad? OK. I get it now.'" That was Kendrick's first brush with the racism that would fuel songs like "Alright" and "The Blacker the Berry," and his first step toward understanding his own identity and racial disparity in the United States.

Kendrick's childhood runs parallel to the heightened tensions in L.A., and on his seventh birthday, retired football star O. J. Simpson—who had spent the past twenty years becoming a global media darling—transfixed the city by cruising through it, from the San Diego Freeway all the way to his house in Brentwood, with a gun pressed to his head. He was wanted for murder, and as his trial unfolded over the next year, L.A. would be strongly divided along racial lines. O. J. was acquitted of the crime, and that was seen as payback for the Rodney King verdict and the decades of brutality and discrimination at the hands of the city's police and justice departments.

The city of L.A. has a long history with such events: In August 1965, a riot escalated in Watts after a traffic stop turned into a massive scuffle between angry residents and white police officers. More than 14,000 California National Guard troops were brought into South L.A. to stabilize the area; in the end, 34 people died, roughly 1,000 were injured, and 4,000 were arrested. In 1991, almost two weeks after the videotaped beating of Rodney King became public, a black teenager named Latasha Harlins was shot in the back of the head by a Korean-American woman in a Vermont Vista liquor store. The woman, Soon Ja Du, had accused Harlins of trying to steal orange juice, a claim that the teenager had vehemently denied before the two tussled at the counter. Du fired the kill shot as Harlins walked away. Though a jury found Du guilty of voluntary manslaughter and recommended the maximum sentence of sixteen years, the judge did not accept the jury's sentencing and instead gave Du five years of probation, four hundred hours of community service, and a five-hundred-dollar fine. The punishment was considered much too light for an offense of that magnitude, and it reinforced the bitter reality that black life simply wasn't valued in the United States. The incident escalated tensions between blacks and Korean-Americans in South Central; many of the businesses targeted during the 1992 riot were Korean-owned.

When Kendrick was five, he saw a teenage drug dealer gunned down in front of his apartment building. "A guy was out there serving his narcotics and somebody rolled up with a shotgun and blew his chest out," Kendrick once told NPR. "It [did] something to me right then and there. It let me know that this is not only something that I'm looking at, but it's something that maybe I have to get used to." Then, at the age of eight, Kendrick was walking home from Ronald E. McNair Elementary School, past the Tam's Burgers on Rosecrans Avenue, when he saw a man get shot and killed in the drive-thru as he ordered his food. As a child, Kendrick toed a fine line between morality and street shit. Too many wrong moves, and Kendrick—the same guy whose music has traveled the globe several times over—would not have made it out of his hometown. Although one could say in retrospect that Kendrick's ascension was ordained, he also needed some luck, a ton of goodwill, and a lot of support from family and friends to pull through.

Kendrick needed a friend like Matt Jeezy, whom he met in the third or fourth grade as a fellow student at McNair Elementary. They lived in the same neighborhood and played basketball with other young kids. Eventually, some of those same friends would kill each other due to their respective gang affiliations. But Matt and

Kendrick weren't thinking red or blue; they simply wanted to have fun playing games they both loved. They weren't gangsters at all, just naturally affable children who knew everyone around the way. "Me and Kendrick used to get picked on because we weren't big bad gangstas," Jeezy recalls. "We hung out with them, we associated ourselves with them, but they knew we weren't gangbanging or anything like that. The girls would pick on us, the fellas would pick on us, but that was part of the territory of living in Compton and growing up around gang culture." In places like Compton (and most inner cities, for that matter), civil rights leaders don't live beyond the pages of old history books. They're contained to paper and speeches on YouTube, making it tough to see the impact they made all those years ago. We see the names Malcolm and Martin scribbled on chalkboards, but most black children don't grow up knowing them. Matt and Kendrick knew the people in their community; they saw them every day, and gang culture was the most visible sign of power in the neighborhood. It was a different kind of influence, equally based in fear and admiration. Gangbangers had unwavering respect, and to make it in Compton was to somehow navigate the culture without being entranced by it. Kendrick's parents did their best to protect him from the streets, even as his father earned money by those means. That kept him pure, but he needed another outlet to express his innermost convictions.

Kendrick was first introduced to creative writing as a seventh grader at Vanguard Learning Center, where he met Regis Inge, an English teacher who brought poetry into the curriculum. Tensions were especially high in the school: a gang war had broken out between blacks and Latinos in a county jail, and those ill feelings made their way to the streets of Compton, then to the Unified School District. The friction seemed to intensify overnight; one day, the students were cordial with one another, then they weren't interacting at all. Inge introduced poetry as a way to de-escalate the intensity. As he saw it, if the kids wrote their frustration, they wouldn't need to express it through physical violence. They were dealing with heavy issues at home, not just gang tension. Some of them were food insecure or had problems with self-esteem. Others trekked to school just minutes after law enforcement stampeded their homes and arrested family members. "Poetry was a way for them to write their emotions down so they wouldn't come to school so angry," Inge recalls. "They'd be ready to *fight* at 7:30 in the morning."

Still, the poetry lesson wasn't an easy sell for the neighborhood boys, who assumed the balladry was all about fluttering hearts and red roses. They weren't comfortable expressing feelings of love, so Inge connected poetry with hip-hop, and let the students know that it isn't always so cloying, that their favorite rappers were simply talking about their lives by putting poetry to music. The kids had a breakthrough: black, brown, red, and blue no longer mattered in the classroom; they started seeing each other as humans and not just rivals. "It broke the color lines down," Inge says. "Hearing poetry from a person of another race helped the students realize that they aren't so different." These weren't just poetry lessons, they taught students how to survive the turbulence. The class had a profound impact on Kendrick, who, in middle school, was still incredibly shy with a noticeable stutter that arose when he got excited. Though that made public speaking difficult at first, he eventually got over it by talking to people more often.

Kendrick was a solid student who earned good grades and put his all into creative writing. Finally, he had an avenue to unpack his feelings—and Mr. Inge would play a major role in his intellectual growth. Kendrick had to work hard to perfect his craft, and Inge didn't take it easy on him. When Kendrick submitted his work in school, Inge would often send it back with visible prompts for the budding poet to dig deeper. Basic language wouldn't cut it; the young man needed to strengthen his lexicon before his prose could truly shine. "I would always circle something and say, 'Kendrick, change this, move this right here,'" Inge says.

Not one to be defeated by hard work, Kendrick took it as motivation to improve. He didn't just want to get by, he wanted to be the *best*, and that meant tapping into a level of focus he hadn't before. It meant pouring everything into his creative being and doing what he could to protect it. If he forgot to do his poetry assignment at home, he'd get to school early and do it there. Kendrick became obsessed with the written word, scribbling rap lyrics on notebook paper instead of finishing assignments for other classes. The lyrics were profane—all "'eff you' and 'd-i-c-k,'" his mother reportedly said—but that was Kendrick mining the seedy aspects of his upbringing to arrive at something more positive. "He was rapping about things he wasn't supposed to rap about," Jeezy says. "He was rapping about what he knew at the time—and that was drugs, gangbanging, and the streets. As we got older and started maturing, I saw him take the craft more seriously."

Kendrick started writing poems about the changes he went through as an adolescent beginning to understand the social dynamics of his neighborhood. His understanding of the world grew exponentially as he began to study other cultures and compare their experiences with his own to strengthen his art. Kendrick stopped writing to make others feel comfortable; instead, he chose to elevate his thinking and make people catch up to him.

By the time Kendrick got to high school, his career path was set. He was going to be a rapper, and nothing could make him veer off the course. One day in particular, Matt Jeezy and Kendrick were walking home from Centennial High School when the budding MC just couldn't stop rapping. He started coming up with rhymes off the top of his head, and he didn't stop until four or five blocks later, when he and Jeezy were close to their respective homes. "It was about twenty minutes' worth of rapping," Jeezy recalls. At that moment, his friend knew that Kendrick had what it took to be a star. All he needed to do was stay away from the pitfalls of street life. "I was like, 'Damn, Kendrick bro, if you just stay out of jail and stay alive, you're gonna make it.' The words that literally came out of my mouth were 'Don't go to jail. Don't die.'" Sadly, prison and death beset many of their friends.

And it wasn't like Kendrick didn't grapple with his own challenges: At age sixteen, he started running with the wrong crowd— partying and drinking alcohol. It was really just kid shit, the same thing teenagers had done for generations. But given Kendrick's neighborhood and family history, his behavior foreshadowed a possible life of crime and gang affiliation. Kenny wasn't having it; he'd come too far to watch his son fall victim to the same habits. "My father said, 'I don't want you to be like me,'" Kendrick told *Spin* in 2012. "He said, 'Things I have done, mistakes I've made, I never want you to make those mistakes. You can wind up out on the corner.' He knew by the company I [kept] what I was gettin' into. Out of respect, I really just gathered myself together." Kendrick adored his father and his loving, no-nonsense attitude. The two bonded over a love of Tupac and gangsta rap. Kenny let him experience triumph and tragedy and was there with real talk when Kendrick lost his way. He playfully coined his dad's advice as "intelligent ignorance." Many of his friends didn't have active fathers at home, but Kenny and Kendrick shared a close bond full of hard lessons and growing pains. He'd caution teenage Kendrick against going with his friends to burglarize houses in the neighborhood, and would be there with a swift "I told you so" when police accosted them before the crime unfolded. At times, Kenny tried to steer Kendrick's friends away from doing wrong. But because Kenny wasn't an actual father to those kids, the advice simply wouldn't stick, and some of them wound up in jail as a result. Of course, Kenny wasn't impeccable—he was a flawed human like the rest of us—but he had a good heart and truly wanted to do right by people.

Having supporters like Matt Jeezy and Mr. Inge helped Kendrick. They saw a light in the young man and helped him nurture it, even if it took the young poet a little while to fully embrace his truth. "Thinking back to when we were walking home from Centennial that one day," Jeezy wistfully recalls. "Look at him now, man. Look at him now."

In hip-hop, it's common for rappers to brag about themselves. It's not enough for them to simply say they're the best; by the end of the verse, you should know they can walk on water and turn it into wine. Or you have to be the toughest dude ever: *Mess around if you want, you can catch a bullet, too*. So Kendrick's earliest rhymes aren't surprising; he was imitating what he'd heard others do since the dawn of hip-hop culture, some thousands of miles away in the Bronx, long before he was born. On YouTube, there's a video clip of teenage Kendrick, cross earrings in each lobe, spitting aggressive rhymes while his friends stand directly behind him. He's in the middle of a cypher, and on certain punch lines, he looks away and smirks, as if he *knows* he's the best. He tugs the hood of his sweatshirt, letting it rest sluggishly on the crown of his razor-sharp waves. He studies the lens, gaping at it with the confidence of a seasoned veteran. This was exercise for Kendrick, who, at this stage of his career, wanted to come off as a street guy. "Creep into ya house, you hear footsteps slowly as I tippy-toe," he asserted through squinted eyes and gapped teeth. "I'm wise like my pops but I'm young, muthafuckas / I'm the one, muthafuckas / Plus around hustlers, you want it? They can serve you like a butler." The claim sends his friends into a frenzy, so much so that Kendrick can't even finish his verse. Their reaction proves that he is very much the people's champion, and that those closest to him truly have his back. He was born to the streets, so his rhymes feel authentic. In those days, maybe he *would* run up in your house.

Still, there was something missing from Kendrick's flow—and that was Kendrick himself. He rapped under the name K-Dot, his fire-spitting alter ego. K-Dot wasn't about uplifting communities; he wanted to decimate everything in sight. The young man had all the technical prowess, the complex sentence structures, and the

natural cadence, but he didn't sound *free*. He was playing a character, and the fastest way to get noticed was to sound like the higher-
profile rappers who dominated hip-hop. He wasn't playing the long
game yet. He hadn't realized that the truest path to immortality
was to be his fully authentic self. Good, honest music has this way
of reaching the right ears; it finds people exactly when they need
to hear it. Though Kendrick would come to understand this years
later, back then he seemed eager to ascend to the top before he had
a full grasp of what it took to remain there.

To understand Kendrick's approach, you have to understand
hip-hop's period of transition at this time. The year was 2003, and
acts like 50 Cent, OutKast, and the Diplomats loomed large in the
music industry. Hip-hop was a global business, and rappers with
the biggest pull were tapped to sell everything from malt liquor to
high-end clothing. "Cool" was in fashion, and no one was cooler
than Shawn "Jay-Z" Carter, a poised, slick-talking MC who went
from selling crack cocaine in East Trenton, New Jersey, to becoming the most popular mainstream rapper in the world. Jay-Z wasn't
only a rapper; he was a paragon of business, lyricism, and swag-
ger. "I'm not a businessman, I'm a business, man," he once claimed
on Kanye West's song "Diamonds from Sierra Leone (Remix)."
He was a king who'd spent the past five years on the throne, and
through albums like *Vol. 2 . . . Hard Knock Life*, *Vol. 3 . . . Life and
Times of S. Carter*, and *The Blueprint*, Jay-Z cornered the market on
all things hip-hop culture. He gave fans everything: moody street
songs, antagonistic battle raps aimed at other lyricists, and polished
pop-leaning tunes made for summertime consumption. He lived
atop the *Billboard* charts, and for a while, it seemed as if his reign

would last forever. No one could defeat Jay; the only way he could lose the crown was if he gave it up himself.

That's just what happened in early 2003, when Jay-Z announced that his eighth studio record, *The Black Album*, would be his last. Retirement was on the horizon and, in Jay's own words, he was headed to a life of golfing and drinking cappuccinos away from the rat race of the music industry. This wasn't just *any* retirement; this was like basketball icon Michael Jordan quitting in his prime, or football legend Jim Brown leaving with a lot left in the tank. It became too easy for Jay-Z to win and he was bored with it all. Rap music was too formulaic; everyone's albums sounded alike, and the singles they released largely fit the same format. It was all too clean—sterile, even. We couldn't hear the grit of old soul samples, the pop and hiss of worn vinyl beneath searing social commentary. But rappers weren't as hungry; hip-hop was a force in the mainstream and it was time to celebrate through the music.

In the early nineties, groups like the Wu-Tang Clan and Mobb Deep made rap dark, but even they couldn't navigate the genre's changing tide, and by the late nineties and early aughts, they struggled to stay relevant and saw their popularity diminish. So while Jay lamented the state of hip-hop, he helped usher its demise: he and Sean "Puff Daddy" Combs made rap sound lustrous, and there wasn't as much soul in the music. In the 1980s, back when rap was a nascent genre, the music had been rooted to the ongoing challenges in poor communities and addressed the hardships of growing up broke and beating the odds to make it out alive. Rap music was born of struggle, tethered to the flames of burning buildings in its native New York City. It was the sound of blackness, in all its unfiltered joy, pain, and celebration. It conversed with those trapped inside cramped apartments with big dreams. Rap was everything, and to young black people who didn't have a voice, it was a way to emote without fear. Hip-hop was counterculture, much like psychedelic rock was in the mid- to late sixties, and punk in the late seventies. Over the next thirty years, rap would slowly replace rock as the expression of disgruntled youth in the United States, even as critics tried to forecast its demise.

Jay's retirement leveled the playing field for everyone else, and Kendrick—the baby-faced rookie that he was—wanted Jay's spot. If Kendrick's ambition wasn't clear in his bars, with all the cocky bravado they exuded, he said it directly on his first mixtape, *Hub City Threat: Minor of the Year (Youngest Head Nigga in Charge)*. He demanded the attention. He *needed* it. He even ripped a few beats from Jay's discography for his own debut project as a way to make an immediate splash. "Jay left, now gimme the crown / *Fuck* later, I'm takin' it *now*," Kendrick declared on "Hovi Baby," over an instrumental that Jay had used for his own album *The Blueprint 2: The Gift & the Curse*.

Hub City Threat was an introduction in the truest sense, a teaser on which the burgeoning MC simply wanted to brag about his ability to put words together. On the tape, credited as Kendrick's DJ, was a guy named Dave Free, whose voice surfaced occasionally to plod alongside the protagonist. Like Kendrick, Free wanted to succeed in the music industry. He met Kendrick in the tenth grade after his friend Antonio told him about the upstart lyricist. "He was telling me he had a friend who went to Centennial that was the craziest," Free once said. "I was intrigued. I told him, 'Bring him through.'"

Free had a makeshift studio in his house, where he first heard Kendrick rap. "Everybody back then was talking about drugs," Free told Google Play in a 2012 documentary about *good kid, m.A.A.d city*. "But he had this one line—'I ship keys like a piano,' or something like that, and I just thought that was the most amazing line for somebody his age." That was the line that made Free want to work with Kendrick.

From there, the two bonded over rap music and a love of *Martin*, a cult-favorite TV sitcom starring comedian Martin Lawrence, and were fascinated with how he created superior black art with limited means. Eventually, Free and Kendrick put that same energy into their visual work as a creative duo. They'd call themselves the Little Homies, and instead of spending tons of money on their videos (at least not at first), they went heavy on vast landscapes and profound imagery that had a much deeper impact on the black community. But back in 2003, they were eager to succeed in music—perhaps *too* eager by Kendrick's own concession—and recorded *Hub City Threat* as a way to escape the dangers of life in Compton. Even at a young age, Kendrick had the technical prowess of Jay-Z and the work ethic of a man with nothing to lose. He'd spent countless hours with his craft—studying, thinking, and becoming one with it.

In Carson, California—some nine miles from Compton—was a guy named Anthony "Top Dawg" Tiffith. He was from Nickerson Gardens, an infamous housing project in Watts known for its wall of names that honored the building's dead residents. Tiffith was an intimidating presence, a tall and stoic dude who'd spent his early days as a hustler. Yet by 1997, he was beginning to grow tired of the lifestyle and wanted to do something more legitimate. Plus, the streets were getting a little too hot. Tiffith decided to get into music after he saw his uncle, Mike Concepcion, have success with it. In 1990, Concepcion produced the song "We're All in the Same Gang," which featured rappers like Ice-T, Dr. Dre, MC Ren, Eazy-E, and MC Hammer promoting a message of antiviolence. Concepcion was an original member of the Crips in South Central who had gone legit in the 1980s and became a quiet force behind some of the most remarkable music from the West Coast. "Uncle Mike helped me with pretty much all of this. I watched him do music, so it made me think, that's a way out," Tiffith once told *Vibe*. "I watched him in the streets; I wanted to do that. . . . He had everything that inspired me. He taught me so many things." Concepcion taught Tiffith how to be stealthy, that true power is quiet and not loud. As he once told *Billboard*, "He was always like, 'Be low-key. Don't be no loud nigga.'" Tiffith governed himself by this mentality, and even as his popularity grew, he remained a mysterious figure in the industry. As a result, he was unfairly compared with another stoic label owner, Death Row Records CEO Marion Hugh "Suge" Knight Jr. But where Suge earned his reputation as a hothead and an erratic leader, Tiffith played the background and let his artists take center stage.

Tiffith constructed a studio space in the rear of his Carson house, and stocked it with high-end recording equipment as a way to attract big-name rappers. He also wanted it to be a hub for burgeoning talent, though it wouldn't be that right away. The streets still tugged at Tiffith and he abandoned the space not long after he furnished it. "It was inactive," Tiffith's cousin Terrence "Punch" Henderson Jr. told *XXL* in 2012. "Top Dawg was doing Top Dawg things."

Tiffith named the company after himself, calling it Top Dawg Entertainment. Once he fully dedicated himself to music, he started working with a producer named Demetrius Shipp, who had made his reputation as an in-house beatmaker for West Coast power-house Death Row Records, and whose son, Demetrius Shipp Jr., would later play Tupac Shakur in a big-screen biopic. That con-nection helped legitimize Tiffith's operation; soon after, rappers like The Game and Juvenile (a southern rap legend who helped put New Orleans hip-hop on the national map) ventured to the upstart studio. "Game came through before he really kicked off," Tiffith told *XXL*. "Juvenile came through there, and a couple of other rap dudes came through. We were just trying to sling tracks to them." Tiffith was trying to win like everyone else, and his work ethic made him an immediate force in the underground scene. He wanted to get his label's music to anyone who'd listen, and his expe-rience as a hustler gave him the fortitude to deal with the ups and downs of life in the industry. Dave Free was equally tenacious; in Tiffith's Top Dawg Entertainment, he saw a man who was incredi-bly serious about building and sustaining a viable company. He had the connections and the willpower to win, and Free needed to get Kendrick's music to Tiffith however he could.

One day, Free—then working as a computer technician—got a call from Tiffith to fix his computer. A few minutes after Free arrived, he realized he couldn't salvage the mogul's machine but didn't want to squander this opportunity. Who knew if they'd be in the same room together again? As Free worked, or at least looked like he worked, he played Kendrick's music loud enough for Tiffith to hear it, and by the end of the job—when Free finally admitted he couldn't repair the device—Tiffith was eager to hear more. Except, next time, it would have to be in a live setting where he could assess the bars for himself. Kendrick had to freestyle for Tiffith and wow him on the spot.

This was the shot Kendrick had been waiting for; his first grand moment. Once in the vocal booth, Kendrick freestyled off and on in Tiffith's studio for what seemed like forever: "Top said, 'Let me see if this is really you,' and I was just freestyling, rapping whatever came into my head, sweating for two hours." Tiffith was so taken by Kendrick's ability, that—at just sixteen years old—he was fully grown as a rapper, even if he didn't know how to write an actual song yet. As Tiffith told *Vibe*: "I put him in the booth and put this double time beat on, trying to throw him off. He went in there and started going off! So I'm trying to play like I'm not paying attention. He notices I'm not moving and starts going crazy. So I look up and I'm like, 'God damn. He's a monster.' So the next day I had a contract for him." Kendrick's signing with Tiffith raised a few eyebrows, though. The rapper grew up on the west side of Compton, and the local Pirus had beef with the Bounty Hunter Bloods, of which Tiffith was a member. "For Kendrick to sign with a dude from the Bounty Hunters and from Watts, people were looking at him like, 'What are you doing?'" says Matt Jeezy. "They were looking at it from the wrong perspective."

By 2004, there wasn't a true King of West Coast Rap like there had been in years past. Ice Cube was focused on acting. Dr. Dre was more concerned with running his record label, Aftermath Entertainment, than putting out his own music. Snoop Dogg was still around, but he was more preoccupied with pimp life than hip-hop.

In a 2006 *Rolling Stone* article, he spoke of how his marriage almost ended due to the lifestyle, until a few pimps at a Players Ball in Detroit told him to go home to his wife. So the icons were preoccupied, leaving the field wide open for new talent to vie for the region's top spot. The epicenter of West Coast rap shifted north—from Los Angeles to the Bay Area of San Francisco and Oakland, where the hyphy—or "crunk"—movement was in full swing, and hip-hop started to blend with dance-oriented genres like funk and "crunk music," which used accelerated rhythms made for vigorous dancing. West Coast hip-hop—and hip-hop overall—was bigger, louder, and more in-your-face, and through the stewardship of Bay Area pioneers like Vallejo rapper Mac Dre and Keak da Sneak, hyphy became the sound of California. It was the subgenre of flash, humor, and bravado, and for the first time since the 1990s, the laid-back aggression of L.A. gangsta rap had taken a backseat in its home state. It seemed the industry didn't have the same palate for the gripping social commentary and tough-minded lyricism that put Cali hip-hop on the map in the first place. That didn't stop rappers like Kendrick from upholding the glory of the past.

A Compton-born lyricist named Jayceon Taylor—known creatively as The Game—would ascend to the fore as L.A. rap's newfound savior. He was considered a throwback, and his arrival recalled the cold-blooded imagery and steely bravado of the 1980s and '90s. He also had something that very few rappers received in Los Angeles: a cosign from the elusive Dr. Dre. By the early 2000s, Dre was a mythical figure, and to have his blessing was to be touched by the right hand of a divine being. His golden ear was proven: In the early nineties, Dre let a skinny unproven kid from Long Beach rap on a number of his songs—including the ominous "Deep Cover," "Fuck wit Dre Day (And Everybody's Celebratin')," and the silky "Nuthin' but a 'G' Thang." His name was Snoop Doggy Dogg. Then, in the late nineties, Dre signed an unknown rapper who'd been making waves in the underground circuit as the talented white lyricist with a penchant for tongue-twisting flows and outlandish imagery. His name was Eminem. In 2005, The Game released his debut album, *The Documentary*, and its commercial success brought renewed interest to gangsta rap in L.A. The glory days were back, and there was a sense that his prosperity would open the door for like-minded rappers to walk through.

The Game served as a mentor to the younger generation of L.A. lyricists, and for a while, he was the main guy looking out for MCs like Kendrick and Nipsey Hussle in the city. The Game was paying it forward, just like the local heroes had before him, and just like Kendrick and Nipsey would do in subsequent years. The Game was an overachiever who believed in hard work as the foundation of everlasting success. Likewise, unfazed by internet buzz and fleeting fame, Kendrick wanted to rule forever, and the only way to do that was to make sure his rhymes were incredibly sharp. He also benefited from the "SoundCloud era" of hip-hop, in which rappers could forgo the old ways of making it in the music industry. Because the internet was the great neutralizer, anyone with Wi-Fi could upload their music to the wildly popular Sound-Cloud streaming service and find immediate celebrity. The internet offered immediate access to fans without the filter of a record label or some tastemaker to cosign the music first. Kendrick didn't have to be visible, and that notion would dictate his career.

Observers in the L.A. rap scene were introduced to Kendrick much like the rest of us elsewhere, as the mysterious kid whose sound was incredibly tough to pin down but was remarkably pleasant to the ear. But that aesthetic cut both ways for Kendrick. Yeah, he could rhyme, but who was he really? Which was the real Kendrick? There was no grand breakthrough for him; rather, he rose through word-of-mouth praise that slowly trickled through the community and made him a cult hero. It was better that way, in fact: this approach gave Kendrick the creative freedom to grow authentically in front of the people who knew him best, the local folks who saw him as Kenny and Paula's son, the quiet, driven boy from the neighborhood. In turn, they wanted only the best for Kendrick, and regardless of the potential fame and fortune coming his way, the people of Compton rallied around the young man—for the most part. Because gangsta rap ruled there, some chided the MC for not honoring the city's musical lineage. To get love from the neighborhood, you almost *had* to be a gangbanger, and Kendrick stopped just short of perpetrating the lifestyle.

Kendrick was actually the second musician Tiffith signed to the label. In 2005, Tiffith had signed a guy named Jay Rock, a rapper and fellow Nickerson Gardens native who'd been recording songs with other local lyricists and generated a buzz. Tiffith heard Jay Rock's music and literally drove around looking for the upstart lyricist to invite him to his studio. "I was chasing him around and he hides, thinking I'm trying to discipline him about some bullshit," Tiffith told *Billboard* in 2017. "I finally catch him while he was getting a haircut: 'Yo, you rap. I'm trying to do this shit. Let's go.'" Jay walked into the deal having known Kendrick from Centennial

High School, where Jay had friends and would skip classes at his own school to spend time at Kendrick's. However, there was slight tension between Kendrick and Jay in the early days, as their respective neighborhoods had beef and the two rappers didn't know how to respond to each other. "With me being the big homie," Tiffith once said, "you guys can bridge the gap between the hood, because y'all can speak to the world now. You can get some money and change all this gangbang shit." The ice soon melted between the two, and soon enough, they spent many hours together in Tiffith's studio, later dubbed the "House of Pain," testing each other bar for bar in the tiny, unassuming space. Jay often tells the story of his first creative interaction with Kendrick, when he caught his first glimpse of the Compton native's transcendent talent. "I'm writing on a piece of paper, and it's taking me damn near 30 or 40 minutes to write like two, three lines," he recalled. "And [Kendrick] just goes in there in five minutes. Dropped my name in the song and all that . . . I'm like, 'Damn, how you just go in there and don't even write this shit down?' From that moment on, I knew he was something special."

That year, Kendrick put out a second mixtape titled *Training Day* under the name K-Dot, and by then he had more real-life experiences to draw from. The bars didn't feel so contrived, and his personality began to emerge. He came into his own inside Tiffith's studio, which became a proving ground for Kendrick and Jay Rock to sharpen their skills, and a safe haven to escape what was happening outside. In 2005 alone, some seventy-two people were killed in Compton, which marked the highest death toll in the city in ten years. One resident was reportedly bludgeoned to death in his home, and a woman—who was eight months pregnant—was gunned down. And those were some of the milder incidents. The sheriff's department's gang officials reported 282 shootings and attempted murders in Compton through much of the year, which led many to believe that city and county leaders were oblivious to what was happening in Compton. Despite the very public spotlight that N.W.A cast on Compton's societal ills, there was a notion that the government simply didn't care about black and brown lives within the town limits. Young black men were dying or going to jail at an alarming rate, and if Kendrick and Jay could just make it to Tiffith's place, they could harness the uncertainty of life in Watts and Compton into beautiful art that could impact generations for years to come. For Kendrick, that harkened back to the teachings of Mr. Inge: *Put your pain into the poetry; transfer that stress to the page.*

Kendrick had time to funnel his angst inside a hub that was completely free to use, and that gave him and Jay Rock the proper space to conceptualize different ideas. Unlike other studio heads who charged exorbitant amounts for the use of their facilities, Tiffith didn't rush his creators to beat a clock before some other dude came through. The music had time to gestate, and in turn, it came out better. In these quiet moments, Tiffith was building a genuine rapport with his artists. It felt more like family than a business relationship. It was there that Top Dawg sowed the seeds of an empire through tough love, fairness, and unwavering respect.

Around the same time, Tiffith opened his studio to another rising prospect: producer Mark Spears, a recent graduate of Compton High School, who made beats under the name Sounwave. He was brought into the fold by Punch Henderson, who'd been a friend of his family for years. Punch used to play basketball with Sounwave's older brother in the backyard, and one day during a break in the action, he heard the then-thirteen-year-old making beats in his room using Sony PlayStation's MTV Music Generator. "He was like, 'Yo, you make beats? My cousin [is] Top Dawg, you know,'" Spears recalled during a lecture with Red Bull Music Academy in 2019. "I didn't know who [Top] was at the time." Spears went to Tiffith's studio and played him a few instrumentals, some of which were "trash," by the producer's own admission. "[He] was like, 'This ain't it, but since Punch is cosigning you, I'm gonna give you a chance. Take these a capellas, see what you [can] do.' I took that as a challenge. I took my time, and the next day I brought it back to him, and he was like, 'Yo, this is better than the original. I'll mess with you.' That was about 2005, and I've just been rocking ever since."

Sounwave met Kendrick the year prior during a talent showcase at a studio in Gardena, California. The producer was asked to cue up one of his beats; he played a remake of an old soul track by a group named Aalon. Kendrick was so taken by the beat that he walked into the recording booth and started rapping for two minutes straight—a freestyle mixed with rhymes he'd already written. "He was the hungriest person I'd seen in my whole life," Sounwave once told *Rolling Stone*. "I had to stop the beat and ask him his name." "K-Dot," the young rapper retorted. A year later, Sounwave was at Tiffith's studio when he saw a familiar face; there was Kendrick sitting on the couch, waiting to audition for the collective. The two had been looking for each other since that fateful encounter at the Gardena space. And while Kendrick deserves credit for seizing the moment, he also has Sounwave to thank for staying in Tiffith's ear: "I looked at [him] and said, 'I met this kid a year ago, you definitely can't let this dude go, it's fate right here. We have to keep him, do whatever you have to do to sign him.'"

Tiffith's studio soon became a sanctuary to other young guys looking to jump-start their careers. In 2006, a guy named Terrace Martin started coming to the studio. He was a prodigious talent who had learned how to play jazz from the great Reggie Andrews at Locke High School, and had been making beats on his own. By the time he started working with TDE in 2006 (though he wasn't signed there), Martin was a producer and multi-instrumentalist in jazz, soul, and hip-hop. He remembers walking through the gate at Tiffith's house, then to the back room, where he'd hear Jay Rock and Kendrick rapping in the studio booth. "It was a fun, everyday creative collective," Martin recalls. "It was also work. It's the ultimate test of humility, because the ultimate ego is the music." He also remembers the phone calls from Tiffith: "If Top give you one of them phone calls, it's serious. When he has a deadline, he means that deadline. And the deadline could be two hours from now. You gotta get it done. With TDE, I learned to always expect the unexpected."

That same year, a twenty-year-old Carson native who rapped under the name Ab-Soul made his way to the famed studio. Two years prior, he'd inked a deal with a small local label called Street-Beat Entertainment that hadn't borne fruit. As soon as that deal expired, Ab went to TDE at the behest of Sounwave, who knew the rapper through his cousin. In a 2012 interview with Complex, Ab remembered why he was so drawn to TDE: "They weren't coming at me talking no paperwork.... We were really just trying to build as a team and try to create a new sound." And if Ab thought he was the best rapper alive when he joined TDE, he soon discovered that wasn't the case at all. Ab met Jay Rock and Kendrick his second time at the studio, where he saw the TDE members working on music for their joint mixtape, *No Sleep Til NYC*. "I hopped right in and we've been a team since then."

Derek Ali, of Gardena, was an All-American football player in high school who used to disassemble his computers just to see how they worked. The seventeen-year-old learned of Tiffith's collective from Dave Free, whom he saw passing out Jay Rock CDs at his high school. Ali told Free that he wanted to get into the music business; Free invited Ali to Tiffith's studio to learn more. He never left. Back then, though, Ali didn't have the skills to engineer; he knew only how to record his friends' raps for custom ringtones, not steer the sound of a full-on hip-hop album. Plus, Ali needed to make personal changes. He'd recently been kicked out of his grandmother's house and needed to be part of something real. "I was doing bad," Ali recalls. "I'm seventeen, wet behind the ears, still stumbling over my left foot." But working with Tiffith, Sounwave, Free, Jay Rock, and Kendrick gave him confidence. It also straightened him up; nonsense wasn't tolerated in TDE's vicinity. "You don't want to bring no shit to [Tiffith]'s house," Ali asserts. "There's the respect that we have for him because of the opportunity he was giving us. All [of] us ran away from the streets to find somewhere else to kind of call home, and he had that for us. If it wasn't for Top, we wouldn't have a house to connect. It was a real collective thing that really happened that kind of catapulted all of us into our respective careers."

Ali had a friend before his TDE days named Quincy Hanley who spit raps under the name ScHoolboy Q. He was a member of the 52 Hoover Crips who gangbanged from the age of twelve until a few months before his debut album, *Setbacks*, was released. Q wrote his first rap verse at the age of sixteen but didn't get serious about the craft until five years later. Around 2006, Ali had Q come through TDE's studio. "I walked in and the beat was playing. Ali told them that I rap," he recalled in a Complex interview. "Punch told me to jump on the beat. It was a record that Jay Rock and Ab-Soul were writing to, so then I wrote [to] it. Punch liked it and he told me to come back through. I kept coming back, kept getting better, and eventually they signed me to TDE."

With his core in place, Tiffith had the makings of a dynasty, and though they had to endure some hardship, that was the truest way for them to grow as men and for TDE to become stronger as a unit. This was boot camp, and domination was the ultimate goal. They convened in the small studio and worked nonstop to fine-tune their music. There was even a list of serious—yet hilarious—rules on the wall outside the studio:

- If you ain't one of the homies don't be Instagramming you creepy muthafucka. I don't wanna look on yo twitter and find a creepy ass pic of me or one of the homies, matter of fact, No Twitter or Instagram in the studio! Act like you been around a bunch of rich niggaz from the bottom before!
- If the homies just met you and decide to clown your bitch azz, sit there and deal with it. It's part of the creative juices.
- Don't touch, ask, or reach for Q's weed, unless he thinks you cool enuff to pass it to you. We only smoke stersonals around here, boy.

- Shut up and look ugly for the homies.
- Remember these rules and you might get a meal out the food budget!

As you can see, the TDE squad wasn't always so poker-faced; they liked to play pranks on each other and ridicule strangers who tried to impede their creative space. Kendrick had a great sense of humor, though you had to be close to him to know it. Like any introvert, the musician wasn't going to show his personality to just *anybody*. No, you had to be in the circle to watch him re-create old MySpace photos by superimposing himself in the shots. And years later, when Twitter became the world's top social media platform, Punch implored Kendrick to flex his humor there—to no avail. By 2013, Tiffith would bring two other top talents to TDE: a Tennessee-born rapper named Isaiah Rashad, and a New Jersey–raised singer named Solána Rowe, who went by the name SZA. Soon enough, TDE would be the most revered crew in music.

Tiffith's mentality came from his own coming-of-age during the height of gang activity in L.A., when many of his friends were dying or going to prison for long amounts of time. But he envisioned something different for the TDE roster. "I had the money to do whatever I wanted, but they weren't going to appreciate shit if I just handed it off to them," Tiffith once told *Billboard*. "So they were rushing to McDonald's to look at what's on the dollar menu, or going to get a River Boat special from Louisiana Fried Chicken. But I was showing them family life because my family lives in this house, too." The rappers survived on greasy poultry, biscuits, and coleslaw, but if they wanted to reach the promised land, they needed to revel in the pain. They had to embrace it to truly value the awards that arrived later. Just like other musical empires—the Beatles, Motown, Dr. Dre—the guys locked themselves in and developed their own distinctive sound, which had never been just one genre. Sure, it was rooted in rap, but TDE never wanted to be boxed in as artists or as black men. "We gave you all of these elements," Sounwave says. "So to this day, [Kendrick] can do whatever the hell he wants to do. It's strategic moves like that, and just the brotherhood of us being in that small little room forever." This was long before TDE had to be great, before fans of black music, then the world, paid attention to the squad's every move. In the House of Pain was the hope of better days and the promise of a brighter future—not just for Kendrick, but for everyone at TDE.

3

The Birth of Kendrick Lamar

In 2007, Jay Rock was the first from TDE to sign with a label when he inked a deal with Asylum Records, a subsidiary of Warner Music Group. The label had a handful of respected rappers at the time, including the Atlanta-based Gucci Mane and OJ da Juiceman. Southern hip-hop had taken off, and Jay Rock, a West Coast gangsta rapper through and through, didn't fit the profile of what label executives wanted at the time. Enter Richie Abbott, an executive at the Warner Group who'd spent years putting out music from his native Los Angeles; he wanted to push Jay Rock as the next big star to emerge from Southern California. The Watts MC was beginning to work with other noted rappers while putting out his own well-received mixtapes. Abbott remembers Jay, Tiffith, Punch, Kendrick, Q, and Ab-Soul working from his office three days out of the week, essentially making his office their own, turning it into a hub for TDE business. Kendrick rarely spoke in the office, only smiling occasionally when he played his music for Abbott. "He loved to get my reaction to it," the executive recalls.

In 2008, Jay dropped his first commercial single, the autobiographical "All My Life (In the Ghetto)," which featured rapper Lil Wayne at the height of his power. The track was receiving radio airplay and TV time, and Jay Rock was poised to be TDE's first breakout star. According to some close to Jay, it became clear that Warner had no interest in pushing him: *XXL*, the tastemaking hip-hop magazine, put him on the cover of its 2010 "Freshmen" issue and dubbed him an artist to be reckoned with, but Warner didn't even pay for him to fly to New York for the shoot. Then the money for Jay's promo was halted and apparently reallocated to OJ da Juiceman. "Top was pissed," Abbott recalls. "This was their chance, this was their time. They flew OJ out to the shoot, but they wouldn't fly Jay Rock. That's when I was like, 'Okay, this shit is over.'" Jay Rock's momentum halted, and so did plans to release his debut album, *Follow Me Home*, which was supposed to be his breakthrough. Disheartened, Abbott started making moves behind the scenes to get himself and Jay Rock away from the Warner Group.

Abbott had started working with a record label out of Kansas City, Missouri, called Strange Music, which was cofounded by a hardcore rapper named Tech N9ne. Tech was a ball of fire, an affable man who took no prisoners onstage and proved several times that he was one of the baddest MCs on the planet. Abbott took Jay Rock's music to him, and while aesthetically it didn't seem like a good fit, signing with Strange Music made the most sense back then. The Strange Music fan base was largely comprised of white kids who liked hard rock, a demographic to which Jay Rock hadn't connected before. But Tech's fans were rabid and they loved deeply. Says Abbott, "It wasn't his core audience, but anything you bring onstage, they'll go nuts for it unless it's shit." By the fall of 2010, Jay Rock found himself in front of thousands of Tech N9ne's fans, opening for the cult favorite during Strange Music's nationwide Independent Grind Tour, gracing the same stages with label rappers Krizz Kaliko, Kutt Calhoun, and Big Scoob, and Oakland stalwart E-40.

During a tour stop in Reno, Nevada, Jay Rock's cousin and hype man, MJ, walked off the tour bus after a show to call his lady. A group of guys, who hadn't even attended the concert, saw MJ wearing a red shirt—the same color the Bloods wore—and decided to cause trouble with the performer. Shots rang out and MJ was hit. Days later, Tech and MJ were on the phone celebrating the fact that he hadn't died that night, and that they'd have to celebrate when he rejoined the tour from the hospital. But MJ never left the building; he died from a blood clot. "It was a bad day, a really bad day," Tech N9ne recalls. Not only had Jay Rock lost his cousin, but he had lost his hype man for the tour.

But Jay had a solution. "He said, 'I got someone else who could help me. He's usually onstage with me,'" Tech remembers Jay Rock saying. "That's the day I met Kendrick." He took over as Jay Rock's hype man, pumping up the crowd during Jay's set and occasionally performing his own music. The time on the road taught Jay and Kendrick how to perform, and how to turn what they'd recorded in the studio into a captivating live show. It wasn't enough to simply go up and shout rhymes to the masses; the TDE guys had to be different. Kendrick studied Tech N9ne to make his set—which, back then, was just a few songs from his first few mixtapes—much more engaging. "He said he watched every night to understand what it meant to be an entertainer," says Tech. Adds Abbott, "Kendrick was legitimately interested in finding out everything he could about the business." He wanted to know everything about everyone, their roles and exact contributions to the concert experience: "He was a sponge. Everybody was on the bus drinking and kicking it, but he was on the side stage, asking a lot of questions."

It's no surprise then that Kendrick became *Kendrick*. Greatness is achieved in moments like these, behind the curtain when no one is looking. It's not enough to simply desire such brilliance; you have to be consumed with it, letting it permeate the core of your very being. It's the old 10,000-hour rule that author Malcolm Gladwell once wrote about, that you master your craft by practicing it over and over again, and true expertise arrives once you reach 10,000 hours of application. Basketball legend Kobe Bryant was well known for this line of thinking; if you're putting up 500 jump shots in a day, he's shooting 1,000. And while you're relaxing, he's on the court—just him and a basketball, practicing his fadeaway, his postgame, and his layups near the rim. For him, basketball was everything, and being good wasn't enough. Kendrick took the same approach with learning the music industry, achieving greatness through tireless dedication to his career. He knew he had something that could change the world, but talent without hard work couldn't get him to the top. Somewhere alone, away from the noise, Kendrick was planting the seeds of a career. "He was Kobe shooting in the gym," Abbott says.

The Butterfly Effect

Before the Independent Grind Tour, Kendrick didn't even know how to dress for the stage: he'd come out wearing knitted, hooded sweatshirts, frayed jean shorts, and Crocs sandals. "Real hippie," Tech N9ne remembers. But those days up and down the road taught Kendrick a lot about discipline and how to operate with quiet, intentional force. The guys at Strange Music operated like the military: go over your set time by a minute and your pay is docked. The Tech crew ran a tight ship, and ten years after the Grind Tour, TDE operated in similar fashion—silent and steadfast, almost machinelike, with the strictest attention to detail and perfection as the ultimate goal. Where other rappers dropped new music at a furious clip, TDE artists stressed quality over quantity, eschewing the speed at which others released their work. The internet was insatiable; anything more than two months old was considered yesterday's news. So there was something quite noble about TDE's nonchalant pace in an industry that craved new material right away. Silence of any sort is deafening, and because the collective didn't say much—or anything, really—between album releases, TDE built a level of intrigue that became its own kind of marketing. Their releases became events; with each new album came a wave of hysteria that ended with massive sales and shiny gold trophies.

Still, it was tough for TDE; the sting of the failed Jay Rock deal lingered and they were unclear where to steer next. Jay had been the first with even the slightest glimmer of shine, and through his opportunity, Kendrick had gotten an early taste of the business alongside men who'd eventually become his brothers. These were the guys with whom he had come into the game, and they were all learning on the fly. That suited Kendrick just fine; he'd always prided himself on loyalty and working hard behind the scenes. He'd sleep on floors, rewrite *hundreds* of rhymes, and stay in the studio until 4:00 a.m. on a school night if that was what it took. It also helped that Tiffith, Jay Rock, and Sounwave were genuine people who wanted only the best for the unit. A win for one of them was a win for all of them, yet in the early days, it was tough to see the road ahead. The Jay Rock experiment hadn't worked as well as intended, forcing TDE to head back to the lab and keep working. There wasn't as much interest in Jay Rock's *Follow Me Home* by the time it was released in 2011. "People don't understand, we did a lot of trial and error with Jay Rock," Sounwave recalls. "He was the first person out of TDE, so a lot of our mistakes happened, unfortunately, on [him]." Jay didn't regret those days, though. As he saw it, he was building up a name for himself and TDE, kicking down doors for Kendrick and company to walk through.

Somewhere around 2009, Kendrick decided to drop the name K-Dot and start rapping under his first and middle names: Kendrick Lamar. K-Dot was a rapper's rapper, a lyrical assassin with a penchant for raw, chase-cutting lyrics. "K-Dot—this was me prepping myself as far as the lyrical ability and being able to go in the studio and say you know what, I want to be the best wordsmith. Anybody who gets on this track I just have to annihilate, however that is, whether it's through rhyme schemes, whether it's through metaphors, whether it's just punchlines, or whether it's wordplay," Lamar told Complex in 2017. "I didn't have the actual technique of songwriting then." Kendrick was the man behind the bravado, still trying to reconcile his insecurities in a world that doesn't reward vulnerability from black men. K-Dot was a freestyle machine ready to battle anyone at a moment's notice. Kendrick was all heart, and with mixtapes *Hub City Threat* and *Training Day* in his rearview, he finally had room to tell *his* story. He saw pushback from some who didn't think he was the guy to take L.A. rap to the next level. "A lot of people in the neighborhood didn't think his music would hit," says Matt Jeezy. "But those same people shout him out now when he comes back home. They were like, 'Man, this shit ain't gon' go. He ain't keeping it gangsta, he ain't talking about the streets.'"

Bloggers weren't feeling it, either: by the time Kendrick released his third solo mixtape, *C4*, in early 2009, it was clear that the K-Dot moniker had run its course, and that it was time for Kendrick to actually talk about something worthwhile. Though *C4* was marketed as an homage to Lil Wayne's recently released *Tha Carter III* album, Kendrick's project felt redundant, and was a weird creative step, given the buzz he had begun to generate on his own. At this point, he didn't need to rip a bunch of beats from a star like Wayne; he had the production team in place to start crafting his own artistic vision. The criticism got to Kendrick in a big way; in interviews and on his subsequent project, *The Kendrick Lamar EP*, he took subtle shots at the naysayers trying to throw dirt on his shine. He was at a cross-roads, and he had to look in the mirror to assess who he wanted to be as an artist.

Then it hit him. "I'mma just be me," Jeezy recalls Kendrick saying. The name change was the rightful next phase of his development, the best way for the Compton lyricist to become a fully realized musician and not just another cool rapper with one foot in the streets. As he once put it, "I think I was put on this Earth just to do music. I think God made me to spread my voice to the world, straight up." It didn't take long for Kendrick to sell Tiffith on the name change; in fact, the Top Dawg leader was on board right away. He joked that the name "Kendrick Lamar" sounded like some sort of designer fragrance you'd find at a Macy's retail store. "Like, that sounds like cologne—we can sell that shit!" Kendrick once told *Billboard* of his conversation with Tiffith. The name change marked not just a shift for Kendrick but a turning point for TDE overall. The idea was to give the public just a little piece of his backstory while saving the rest for his proper debut album, *good kid, m.A.A.d city*, which he'd already started preparing three years before its eventual release.

In December 2009, *The Kendrick Lamar EP* drew listeners into the singular talent who'd grow to become the world's best rapper. This was the first step toward that lofty acclaim, and was the first time he'd discuss himself and those closest to him in any kind of detail. "It's like I don't think y'all fully understand who I am, ya know? / I'm just a good kid from Compton who wanna rap," he declared on "Wanna Be Heard," a standout from the EP. "I don't represent no colors, I represent my little sisters and brothers." For the first time, people got a true glimpse of the kid who had watched the film *House Party* on TV and eaten Apple Jacks cereal in his parents' house. He had sold Sega video games while other family members sold illegal drugs. We heard about his beloved uncle Bobby, who got his life together after fifteen years in prison, only for it to change for the worse following a claim of domestic violence. Then there was the story of Jason Keaton, a West Side Piru who wrote a letter to Kendrick from prison. He was twenty-one and facing some serious time, and through the rapper's lyrics, we heard the pain of Keaton's separation from the outside, where his grand-mother and brother were getting older, and it was possible he might not see them again: "Said that they tried to give him like a hundred years," Kendrick raps. "Sleeping in a cell, it's been thirty weeks / Ain't received any mail / It's cold and the hole stinks."

These revelations speak to the dichotomy of Kendrick Lamar—the shy kid in a tough environment, surrounded by strong black men who did what they could to survive. He'd been around the vices that had ensnared so many, yet his family—uncles, cousins, and dear friends—had shielded him from those trappings. It was as if they knew who he would be long before he did.

On *The Kendrick Lamar EP*, the rapper unpacked a childhood steeped in mischief and driven by the will to do right. Where *Hub City Threat* found Kendrick staking his claim as the world's top rapper before he had any real credentials, the song "Is It Love"—the opening track of *The Kendrick Lamar EP*—outlined his wants in specific detail: he wanted the Grammys, the fame and fortune, the proximity to generational wealth. He also wanted to play golf with real estate mogul Donald Trump; that didn't age well. Back then, Kendrick was driving his mother's van to the studio with almost no gas in it. Around this time, his father started to wonder where Kendrick's career was headed, and how long it would take before he'd earn money from it. He was twenty-two years old, and when his dad was the same age, he had had his own place and two cars in the driveway. Meanwhile, Kendrick was still living at home, and his career path was more of a slow burn. It took great patience to watch the young rapper make gradual gains when others seemed to make longer strides. His dad knew his son had a gift that the world needed to hear, and in his own gruff way, Kenny was simply expressing the frustration of having to watch bullshit be celebrated on the tube when Kendrick had what it took to outshine those same rappers.

But Kendrick was playing the long game; he was his own man, and it was clear by listening to the EP that he wouldn't beg old-school West Coast rappers for fleeting cosigns. That had become an issue in the area, so much so that Ice Cube publicly lambasted the younger guard for trying to jump onto what his generation had established two decades prior. As he saw it, the new guys simply weren't willing to put in the sweat needed to win on their own. He also didn't think it was his responsibility to usher them along their journey. "They ain't on my level," Cube wrote in a blog post. "They can't make a name for themselves so they need help from the OGs. I refuse to throw them a life line. It ain't my job to make nobody famous."

Though Kendrick's friend Jay Rock was angered by Ice Cube's comments, Kendrick eschewed acknowledgments from older MCs like Cube, DJ Quik, Snoop, and the like. "Do I need a cosign from Dre or Jigga?" he asked on the EP track "Celebration." "They can make me much bigger, but do I need 'em, though? / I just need a flow / The type of shit that make you think you seen Pac ghost." For the vets to give a thumbs-up would've been substantial, but Kendrick knew he wasn't like those who'd come before. He was a nuanced mosaic of varied influences, pulling into one body the lush humility of southern rap stalwarts like OutKast and Goodie Mob, the lyrical dexterity of Nas and Eminem, and the straight-ahead tough talk of Pusha T and Killer Mike. He also had a golden ear for all kinds of instrumentals—from the off-kilter soul of J Dilla and Madlib to the jazz-based orchestration of the Roots. Kendrick wasn't classically trained, but he had instinctive musical awareness; he just knew what sounded good, and he knew how to articulate his vision for his art, no matter how weird it seemed to others. Though he didn't play traditional instruments, he turned his voice—a nasal, almost childlike timbre—into its own instrument, sliding up and down the register like a singer to convey the right emotion. Critics of hip-hop like to chastise rappers because they're supposedly not musical, that maybe they can't pluck an upright bass or tell you what key the composition is in. Such thinking isn't fair; it takes tremendous poise to spin words into vibrant poetry. Kendrick was theatrical in that way; listeners never knew what they'd get from one verse or song to the next.

He didn't close himself off to disparate art to hold up some make-believe narrative of Compton rappers being drawn only to gangsta shit. And that was why, ultimately, he gained the respect of L.A.'s rap elite, because he had the courage to be himself in a town that didn't always reward such bravery. Kendrick remained true to the music that *he* wanted to create; that the rapper stood on his own two feet made him much more intriguing to the artists he admired.

Still, the pangs of his father lingered, and eventually the self-doubt spilled into a song called "Determined," the closing track from his 2009 EP. Here, Kendrick recalls a simpler time, when he and his girlfriend were splitting a bucket of Kentucky Fried Chicken, looking forward to the days when his name would be mentioned alongside the greats. In those days, Drake was the guy; through his popular single "Best I Ever Had," the Canadian rapper and Lil Wayne affiliate was quickly becoming the "it" guy in hip-hop. And though Kendrick's partner was listening to Drake's music back then, she knew it was only a matter of time before Kendrick's reign kicked in. "You know you the best, boy, you gotta keep doing it," Kendrick remembered her saying. "But don't forget when you do, just keep you in it."

That plea stuck with Kendrick, and even after he started racking up awards and became a transcendent figure in music and pop culture, he never let fame get to his head. "He's the same person. Nothing has changed," the experimental producer Flying Lotus said in 2019. "He [don't] be coming in no designer shit. This motherfucker came through to the crib a few months ago with the hoodie and some shorts on. Socks and slides on. He's just the same cat. It didn't feel any different." Matt Jeezy concurs: When he worked in a homeless shelter near Skid Row in downtown Los Angeles, Kendrick would come through—at the height of his popularity—without any cameras or an entourage in tow. "He took care of some of the kids I worked with down there," he recalls. "Even the first time he called, I was crazy busy dealing with some traumatic stuff at the center and Kendrick insisted on coming down to help."

Though *The Kendrick Lamar EP* was a breakthrough, the public still wasn't paying attention. Surely he'd amassed some fans on the road, but Kendrick was still unknown to much of the press and to listeners at large. His name was being whispered on blogs and in underground rap circles, not shouted out loud like Drake's, Wayne's, and Kanye's. But in lieu of critical acclaim, the EP reset the palate of those who may have written him off after *C4* and set an emphatic tone for what his career would be going forward. It was the first to display Kendrick as the deep critical thinker, and offered a glimpse into the family dynamic that made up his character. For the first time, Kendrick dropped the veneer of simply being a good rapper and let us into the personal torment that drove his hunger to be the best. Here was where he first let listeners into the depression and nagging self-doubt that haunted him well into his prosperity. But Kendrick never let it define him; instead, he used it as fuel to propel moments of unvarnished truth. This was his narrative, his history, and whether or not he succeeded, Kendrick vowed in 2009 to go out his way and no one else's. Little did he know, there was a life-altering phone call just around the corner.

Imagine you're out with a friend and the phone rings. It can be anybody—your girlfriend, your boy talking trash about sports, or your mom wondering when you're coming back with the van. Instead, it's a number you don't recognize, and the voice on the other end claims to be a member of Dr. Dre's team. *The* Dr. Dre. The pioneer. The dude who was partly responsible for the hip-hop you danced to shirtless in your living room as a kid. The dude who you saw with your hero, Tupac Shakur, at the Compton Swap Meet all those years ago. That guy. Now take Dre out of the equation; how would you feel if the ayatollah of your profession reached out just because he thought you were dope? That was what happened to Kendrick in 2010 during a stop in Los Angeles for the Independent Grind Tour. He was still Jay Rock's hype man, and as he remembers, the call came while he and TDE engineer Ali were eating at Chili's. Kendrick didn't think it was real, so he and Ali laughed it off and hung up the phone. "We got a call like, 'Yo, Dr. Dre likes your music.' And we were like, 'Yo, who the fuck is this on the phone?'" Kendrick once told Howard Stern on SiriusXM. "Another call came in from somebody else. Then another call came in from somebody else like, 'Yo, they trying to reach out and figure out who you with.'"

It's a good thing Dre's people were consistent; they eventually convinced Kendrick they were legit, and the rapper was in the studio with the producer the following week, laying down vocals for Dre's long-simmering *Detox*. Everything Kendrick had done in his short rap career had led to this one moment. Kendrick walked into Dre's studio, still beaming from the opportunity to work with his idol. Once in there, Dre—a hulking presence at six feet, one inch tall and two-hundred-something pounds—introduced himself to Kendrick, then quickly pressed play on a beat that Dre had received from the noted producer Just Blaze. It was for a song called "Compton," which would appear near the end of Kendrick's *good kid, m.A.A.d city*. "We had the overall concept and it already had verses and everything on it, it was all done," Just Blaze says of the song. "This was right when Dre became aware of Kendrick and was like, 'Well, bring him down to the studio.' So he had brought Kendrick in to add onto whatever he felt. 'Compton' was one of the things that he gravitated toward, it was one of the stronger songs that we had in that batch, so Kendrick wound up jumping on it." "I remember that shit sounded so loud," the rapper said to *Vice*. "Compton" wasn't just a crowning achievement for Kendrick, it was an achievement for hip-hop as well: Dre wasn't really rapping that much at the time, so for him to jump on the microphone, the vibe truly had to be something special.

Once in the studio with Dre, Kendrick was so overwhelmed by Dre's presence that he nearly missed his chance to shine. "It came to a point where I had to really snap out of fan mode and become a professional after we were introduced," he told BBC Radio. "Then he said, 'Okay, now write to this, write a full song to this.' Right after I said, 'Man, Dr. Dre, you're the greatest,' and he was like, 'Yeah, man, you're good too, you could be something, all right now write to this beat.'"

Dre and Kendrick worked nonstop for almost two weeks on songs for *Detox*, and Dre—who'd never been one to cosign much— saw greatness in Kendrick right away. The young rapper flashed back to the moment when he had seen Dre and Pac from his father's shoulders in Compton. The producer remembered all the children who were out there, and the duo reminisced on the destiny that brought them both to the studio together. It was wild that, out of all the people at the video shoot for "California Love" that day, Kendrick was the one to ascend.

In Dre, the young rapper saw a reflection of himself—the upstanding dude in a precarious situation who was able to escape through music. But while Dre had already ascended, Kendrick was just getting started on his path to prominence. From the producer, he'd take in great gems, like how to stay low-key in the limelight when strangers wanted to know your whereabouts. Dre and Kendrick weren't just collaborators, they grew close enough to be family. "It was more like a uncle-nephew kind of vibe," Kendrick said in a Complex interview. "When we sit in the studio, we talk about these different streets that we both lived on and experiences he had that I can relate to being two generations younger." Dr. Dre's studio sessions have become the stuff of legend in rap music, with everyone from Kendrick to 50 Cent to Eminem singing the Doc's praises once their work together is done. They all proclaim Dre the perfectionist, whose studio sessions can go seventy-plus hours if the vibe is right. He's also a stickler when it comes to words, nitpicking the inflection of the rappers he works with hundreds of times and recording hundreds of takes. It's a grueling test of will for the privilege of having the Kingmaker's stamp on your music. He's been called a coach, much like basketball's Phil Jackson, the rapper Mez once told the webzine Pitchfork—the most decorated club leader in NBA history. Dre had this way of bringing the best out of everyone with whom he worked. And though the producer didn't write his own lyrics, he knew how to instruct rappers in his studio to inflect his voice in the rhymes they wrote for him. *Chemistry* is the word that arises when discussing Dre. As Eminem once said, "I don't have chemistry like that with anyone else as far as producers go—not even close."

Eminem's manager, Paul Rosenberg, put Dre onto Kendrick's music. "I was in Detroit and he was like, 'You gotta hear this kid from Compton,'" Dre once told Kurt "Big Boy" Alexander on his radio show, *Big Boy's Neighborhood*. "So I went online, and the thing that really turned me on in the beginning was the way he spoke during an interview. It wasn't even the music at first. It was just the way he spoke, and the way he showed his passion for music. It was something in that. Then I got into the music and really realized how talented he was." Once online, Dre found a video that Kendrick did for his song "Ignorance Is Bliss," one of several great tracks from the rapper's 2010 mixtape, *Overly Dedicated*.

Some of hip-hop's all-time greatest MCs have a "Dre discovered me" story. In 1992, the producer found Snoop through a song he'd recorded that year called "A Gangsta'z Life." Collaborator Warren G played the song for Dre, who showed immediate interest in the Long Beach rapper. "It was a rock, it wasn't shined up yet," Snoop once said of the song during a conversation with Kendrick. "He sees something in you, and by you being around him and being with him, he just gon' tighten your shit up."

Dre and Eminem found each other when they both needed a lifeline. The year was 1997, and Dre was coming off his biggest commercial failures as a leader, when two albums he helmed in 1996—the Firm's *The Album*, and *Dr. Dre Presents the Aftermath*—both flopped. Dre was at the home of Interscope Records cofounder Jimmy Iovine; in his garage were piles of cassette tapes. Jimmy picked up one particular tape, popped it in, and pressed play. It was Eminem freestyling in a cypher over the kind of West Coast G-funk beat that Dre would've created. On the day they met in Dre's home studio, the producer quickly compiled an instrumental to see what Em could do on the spot. "I hit the drum machine, and maybe two or three seconds went by, and he just went, 'Hi, my name is! My name is!'" Dre recalled on his HBO docuseries, *The Defiant Ones*. "My Name Is" was a smash hit and the track that introduced Eminem to the world as a wrecking-ball force, the likes of which the world had never seen.

Kendrick had that same potential, and "Ignorance Is Bliss" was the perfect marriage of technical skill and content. It was also another example of Kendrick trying to change the public perception of who he was: a mix of gangsta rap and introspection, he wasn't *just* a Compton rapper and he wasn't *just* a conscious MC like Common, Yasiin Bey (who, back then, went by the name Mos Def), or

Talib Kweli. He *was* conscious, he *was* a student of hip-hop culture, and he *was* gangsta—when he wanted to be. But Kendrick was able to marry these aesthetics without having to adhere to one style in particular, and as a result, he didn't fit any of the man-made boxes in which critics tried to put him. Instead, he glorified the gangsta aesthetic by acknowledging that Compton natives might not have known why they banged in the streets. In some cases, that was all they'd known; their uncles and fathers had been born into it, and they passed it down to their kids, and so forth.

The video for "Ignorance Is Bliss" portrayed this history; in the one-minute, fifty-two-second clip, Kendrick swigs from a forty-ounce of Olde English 800 malt liquor and pours some on the grave of his dead friend, then he hops in the back of a car driven by TDE mate ScHoolboy Q and they drive up on the person who killed his friend. The video ends with us (the viewer) in the antagonist's shoes, staring down the barrel of Kendrick's gun. There's a sudden pop, then darkness, and we're left to believe that the good kid has succumbed to the treacherous city, and that he couldn't survive the minefield that's entrapped so many young black men before him. Kendrick, much like his uncles and cousins, was forced to make a life-altering decision long before any teenager is capable of doing so.

A song like "Ignorance Is Bliss" helped define Kendrick's expression. The rapper made a career of taking common themes and looking beyond the veil to assess human behavior: *Yes, gangbanging is a culture, but why? Why are black men left without choices in places like Compton and South Side Chicago? Why are we left with only liquor and weed to soothe our angst? How do these dependencies impact communities?* Questions like these became the foundation of the Kendrick Lamar era, and by detangling the fabric of Compton and Los Angeles as a whole, he was unraveling assorted aspects of his own being. Kendrick was still a young man (age twenty-three at this point), and while he was forced to grow up quickly, he was getting to know himself in an increasingly public way.

Kendrick's evolution from *The Kendrick Lamar EP* to *Overly Dedicated* was astounding; in just one year, he had grown from a promising lyricist with a decent grasp of songwriting and complex song structures to a full-fledged artiste who could execute circuitous concepts with ease and flair. There was an actual theme to *Overly Dedicated*, not just a mere collection of songs being thrown into one set. Ali tinkered with different sound frequencies for Kendrick's voice—warping it, slowing it down, making the rapper sound alien. TDE's in-house producers—Sounwave, Tae Beast, and Willie B— also stepped up their game: the beats felt dense and spacious, and that gave Kendrick the vast canvas he needed to unpack his views on religion, gun culture, and social and economic disparities, while namechecking Patrón tequila, NASCAR legend Dale Earnhardt, and R&B/pop icon Beyoncé. He dug deeper and got even more personal on this project; on "Average Joe," Kendrick talks about the time someone shot at him during a walk home from Centennial High School. A car pulls up and asks him where he lives. "Westside," he responds. That's Piru territory; the guys in the car wore blue hats, a Crip color. Kendrick dropped his backpack and ran to a neighborhood cul-de-sac. Shots rang out, but the rapper wasn't hit.

In later interviews, he'd brush off the incident as yet another by-product of living in Compton, where safety isn't a luxury people have and violence can pop off at any time. Something as simple as walking home from school could lead to gunshot wounds. "You're going to get into situations, you can't escape that," Kendrick once said. "You can either take action or fall back. In most cases, I have to take action because that's just how it goes when you're put in a situation where you have to defend yourself. I think a lot of kids can relate to that story on 'Average Joe' because it's real. A lot of these mother-fuckers are good kids. The influence is making them fucked up."

Elsewhere, the song "P&P 1.5" was the best example of Kendrick's artistic growth from one project to the next: the initial version—called "Pussy and Patrón" on *The Kendrick Lamar EP*—was a straightforward ode to sex and liquor over a repurposed beat created by the Roots for their 2006 album, *Game Theory*. On *Overly Dedicated*, the song becomes a shape-shifting epic with a full break-down, modulated vocal shifts influenced by southern rap, and a changing rhythm midsong. The instrumental drops out and skips in certain parts, a subtle effect by Ali that accentuates the ferocity of Kendrick's battle to reconcile his grandmother's death and his uncle's murder at Louis Burgers. Kendrick played the song for Tech N9ne on tour, and that was when the Kansas City lyricist knew just how dope the young man was. The track precedes a song like "Swimming Pools (Drank)" from Kendrick's *good kid, m.A.A.d city* as a sprawling sermon about the joy and pain of worldly vices. On "P&P 1.5," the rapper dives head-on into the thrill; in a world made increasingly tougher for black men to survive, pleasures like "pussy and Patrón" can combat the stress of just being alive and black in Los Angeles. On "Swimming Pools," Kendrick toes the line between that same struggle and ecstasy; the same liquor that brought joy can cause tremendous pain, and given his family history of alcoholism, Kendrick peers at the bottle askance, fully aware of the havoc soaked within its forty ounces.

Overly Dedicated was easily Kendrick's best project to that point, and the one that *finally* got the attention of larger press outlets and bigger groups of fans. Unlike the EP and the previous work before it, *Overly Dedicated* exhibited a level of complexity and freedom that, from the outside looking in, seemed to have been brewing for a lifetime. It was the little things that made *Overly Dedicated* what it was and further demonstrated just who Kendrick was as a person: he didn't care about arbitrary rules that claimed an EP needed to be a short set of songs, or that an interlude couldn't be a quick rhyme just because. "They said seven tracks, I said fifteen / Called it an EP, they said I'm trippin'," he rapped on "The Heart Pt. 2." Kendrick wanted to change the norm of what rap music could be. After years of tapping on the glass ceiling, TDE finally created a crack, and years later, Sounwave and Ali would admit that *Overly Dedicated* was the first TDE album to wake people up to what they were doing at the House of Pain in Carson. It was the first project of Kendrick's to make the *Billboard* charts, where it peaked at number 72 on its Top R&B/Hip-Hop Albums chart.

At the time of its release in September 2010, Kendrick was still on the road with Tech N9ne and Strange Music as part of the Independent Grind Tour. But he was no longer just a hype man; while he was still down to support Jay Rock, his musical brother, Kendrick was quickly gaining steam and becoming his own entity. Yet there wasn't anything about *Overly Dedicated* that screamed "greatest rapper of his peer group." It was a building block, and looking back at the project years later, it doesn't compare with the cinematic *good kid, m.A.A.d city*, the seismic force of *To Pimp a Butterfly*, or the dark, claustrophobic tone of *DAMN.*, and is often forgotten when debating Kendrick's best recordings. That's not a diss to the rapper or *Overly Dedicated*; rather, it's a testament to Kendrick's unconventional brilliance, and how—just two years after the mixtape's release—the songs on it felt obsolete. His collaborators willingly called him a genius whose old-school ways of creating meant he'd come to your house unannounced with a rhythm in his head and clear-cut ideas for albums that weren't even next in line to be released. Kendrick was always thinking two steps ahead, and even in 2010, he was already thinking about 2012 and beyond, strategizing on what his music would sound like, long before he'd put pen to paper. "He's the most hands-on person I've ever, ever dealt with," Sounwave once told Red Bull Music Academy. "I can be in the bathroom, on the toilet or something, and he'd just knock, 'Yo, I got this melody. Can you do this for me real fast?'"

Indeed, you couldn't rest around Kendrick; he was an ambitious creator. So it's no surprise that he eventually became the best, because while other rappers might've held *Overly Dedicated* as their landmark project, Kendrick and TDE weren't resting until they released the very best record possible. It's a fool's errand, really: Kendrick was a perfectionist, and people like him don't always fare well in creative arts. Even Dr. Dre fell victim to such perfectionism; after years of tinkering with *Detox*, adding and subtracting verses, deleting drafts and fine-tuning new ideas, the album still hadn't come out as of this writing. Kendrick's drive ran close to Dre's; he'd record two or three albums' worth of material just to release one LP, and the unreleased work would sit somewhere on a hard drive. The jazz pianist Robert

Glasper, who contributed to Kendrick's *To Pimp a Butterfly*, laments having what he thought was an incredible Kendrick verse for one of his *Black Radio* LPs, only for the rapper to deny its usage because it wasn't up to his incredibly high standard. Kendrick had the type of sensitivity that could ruin him if he didn't protect himself. To be black in America is to feel like whatever you do is never good enough. And he was a deep thinker, creatively attuned to personal and cultural struggles. He wanted to absorb those problems and address it through his art. In doing that, it was easy to lose himself in the process if he didn't take time to replenish his energy.

A project the magnitude of *Overly Dedicated* should've landed with more force than it did, but it entered a crowded space in which rap heavyweights like Nicki Minaj, Kanye, Drake, and T.I. were taking up all the creative real estate, and there wasn't much room for underground rap to break into the mainstream. Kendrick's project was released just two months before Kanye's earth-shattering fifth studio album, *My Beautiful Dark Twisted Fantasy*, was dropped into a universe that craved new music from the eccentric rapper/producer who'd disappeared from the public eye to craft that thick, sprawling opus. Kanye dominated the news cycle for the better part of three months leading up to the record's release—from the Twitter account he launched in July, to his return to the MTV Video Music Awards, where, just a year earlier, he had hopped onstage and interrupted Taylor Swift's victory speech to proclaim Beyoncé's "Single Ladies (Put a Ring on It)" as "one of the greatest music videos of all time." The listening public not only craved new music from Kanye, but relished his antics as well. He was the villain they loved to hate, and though they complained about his public rants and mic-snatching decorum, the fans still sought his creative acumen and stadium-sized rap anthems.

With the public's eyes and ears trained on Kanye, Kendrick—and, well, a lot of rappers—flew under the radar, perhaps unfairly. Mixtapes are often denounced for sounding rough, or even unfinished, but Kendrick's *Overly Dedicated* had a level of polish not often heard from up-and-coming musicians. That he wanted to make it available for free spoke to his humility. In his mind, he hadn't done enough yet to warrant any sort of profit, but the TDE brain trust—namely Top Dawg and Punch—felt he, engineer Ali, the in-house producers, and the mixtape's features had finally done enough legwork to generate income from the record. At last, it was time to level up to new ways of living, to get paid for all the grunt work, the sacrifice, the moments alone with just a little bit of money and the dreams of giving the world something it didn't know it needed at the time. The general consensus was that *Overly Dedicated* was *good*, but there was still something missing from it. Kendrick was close—*very* close—but he needed to keep pushing toward his full potential. He needed a signature project of fresh ideas, devoid of rehashed songs from previous projects. For his next act, Kendrick would have to dig even deeper to summon undeniable work. It had to be even better than *Overly Dedicated*, light-years beyond *The Kendrick Lamar EP*, and a far cry from anything before that. For his next feat, Kendrick blacked out in ways that truly surprised rap fans.

No one saw *Section.80* coming, and those who claim otherwise might be revising their own history. Kendrick released his first official album in the heat of the U.S. summer, on July 2, 2011, right as his demographic was more preoccupied with eating grilled meat and drinking cold beer along the coastline. By the time Kendrick started recording *Section.80*, the TDE team had gotten bigger, and more producers were brought in to cultivate a sound. For Kendrick, that sound meant—well—everything: jazz loops, atmospheric R&B, and spellbinding drums. The atmosphere was more competitive, as each composer wanted to create the most-talked-about song on the record. Of course the competition was friendly; as Terrace Martin says, it was all for the greater good of *Section.80* and TDE as a whole. "We just wanted to make sure Kendrick had the best music possible, because he was younger than us, but he was our leader in that aspect," Martin recalls. "We wanted to make sure he had the best art to get his shit off properly so the world could hear it. It was his time." Indeed, there was a team-first mentality at TDE: if you were working on an album, everyone in the collective would concentrate solely on your project to make sure it was high quality. "It was Kendrick's time, so everyone was focused on Kendrick. If it's your time, you're the leader of that time. We believe that's how great records are done."

To those who weren't in TDE or close to the camp, everyone seemed to have the same question upon *Section.80*'s release: *Who is this kid?!* Of course, if you'd seen him perform or listened to the previous music, you knew he had potential. But very few people saw *this*—this being the flawless double-time flow of "Rigamortus," this being the raw, "ready for war" aggression of "Ronald Reagan Era (His Evils)." Kendrick wrote the songs for *Section.80* in the spring of 2011, just four months before the album came out, and just a few

months after the end of the Independent Grind Tour with Tech
N9ne, Jay Rock, and Strange Music. Once off the road, Kendrick
retreated to the places where he felt most comfortable: to the House
of Pain in Carson, and to the kitchen and couch of his parents' house
in Compton. These places, far away from the bedlam of rowdy tour
buses and crowded venues, represented home for Kendrick, where
he could regain some peace of mind. It's hard to write when exter-
nal forces tug at you, pressuring you to conform to them. Though
he wrote on the road when he could, he found it tough to concentrate; he needed solitude to fully connect with his intentions, and to
conceptualize what he wanted *Section.80* to be.

So he went home to where it all started, back to the dungeon,
back to familiar settings. It was his way to reset, to remind himself
that, despite the shows and the fan support, there was still plenty
of work to be done, and that—as a creator—you're only as good
as your last project. Much like *The Kendrick Lamar EP* and *Overly
Dedicated*, *Section.80* was equally about Kendrick and those closest
to him. But where his previous two projects were more about his
own peaks and valleys, *Section.80* widened the scope to discuss his
generation as a whole—the kids born in the mid- to late 1980s who
were around when crack cocaine flooded the streets, but were too
young to understand what was happening to their friends, families,
and neighbors. The song "A.D.H.D" speaks to this: here, Kendrick
dissects the natural connection that he and his peer group have to
drugs and dependency as a whole. It's not just age-old addictions like
marijuana and liquor; his peers are now addicted to cough syrup,
pills, and video game consoles. Compare that with the song "No
Makeup (Her Vice)," where Kendrick questions why a woman he

knows hides her natural beauty beneath layers of cosmetics. "Damn girl, why so much?" he asks. "You 'bout to blow your cover when you cover up / Don't you know your imperfections is a wonderful blessing?" We learn later in the song that she's a victim of domestic violence, and the makeup is covering black eyes.

Then there's "Keisha's Song (Her Pain)," on which the rapper tells the story of a young woman fighting against societal ills: Keisha was molested as a child and later works as a prostitute. After a short life of fighting crooked cops and overzealous johns, she was found dead—raped and stabbed. *Section.80* is where Kendrick became a masterful storyteller who could elicit joy, deliberation, and sorrow in equal measure, and where he merged his two very distinct personas—the aggressive K-Dot and the introspective Kendrick Lamar—with the best results to that point. On a song like "Ronald Reagan Era," Kendrick summoned K-Dot to a certain extent, leaning upon the unfiltered aggression of his old persona to salute city gangs as one united front. To him, colors didn't matter; this was him declaring once and for all that Compton was *one* city. Crips, Eses, and Pirus, it didn't matter, he said they all had his back. The same went for "Fuck Your Ethnicity," *Section.80*'s opening track. This time, he flips the notion of color, broadening it from gang culture to race, lumping all ethnicities into one group. Everyone was the same; when he looked into the crowd from the stage, he saw black, white, Asian, and Hispanic faces all in one place. The song also finds him trying to embrace God, a theme that would define his career. In this moment, it was as if he were rushing to find Him before the sins of his past caught up.

With *Section.80*, the rapper wanted to achieve balance in his music and in life, with art that addressed all facets of the city's culture while paying homage to the men in his family who were still active in the streets. Kendrick pulled from these experiences—from the hard lessons he learned from his uncles and cousins, to the nurturing he got from his mother and father, who always encouraged him to dream and live life abundantly. "They taught me the world is bigger than Compton and to go out and explore it," he once told *Billboard*. "That made me an individual. I actually know who I am, where I come from, and what I got to do to represent and connect people." *Section.80* was partially influenced by a close friend of his who was given a sentence of twenty-five years to life for a violent crime. "He had no guidance and was caught in that negative stigma of our generation that [we] don't care about anything and don't listen to anybody," Kendrick told the publication. "He was so young and his life is almost completely gone, it's like he missed the whole world. Just the fact that's gone from him at such a tender age shows me that we have a lot to go as far as listening and being able to critique ourselves as individuals. That's what *Section.80* represents. [It's] that particular moment [in which] I thought back to the pain I felt when one of my friends was about to be gone for a minute. That's the creation process going into the studio, thinking about those emotions."

With *Section.80*, Kendrick portrayed his peer group as actual human beings with real concerns. They're not apathetic and only addicted to themselves and their cell phones. They hurt and they bleed like everyone else. They lament the state of the world, and just because they don't protest the way their parents did doesn't make them any less thoughtful. *Section.80* was an exercise of duality, a walk through the pleasures of pain and the dark sides of temptation. It was a story about real life and good times, and the uncertainty looming at every corner of the inner city. It was also an album of self-discovery, of Kendrick trying to evade the pitfalls waiting for him. The rapper spoke to this in detail on "Poe Mans Dream (His Vice)." Here he unpacks his own flawed thinking, that he once believed going to jail was cool. That was until he saw the stress and strain that prison had put on his family.

A story like this doesn't just apply to Kendrick; it addresses the plight of many young black men who've seen their uncles, brothers, and fathers ushered to prison so much that the path seems glamorous. Jail is far from utopia, and some of these men have spent so much of their adult lives in custody that a culture behind bars is all they know. Kendrick tapped into the isolation that his family and friends felt in jail, when all they had were the memories of freedom, a pen, and just a few sheets of paper to write their loved ones back home. With *Section.80*, you can feel Kendrick become more serious, more reflective, somewhat more isolated. Though the album was tailored specifically to Compton, Kendrick kept the stories open-ended, so those close to his age group in Philadelphia, Houston, New Orleans, and elsewhere could relate to the narrative. This is where he started to move to the forefront of TDE and become its star player, and where his buzz grew so palpable that he could no longer be denied by the public. In fact, 2011 was a big year for Kendrick: that February, he was named to *XXL*'s eleven-member Freshman Class along with other soon-to-be-big rap stars: Meek Mill, Mac Miller, Big K.R.I.T., Lil B, and YG.

Then in August, a group of Cali rap icons gave Kendrick the

biggest cosign of his career. During a show in his native L.A., they passed him the torch, dubbing him the King of West Coast Rap. It was an emotional moment for Kendrick, so much so that he cried onstage. The moment was greater than anything the rapper could've imagined, and more valuable than any accolades given to him by an outsider. "You great at what you do. You ain't good at what you do, you great at what you do," Snoop said to Kendrick. "You got the torch, you better run with that muthafucka. You better run with it, nigga, 'cause it's *yours*." Eight months later, it was announced that Kendrick was going on the road once again, this time with Drake as part of his four-month Club Paradise Tour. The intrigue surrounding Kendrick arose, and he became an enigmatic figure in the eyes of the media. They couldn't quite figure him out or describe his music; it was equally fascinating and strange to the ear. Compton rappers weren't supposed to rhyme over jazz breaks, but he did. They weren't supposed to evoke the piss-in-the-hallway, roaches-in-the-cereal, rats-in-the-subway aesthetic of New York's Wu-Tang Clan, but he did. They weren't supposed to summon the warmth and gospel-infused essence of the Dungeon Family, but *he did*. That he could pull from these disparate aesthetics and remain overtly Compton was his greatest feat.

Pitchfork, the popular music site known for its tastemaking album reviews, gave *Section.80* a positive score of 8 out of 10. In his assessment, critic Tom Breihan called Kendrick "a weird kid" and "an introverted loner type," but noted that the album stood "as a powerful document of a . . . promising young guy figuring out his voice." Over at *XXL*, critic Adam Fleischer trumpeted the rapper's humility and artistic flair, highlighting the fact that he could examine money, history, and religion—all at the same time—with "passion, focus, and sincerity." Still, Kendrick wasn't buying into the media hype; everyday people were feeling it, and that meant more. "When I go out to do these shows, these kids actually believe in what I talk about because they understand the look it's been getting from people I looked up to," Kendrick once said. "I love the acknowledgment as far as the music and the stamps [of approval], but at the end of the day, those stamps gonna carry no weight unless I put the work ethic behind it. . . . I wanna make the best music in today's world, period. Once I do that, I'll feel like I've accomplished something."

In a year of notable hip-hop releases from the likes of Jay-Z and Kanye (*Watch the Throne*), Drake (*Take Care*), and fellow upcoming rapper J. Cole (*Cole World: The Sideline Story*), *Section.80* stood apart. If *good kid, m.A.A.d city* presented Kendrick as a fully formed human with very visible blemishes, *Section.80* was paint strewn on the canvas—his visage and ideas still broadly taking shape. It was a masterpiece in its own way, the record on which he started to embrace his genius before he started taking himself so seriously. "We look at *Section.80* and how different that was compared to everything in that time," TDE engineer Derek Ali has said. "It just showed me—if you just be yourself and stay true and loyal to yourself, then there's nothing you can't do, and there's nowhere you can't go."

4

A Star Is Born

By early 2012, Kendrick was a budding star rubbing elbows with the hottest rappers in the industry. In mid-February, he and another promising lyricist, Harlem's A$AP Rocky, hit the road with Drake as part of his Club Paradise Tour. Kendrick got the opportunity after he spoke with Drake in person following his first show ever in Toronto. "He called me up and we had a few drinks and he always said he was appreciative of my music," Kendrick reportedly said. "I've always been a fan of his music. We just been chopping it up since." Drake handpicked Kendrick to open for him on the road: "There's a lot of artists out there who could have been out there on tour with him, for him to sit there and respect my music. We have the same mutual respect." This was before the 2013 "Control" verse, and years before they greeted each other with passive-aggressive tension, begrudging smiles, and forced pleasantries backstage.

Across thirty-eight dates and in cities like Austin, Oklahoma City, San Diego, and London, Kendrick performed to bigger crowds in bigger arenas, this time as a solo act and not as someone else's hype man. He was taking *Section.80* to fans who somewhat knew his work, but because he was an opening act, he was performing monumental tracks like "HiiiPoWeR," "Hol' Up," and "Blow My High (Members Only)" to somewhat uninterested fans who were there to see the headliner, or even A$AP, before him. A$AP was riding the wave of an incredibly popular mixtape called *LIVE. LOVE. A$AP*, a tough-minded street record that introduced the rapper as a weed-smoking disciple of UGK and DJ Screw. He wasn't as lyrical as Kendrick, but because the majority of rap fans didn't prioritize complex wordplay like the previous generation, A$AP's star shone brighter than Kendrick's at that time. Still, these were the biggest crowds that Kendrick had ever seen, but with a limited budget and only a few minutes to make an impression, some of the early shows felt a bit rough. On the first gig of the tour, at the BankUnited Center in Coral Gables, Florida, Kendrick and Ali didn't have much: just a white folding table, an Apple MacBook, and a TDE banner draped across the front monitors. That setup could work at a tiny hole-in-the-wall club with hundreds of people crammed into it, not in a midsized basketball arena with thousands of seats. But the rapper had toured arenas of similar size, with Tech N9ne and the Strange Music crew as part of the Independent Grind Tour. And being a disciple of Top Dawg Tiffith and TDE's "Hustle Like You Broke" mentality helped as well. He knew there was no way to convert every single concertgoer into a Kendrick-loving follower, but if he could get a few of them, that could go a long way toward building a sizable fan base. "I know it's fifteen thousand people out there, I'm used to two thousand," Kendrick once told Fuse TV. "I'm finna work. I'm finna get at least a hundred of these folks to understand what Kendrick Lamar was." Slowly, he was building momentum toward his first masterpiece, gathering fans in dribs and drabs.

The first taste of *good kid, m.A.A.d city* came in February 2012 with the release of the song "Cartoon & Cereal," a methodical cut that, in hindsight, is essential to understanding Kendrick's creative aesthetic for the years to follow. Through modulated vocals and complex imagery, the rapper walks through family history—not just his, but those of his peers who grew up around gang culture. He speaks of male mentorship, of fathers and sons being connected physically and emotionally, and how little boys ultimately want to be like the grown men in their homes. But what happens when the role model is knee-deep in the streets, or locked up in jail? Here, the man is literally holding the gun as the woman gives birth to the little boy. Inadvertently, the armed man is the first image the boy sees, which informs his childhood perspective. "You told me, 'Don't be like me, just finish watching cartoons,'" Kendrick raps. It was supposed to be a single for *good kid*, though after it leaked to the internet, Kendrick and TDE decided to leave it off the album; as such, it has become a cult favorite for fans.

The next month, it was announced that the rapper had signed a joint venture deal with Interscope Records and Dr. Dre's Aftermath Entertainment imprint to release *good kid, m.A.A.d city*, his major-label debut album. Kendrick signed the deal not only because of Dre, though that was surely a big reason, but because Interscope had a reputation for putting out *albums* in the truest sense. "It was about who understood the vision, and Dre and [Interscope CEO] Jimmy Iovine understood," Kendrick once said. "They were just banking off talent, like Eminem. They understand how the growth of an independent company, like Aftermath, can develop into something that becomes its own Interscope, and that's what we're doing with Top Dawg Entertainment. We want to develop artists and put out solid albums like Eminem did with *The Marshall Mathers LP* and 50 Cent did with *Get Rich or Die Tryin'*—they're records that stood the test of time. They understood that."

But having a deal didn't mean he was going to submit to pressure from record executives; Kendrick still had a unique vision for his music, and *good kid, m.A.A.d city* was going to fulfill it. He wanted to carry out Snoop's directive as the next great savior of West Coast hip-hop, and to make believers out of those who claimed that L.A. rap had fallen off. Kendrick didn't think the city had lost a thing, but compared with the earth-shattering force of his creative forefathers, Southern California hip-hop needed a new voice to carry it back to prominence: "If I'm the shining light that can branch that off then so be it, I'mma do just that." By the summer of 2012, there was a legitimate buzz surrounding Kendrick, but he still hadn't broken out on his own; on the Club Paradise Tour, he was just the opening act; now it was time to command stages by himself. That July, just three months after his gig concluded on Drake's tour, Kendrick was in Chicago, some fifteen minutes up I-90W from where his parents lived before they picked up stakes and moved to Compton in 1984. It was a full-circle moment: His folks had to leave to escape street life and make a better way for themselves. Now their firstborn son was in their home city, on the verge of becoming a star.

The Butterfly Effect

Kendrick was booked to play the annual Pitchfork Music Festival in Chicago's Union Park, where prominent rock artists like Modest Mouse and the National, and rap acts like Public Enemy and De La Soul once graced its stages. Kendrick was part of Pitchfork's most rap-friendly lineup ever to that point, where even his TDE partner ScHoolboy Q—who'd released a really good LP, *Habits & Contradictions*, in January—had a slot to perform. Up-and-coming rappers Big K.R.I.T., Danny Brown, and experimental producer Flying Lotus were also on the bill that year. Kendrick was easily the weekend's star, even if his name wasn't the biggest on the flyer. Chris Kaskie, the then-president of Pitchfork Media, says he knew he wanted to book Kendrick to play the fest the year prior—in 2011—but the lineup was already locked in by the time *Section.80* was released. Kaskie says Pitchfork paid Kendrick five thousand dollars to play its Blue Stage in 2012. "There probably wasn't a day from spring 2012 to the fest I didn't worry about him getting too big and move away from [it]," Kaskie says. Ryan Schreiber, the founder and CEO of Pitchfork, remembers the Pitchfork crowd being especially excited to see Kendrick. There was an eight-month period from when the company booked the rapper to play the festival to when he actually set foot on the stage, so the buzz only heightened. "I remember watching people flood from other stages mid-set over to this tiny blue stage," Schreiber says. "And seeing these massive throngs of people stretching out, way past the food stands and everything else. For us to see Kendrick having that kind of pull that early on was pretty impressive."

Somewhat inexplicably, he'd made a fan out of Lady Gaga, who by 2012 had become a mega pop star with the type of box office fame we hadn't seen since Madonna in the mid-1980s. From the outside, the friendship felt odd: she was an eccentric personality who had worn a meat dress to the MTV Video Music Awards just two years prior. Kendrick was introverted, didn't like drama, and was more content living in his own head. Nonetheless, Gaga came to the festival in a mini motorcade, and pulled up to the rear of the Blue Stage, where he was performing. There were rumors that she might even perform with him. Gaga's appearance was a big deal for Kendrick and the festival itself: Pitchfork was known for attracting niche artists with sizable cult followings, not ones with Gaga's gravitational pull. "We didn't have any notice of her showing up and being sidestage until a half hour beforehand," Schreiber recalls. "She just rolled up and there she was."

Rappers with bigger names and bigger budgets couldn't land a Gaga cosign, so for Kendrick—a nascent MC who was anti-industry—to garner that level of interest meant he really had something worth hearing. That he didn't care about the fame likely attracted Gaga to his music. "She's a regular person," Kendrick told Pitchfork. "We became friends off of the genuine love for the music. She just hit my phone one day and said that she had a respect for the hip-hop that I was doing, that it wasn't like anything she heard on the radio. Then chemistry collided from there."

The energy was hectic backstage at the festival. Pitchfork staffers had to somehow sneak in one of the biggest pop stars in the world without disrupting Kendrick's set. "By the time the show happened, you could see her sidestage jamming out to each song, but very clearly not planning to come out," Kaskie recalls. "After some talks with [my business partner] Mike

Reed and some folks on their team, it sounded like Gaga saw his set as 'his moment' and didn't want to take the spotlight off of him. I thought that was fucking awesome of her, because it definitely would've made the show all the more frenzied." There was something electric about Kendrick, something engaging yet somewhat foreign. No one could figure him out or make sense of the connections he made in such a short time. And because the rapper didn't divulge a lot when he spoke made him even more mysterious, and thus, more intriguing. Two questions followed Kendrick as he rose up the ranks: *Of all the budding lyricists in the world, how did he get Dr. Dre's cosign? And just how the hell did he get* Gaga's *attention?!*

In the whirlwind that his life quickly became, the rapper struggled to reconcile his ascendance. Yet to those closest to him, the love wasn't surprising at all. He was a genuine dude who had worked *incredibly* hard in silence to finally reach this point. People like Kendrick don't stop to smell the flowers or revel in the love that they've rightfully earned; they're obsessed with getting better. Good work is the foundation of success, and even if Dave Free, Sounwave, "Top Dawg" Tiffith, Dre, or Gaga hadn't seen greatness in Kendrick, he was destined to win anyway. He had his head on straight; he wasn't going to cheat the process. "He put in his ten thousand hours to be an ascendant master at his craft. He's incredibly disciplined," says vocalist Anna Wise, one-half (or one-third, depending on who was in the group) of Sonnymoon, an alt-soul and bedroom pop outfit of which Kendrick became a fan after watching clips on YouTube. Kendrick reached out to Wise because he liked the different characters she portrayed in her music. Within the course of a song, she could flip her falsetto from sultry to cartoonish. The two sang on "Cartoon & Cereal" and became frequent collaborators.

The genesis of Kendrick's legend can be traced to that stage, in Union Park, on a sweltering ninety-two-degree day on Chicago's North Side, where fans chanted his name with a vigor that they hadn't before. Somewhere along the way, Kendrick became a household name; they *knew* these songs and yelled the rapper's bars back to him when his DJ, Ali, cut the instrumental for their voices to shine through. *Section.80* tracks like "HiiiPoWeR," "Hol' Up," and "Fuck Your Ethnicity" had suddenly become cult favorites. "I remember watching him just cut *loose*," Schreiber recalls. Fans—and, yes, even Lady Gaga—saw Kendrick sweat through a forty-five-minute set and become a leading man in real time. In the summer of 2014, Kendrick returned to Union Park and the Pitchfork Music Festival, this time as one of its three headliners. This time the money was much better (roughly three hundred thousand dollars) and the stakes were much higher. Plus, Kendrick was earning serious clout. "We wanted him to feel not just that he was here to headline, but we were also about his people and community," Kaskie says. "We booked ScHoolboy and SZA not to appease, but to also celebrate what we know to be a powerful thing growing on the West Coast." Indeed, there was a renaissance of sorts happening in West Coast rap, due in part to Kendrick and TDE. Around 2010, a collective of L.A.-based rappers captivated pop culture with shocking antics and hardcore rhymes. They called themselves Odd Future, and they were led by the garish Tyler, the Creator—a fire-breathing producer and MC who once bit into a cockroach in a music video. Also in the group were rapper Earl Sweatshirt and singer Frank Ocean, two superstars-in-waiting who would become respective cornerstones in underground rap and R&B. Sweatshirt birthed a movement of heavy-eyed, conversational rap that paired weed-induced flows with obscure soul-sampling loops. In 2012, Ocean released *channel ORANGE*, his spectacular major-label debut album, and was quickly dubbed an R&B savior. Then there was YG, a Compton-born gangsta rapper whose work with producer and fellow L.A. native DJ Mustard was a glossy alternative to Kendrick's heady approach.

On July 31, 2012, Kendrick released "Swimming Pools (Drank)" as the first official single from *good kid, m.A.A.d city*, and his life changed forever. On the surface, "Swimming Pools" seemed to celebrate the joy and eventual crash of excessive drinking, with its unforgettable hook that crowds love to recite. "Pour up (Drank!), head shot (Drank!)," the chorus goes. When performed at open-air festivals like Pitchfork's, and after several hours of guzzling beer and eating street food, "Swimming Pools" hits like a party song, with its deep, vaporous bass line and sledgehammering drum loop. Dig into the lyrics and you hear Kendrick wrestling with his family's history of alcoholism, and how their struggles led to his own complicated relationship with the drug. "Now I done grew up 'round some people livin' their life in bottles," he raps. "Granddaddy had the golden flask / Backstroke every day in Chicago." When he was younger, Kendrick wanted to fit in with the popular kids, so he drank solely for that reason.

The song also addresses the peer pressure associated with drinking, that if you're out with friends, you're expected to get drunk. If you don't, you're somehow considered soft and clowned for "babysittin' only two or three shots." This speaks to the genius of Kendrick Lamar: on this song and others, the rapper knew how to weave serious themes through pop-infused beats, educating listeners without preaching to them. He wrote illusively and buried the message, thus making it connect with passive and active listeners. "Swimming Pools" was a dark song teeming with Kendrick's personal torment, but because he talked *to* you and not *at* you, the rapper was able to relate on a human level. Many of us have some sort of connection to alcoholism, so the lyrics hit home in a way that simply wasn't on Top 40 radio at that time. It was just *different*, much like Kanye West's "Jesus Walks" in 2004; with its backing choir and marching drums, that song was gospel masquerading as hip-hop. (In 2019, Kanye leaned heavily into that aesthetic; his ninth studio album, *Jesus Is King*, was essentially a Christian rap record.)

"I wanted to do something that felt good, but had a meaning behind it at the same time," Kendrick once told Complex regarding "Swimming Pools." "I wanted to do something that's universal to everybody but still true to myself. What better way to make something universal than to speak about drinking? I'm coming from a household where you had to make a decision—you were either a casual drinker or you were a drunk. That's what that record is really about, me experiencing that as a kid and making my own decisions."

People never address alcoholism in mainstream music, said producer T-Minus, who compiled the beat for "Swimming Pools." "A lot of people, when they first hear it, they think it's just about drinking and the positive effects of getting drunk," he told Complex. "But this record talks about the negative effects as well. Which is really dope because not a lot of people want to touch on all the other things." Because Kendrick went against the grain, and because he was a real person talking about real topics, and because he appreciated the spotlight (yet wasn't seduced by it), "Swimming Pools"—and his music overall—gave us energy. It peaked at number 17 on the U.S. *Billboard* Hot 100, making it Kendrick's first big hit. Almost overnight, he'd broken away from underground rap.

From there, it was full speed toward the October release of *good kid, m.A.A.d city*, now one of the most anticipated albums of 2012. Though the rapper played it cool during the press run, there was a lot riding on *good kid* for him and TDE as a whole. The memory of Jay Rock's failed Warner deal was still fresh in their minds. Coupled with the critical success of *Section.80*, along with the Dre and Gaga cosigns, Kendrick's major-label debut had to be a home run. There were too many eyes on him; no way this could flop. "We've done a lot, but we haven't sold any records," Tiffith said at the time. "This is our real first release. This is going to set the tone for TDE."

Kendrick's interviews leading up to the album release only heightened anticipation: after listening to the record, he declared, we were going to know why he didn't drink too much or smoke at all, and why he held his family and friends so closely. He only gave us a little bit in these interviews, and in some instances, he'd start to unpack the album's concept before stopping himself. He'd been planning this album since his days of dropping mixtapes and he didn't want to give too much away. He wanted us all to be surprised, to see his hometown in all its nuanced splendor. The *good kid* album was Kendrick's crowning achievement; now it was time to unleash it on the world.

Released October 22, 2012, *good kid, m.A.A.d city* wasn't just a dope album; it was an exquisite masterpiece that far exceeded everyone's already grand expectations. It didn't sound like a West Coast rap record, at least not completely; songs like "Sherane a.k.a. Master Splinter's Daughter," "The Art of Peer Pressure," "Sing About Me, I'm Dying of Thirst," and "Real" had the lush openness of a Southern rap cut, and Kendrick sounded a lot like André 3000. He had the same breathless, conversational flow as the OutKast rapper and peppered his rhymes with the same rich symbolism. In fact, Kendrick played the album track "Bitch, Don't Kill My Vibe" for André before the album came out, since TDE's Punch Henderson wanted him on the song, but André, who was shooting the Hendrix biopic *Jimi: All Is By My Side* at the time, wasn't in the headspace for it.

Nonetheless, *good kid, m.A.A.d city* was a cinematic marvel that unfolded like a Quentin Tarantino movie: subtitled *A Short Film by Kendrick Lamar*, the listener is dropped into a cliff-hanger right away, on the opening song, "Sherane a.k.a. Master Splinter's Daughter," then the album slowly unpacks the details leading to the protagonist's dilemma. It was a beguiling puzzle in which scenes are out of order but the story still flows. Above all, it was incredibly *visual*; on "Backseat Freestyle," you could almost see Kendrick rhyming in the backseat of a friend's car at the behest of his crew. Set in 2004, he was still K-Dot, and the song—the third single from *good kid, m.A.A.d city*—was an unbridled lyrical assault akin to his early mixtapes. The album moved methodically with great subtlety and care, not wasting any audio, delving into the fun and trouble that young black kids in Compton can get into. The cover art is also essential to the narrative: the album's deluxe version—with six bonus tracks, including the "Bitch, Don't Kill My Vibe" remix with Jay-Z and "Now or Never" with Mary J. Blige—consists of an old Polaroid photo of his mom's van parked in front of their house. The regular twelve-track version is covered by an equally nostalgic pic of young Kendrick sitting on his uncle's lap at a white table. His grandfather is to his left and another uncle is to his far right. It perfectly depicts the dichotomy that characterized Kendrick's life and music: his eyes are innocent, not knowing that the uncle who's holding him throws up a gang sign underneath his tiny arm. On the table is Kendrick's milk bottle near a forty-ounce bottle of beer. "That photo, it says so much about my life and about how I was raised in Compton and the things I've seen," Kendrick said in 2012.

The album began with a song about "Sherane," a girl Kendrick met at a house party and with whom he wanted to have sex. She lived "down the street from Dominguez High / . . . borderline Compton or Paramount." According to the song, her mother was a crack addict and her family had a history of gangbanging. The story begins with seventeen-year-old Kendrick driving down Rosecrans Avenue in his mother's Caravan, with a fifth of Grey Goose vodka in the trunk and barely enough gas to get to his destination. He finally gets there, when he sees two dudes in black hoodies looking to start trouble. This could be a setup, or maybe Kendrick was simply in the wrong neighborhood at the wrong time. Just as he sees them, his phone rings: It's his mother, Paula, wondering where the hell Kendrick went with her van. "You told me you was gon' be back in fifteen minutes!" Paula exclaims, her voice racked with frustration. "I gotta go to the county buildin', man / These kids ready to *eat*! / I'm ready to eat, *shiit*." Kendrick's father, Kenny, doesn't care about any of that; he only wants to know what his son did with his damn dominoes: "This the second time I asked you to bring my fuckin' dominoes / Keep losin' my goddamn dominoes, we gon' have to go in the back-yard, and squab, homie!" This exchange, right near the end of the song, quickly shifts the mood, bringing levity to a tense scene. As his parents leave a comedic voicemail, we don't know if Kendrick made it past the guys, or if they were even worried about him in the first place. And after all that, did he even link with Sherane?

Then there's "The Art of Peer Pressure," which delves into the home invasion that almost got him arrested. Here we see Kendrick and his friends rolling down the street, "four deep in a white Toyota / A quarter tank of gas, one pistol and orange soda." They're speeding down the 405 at two thirty in the afternoon playing a CD by rapper Young Jeezy. Later, when the sun begins to set, they get to the house they'd been plotting to rob for a couple of months. Kendrick goes through the back window looking for anything—a Nintendo video game system, DVDs, and plasma-screen televisions. Then they dash out of the neighborhood as cops give chase—or so they thought:

> *We made a right, then made a left, then made a right*
> *Then made a left, we was just circlin' life . . .*
> *But they made a right, then made a left*
> *Then made a right, then another right*
> *One lucky night with the homies*

This was also the first time that Kendrick ever smoked weed. "Usually I'm drug-free," he declared, "but, shit, I'm with the homies." We learn four tracks later, on "m.A.A.d city," that the blunt was laced with cocaine, which explains why he didn't do drugs as an adult: "Imagine if your first blunt had you foamin' at the mouth."

The album featured Jay Rock, Drake, Anna Wise, Mary J. Blige, and Dr. Dre, but the guest star on "m.A.A.d city" was easily the most surprising. As the beat flips from a dark, menacing stomp to a bright, headbanging trunk rattler, a Compton OG named MC Eiht announced his arrival in the most MC Eiht way possible. "Wake yo' punk ass up!" the veteran rapper implored. "It ain't nuthin' but a Compton thang / G-yeah." MC Eiht was considered a legend in Los Angeles and West Coast hip-hop overall. The rapper was perhaps best known for his 1993 song "Streiht Up Menace," which told the semi-imagined tale of a young black man growing up in Compton, whose father was killed and whose mother struggled to put food on the table. Ultimately, the character—loosely based on the protagonist in the film *Menace II Society*, which Eiht also starred in—joins a gang and dies while protecting his block. Eiht, with his trademark baseball cap and long braids, was known for these sorts of voyeuristic rhymes that warn listeners against bloodthirsty cops and gun-toting gangbangers. In Eiht's world, Compton was a dark place where death and jail sentences awaited young black men at every turn. He'd been pretty quiet until he resurfaced on Kendrick's album, showing up on "m.A.A.d city" to "teach you some lessons of the street" while letting the good kid know that the bullshit he had endured in Compton had been going on since the 1980s. On the song, MC Eiht sounded like his old self: chill, no-nonsense, brotherly but not preachy. Kendrick grew up listening to hip-hop like this, so to have a legend like Eiht on his major-label debut was a big accomplishment.

"Some people of mine knew Kendrick. They contacted me and said that he wanted to do a song with me. I said, 'Cool,' and told them to slide him my number," Eiht tells me. "He hit me like two weeks later." From there, Eiht and Kendrick met at the studio, where the younger rapper laid out the concept of "m.A.A.d city." Kendrick wanted to pay homage to the old days of Compton and the golden age of gangsta rap: "We sat down, he played me the song and let me hear the hook. I came up with my verse and everything went like clockwork. He could've gotten anybody from Compton to be on the song, but because of the type of music I had put out, which always referenced Compton and the streets, that was the type of flavor he wanted on it. He was trying to bring an authentic cat who used to do rap back in the days, who came from that era. It was basically a studio conversation and him telling me that he wanted me to do what I was known for."

Kendrick wasn't like some other rappers with whom Eiht had collaborated. He was about the work and that was it. "He's a real laid-back kid, humble, wasn't too demanding for somebody who was making his first major project," Eiht says. "Usually, cats don't really have a direction of what they wanna do. They just have me come in the studio and be like, 'Hey, Eiht, bust a verse.' And usually I ask dudes, 'What's the concept? What's the direction?' and they say, 'Hey, just do what you do.' He had the time to sit down with me and explain, so that shows the great respect he has for the craft of hip-hop. He's not one of them guys with fifty million people in the studio with drank and smoke and all that type of shit. Everything was basically just work. Some people need the props or whatever, the ambience of the stereotypical hip-hop scene, but true artists bypass a lot of that. When you're somebody like Kendrick, who's really articulate about what you want to produce and put out to the people, you have to be serious-minded."

For *good kid, m.A.A.d city*, Kendrick tapped deeply into a tumultuous past that he'd moved beyond. And where other musicians might only present the best of themselves, he told his entire truth, imploring kids in Compton to dream beyond the city. On "m.A.A.d city," we learn that he had a real job for only a month; he was a security guard, but got fired after he staged a robbery there three weeks into the gig. Sure, he was a burgeoning star with a record deal and big affirmations, but Kendrick was still part of the community and felt the same pain that they did. On "Money Trees," he remembered leaner times, of putting hot sauce on cheap ramen noodles, and rapping in cyphers even when cash wasn't in the picture. He honored his uncle Tony, who saw big things for his nephew's career but was shot twice in the head at a local Louis Burgers before his prediction came true: "He said one day I'll be on tour, ya bish . . . / A Louis belt will never ease that pain." We learn near the end of "Poetic Justice," a sultry R&B-focused cut that samples pop icon Janet Jackson's song "Any Time, Any Place"—and is named after a film in which she and Tupac starred—that Kendrick was jumped before he ever got a chance to link with Sherane. "I'mma tell you where *I'm* from," declared one of the men who interrogated Kendrick in his mom's van. "You gon' tell me where *you* from, okay? / Or where your grandma stay, where yo' mama stay, or where yo' *daddy* stay." In most cities throughout the U.S., these kinds of questions will never come up; but in Compton, where claiming the wrong neighborhood will get you beat up or killed, they're incredibly common. The attack on Kendrick led to a shootout and the subsequent death of one of his friends.

The incident and its aftermath is laid out masterfully on "Sing About Me, I'm Dying of Thirst," *good kid*'s centerpiece and one of Kendrick's most powerful songs ever. On this two-part, twelve-minute epic, the rapper unpacks the anger of watching one of his friends die in front of him, and how a chance run-in with an older woman changed his life forever. The first verse is easily the most sobering: he rhymes from the perspective of a friend named Dave, whose brother was killed and Kendrick was there to see it. The friend was in the streets, still trying to find a passion that could take him away from that life. But he was in too far at that point, and just couldn't change his ways. If Dave died, he wanted Kendrick to memorialize him and his brother in a song. Sure enough, Kendrick's friend was shot and killed before *good kid, m.A.A.d city* dropped. The second verse revisits "Keisha's Song (Her Pain)" from 2011's *Section.80*, where Kendrick details the story of a prostitute who was raped and killed by a john; it was a tragic tale that Keisha's younger sister didn't want to be told. "I met her sister and she went at me about her sister Keisha," Kendrick once told MTV News, "basically saying she didn't want [me] to put her business out there and if your album do come out, don't mention me, don't sing about me." Going against the demands of Keisha's sister, Kendrick rapped the second verse from her vantage point, his voice defiant, then fading away. On the third verse, Kendrick raps from his own perspective as he tries to comprehend his own demise and what that could mean in the afterlife. At that point, he still hadn't found the God he sought, but with death chasing him so steadily, he put his burdens in the hands of Jesus Christ, dousing himself in figurative holy water before it was too late. In this moment, Kendrick was physically and spiritually drained; he'd been running down his dreams so fervently that he truly needed rest. He let those emotions build up, taking each murder, every jailed friend and relative, and putting it all on his back. He was determined to carry the load and somehow make it better for everyone. But that cuts both ways: *With Kendrick looking out for so many people, how could he possibly look out for himself?* The third verse is prayerful and carried by Kendrick's inferiority complex. "Am I worth it?" he asks. "Did I put enough work in?"

The song's second half, "I'm Dying of Thirst," gives Kendrick the cathartic release he needed. A riveting gospel-focused cut with haunting choral moans and cascading bass drums, the track is vengeful at first, and represents the moment when fight or flight kicks in. Everything in Kendrick says, *Go kill the niggas that killed my friend*, but a chance encounter with an elder changes all of that. "I don't want to say she was religious, but she was a spiritual lady who broke down what life is really about to us," Kendrick told Complex in 2012:

"I'm Dying of Thirst" represents being in a situation where all this happens throughout the day, but at the end of the day we run into this particular lady and she breaks down the story of God, positivity,

life, being free, and being real with yourself. She was letting us know what's really real. Because you have to leave this earth and speak to somebody of a higher power. That song represents being baptized, the actual water, getting dipped in holy water. It represents when my whole spirit changed, when my life starts—my life that you know right now, that's when it starts.

The woman is calm, resolute, and a blessing, not at all intimidated by the fury of the young men. She settles their spirit and makes them recite a prayer to wash away their past:

Thank you, Lord Jesus, for saving me with your precious blood
In Jesus' name, Amen

Without that elder, who knows what would've happened. Maybe Kendrick and his friends kill the dude who smoked one of their own. Maybe they get away with it or maybe they don't. Maybe their friends come back and pop more of Kendrick's friends. Or maybe they pop Kendrick. Then there's no mixtapes, no tours with Tech N9ne and Drake, no meeting Dre and Snoop, no record deal, no *good kid, m.A.A.d city*. He'd be just another dead black boy in a city and country that doesn't care about black life. He'd be another statistic, one more cold body beneath a thin white sheet. More important, Kenny and Paula's son would be gone. Despite his dad's loving real talk and his mom's wide-eyed optimism, it took the voice of a person outside the home to set Kendrick on the right path. The elder was there just when he needed it and saved his life as a result. His parents guided him, but she was the angel that arrived at the very second things could've gone horribly wrong.

The next song, "Real," represents Kendrick's divine awakening. This is where the rapper understands—with the help of his father—that running the streets didn't make him cool, that "realness is responsibility, realness is taking care of your . . . family, realness is God . . ." If "I'm Dying of Thirst" was Kendrick's baptism, "Real" is the moment he rose from the water, fully anointed as a new man, much to his mother's delight. "Tell your story to these black and brown kids in Compton," Paula implores on his voicemail. "Let 'em know you was just like them, but you still rose from that dark place of violence, becoming a positive person. But when you do make it, give back with your words of encouragement, and that's the best way to give back to your city . . . And I love you, Kendrick." Songs like "Sing About Me, I'm Dying of Thirst" and "Real" fulfill the prophecy of "Jesus Saves," a one-off tune floating around the internet. On it, Kendrick wondered why his God kept blessing the song's protagonist, even after he's cussed out his mother, hit his girlfriend, and fired a handgun. As the song plays, his voice cracks, sobbing through his testimony while a good friend suffers through a string of bad luck.

The *good kid* album ends with "Compton," the vaunted Dr. Dre and Kendrick collab. Where the album's other songs felt tethered to Kendrick's coming-of-age in 2004, that track seemed to merge all eras of Compton, the teacher and the student. Just Blaze admits that he wasn't impressed with Kendrick's music at first; he'd downloaded *Section.80* but hadn't played it before the rapper's session with Dre, then he'd heard another song—though he can't remember which one—and wasn't feeling it. But then Just Blaze heard an advance of *good kid, m.A.A.d city* in the studio while mixing "Compton" and was hooked. "I was like, 'Okay, this is different,'" the producer recalls. "When I heard the fact that it was a story line that was woven through the album, which is something that had been missing in hip-hop for a while, and then when I heard that mix of more traditional hip-hop sounds with what was considered more contemporary at that time, then you had MC Eiht on the album. All of that together, you could tell this was a kid who was young and on the cutting edge of what the next group of young artists were gonna be. But it was also a kid who understood and respected what came before him. And that's what made it special to me. Just how he embraced both sides of it, from the production to the song references to the slang and the language. Not too many artists in his age group were doing that in hip-hop at that time, with the skill and the caliber with which he was doing it. I did not expect it to become this new wave of hip-hop only because I wasn't sure the climate was ready for it. So when it became successful, I was that much more happy for him."

The Kendrick heard toward the end of *good kid* is the guy we'd see for years, the intensely private guy who took time for himself and eschewed the approval of others. The album chronicled his evolution from a cocky child who was quick to succumb to peer pressure to an independent, self-assured person. This is where he put God in control of his life and art, and where his work became therapeutic for himself and listeners at large. Close your eyes, and the combination of "Sing About Me, I'm Dying of Thirst" and "Real" play like old church records, the feeling of stress relief in harmonic form.

In its totality, *good kid, m.A.A.d city* presented the full spectrum of Compton and its people, not just the negative aspects you'd see on the news. By presenting the good and the bad, the light and the dark, Kendrick triumphed; the world caught on, and it became a massive critical and commercial hit. *Rolling Stone* praised the rapper for "setting spiritual yearnings and moral dilemmas against a backdrop of gang violence and police brutality." Pitchfork lauded the album's "autobiographical intensity." "Listening to it feels like walking directly into Lamar's childhood home and, for the next hour, growing up alongside him," music critic and author Jayson Greene wrote.

Upon its release, *good kid* hit the *Billboard* 200 chart at number 2 and sold roughly 241,000 copies in its first week. It marked the second-highest opening for an R&B/hip-hop album that year, with only Nicki Minaj's *Pink Friday: Roman Reloaded* selling more in its first week of release. Still, *good kid, m.A.A.d city* went gold by the end of 2012, selling 500,000 units, and platinum a year later, with more than one million units sold. As of September 2019, the record surpassed Eminem's 2002 record, *The Eminem Show*, as the longest-running hip-hop album on the *Billboard* charts. It was fitting that Kendrick shared the same milestone as Eminem; when *good kid, m.A.A.d city* came out, Em was one of his biggest supporters. "When I first heard Kendrick's debut on Aftermath, I couldn't believe it," he said in 2016. "The fact that it was his first real album and he was able to make it into a story [that] intertwines with the skits like that was genius. That hasn't really been done that many times, let alone on someone's first time up. The level of wordplay, the deliveries, the beats—it's just a masterpiece."

The album also drew praise from another acclaimed storyteller in hip-hop: Nas. "No disrespect to nobody else in rap music, but Kendrick Lamar," the rapper told the Associated Press; his 1994 debut album, *Illmatic*, is considered by some to be the greatest rap record of all time. "I'm really happy about his record. I needed that. His record reaches you. It gives you hope." In an interview with *Vibe*, Kendrick revealed that he wanted Nas to rap on "Sing About Me, I'm Dying of Thirst," but didn't have time to reach out. "I was so wrapped up in getting the music done, samples cleared and mastered," Kendrick said. "I didn't really wanna rush the process. I actually wanted to sit in the studio and vibe with him." Nas was right: *good kid, m.A.A.d city* connected because it came from such an authentic place, and it used a wide array of beats, vocal manipulation, and personal history to make it resonate with listeners everywhere. There are strong parallels between *Illmatic* and *good kid, m.A.A.d city*, from the baby pictures that don the front covers to the filmic way the music unfurls. Both rappers wanted you to see the world with their eyes: in Nas's case, it was the drugs and devastation in New York City's Queensbridge projects; with Kendrick, it was the trauma beneath Compton's bright sunshine. Nas and Kendrick wrote incisively about their respective cities, uncovering vast worlds through subtle imagery that puts you in the scene they're narrating. *Illmatic* transported us to the subway and the block; *good kid* put us in the car on the freeway.

Privately, though, Kendrick wondered if listeners would understand his debut album. "I'd be lying to you to say I knew *good kid, m.A.A.d city* would be as successful as it has been," the rapper wrote in a *XXL* cover story in 2015:

In the beginning I was very doubtful. Once I was done, the jitters hit me so fast. I was so confident in making it, because I was like, "This is it, man. Nobody heard this story and if you heard it, you heard it in bits and pieces but I'm finna put it to you in a whole album—from Compton, from the hood, from the streets—it's a whole other perspective and light, I'ma go back and do the skits just like how Biggie and Dre and Snoop and 'Pac did it. And I'ma tell my story." Then I wrapped up with it and said, "Man, what's on the radio right now? I don't think they doin' skits and things like that." I don't know if the people are gonna understand what I'm talkin' about on this album because it's almost like a puzzle pieced together, and albums ain't been created like this in a long time.

The rapper was nervous until he got a call from producer Pharrell Williams that shifted his perspective. "He said he had a copy of the album and it's amazing," Kendrick wrote. "That call was right on time because that was when I was feeling super insecure about it. Pharrell said, 'Never feel that way again. When that little negative man come behind your head, always follow your first heart, and that was your first heart, to put the album out like this.' . . . He said, 'Watch what's gonna happen.'"

Suddenly, Kendrick was famous. Fans trekked to his childhood home to take pictures of his mom's van, so much so that she had to hide the vehicle. Go to Google Maps and type "Good Kid M.A.A.D City House"; pictures of the home pop up like some sort of Graceland for rap fans. The album became source material for an English composition class at Georgia Regents University, where

Professor Adam Diehl used it as a gateway to study authors Gwendolyn Brooks, James Joyce, and James Baldwin. "With Kendrick's album," Diehl told *USA Today*, "you've got gang violence, you've got child-family development in the inner city, you've got drug use and the war on drugs . . . a lot of the things that are hot-button issues for today are just inherent in the world of Compton, California." The professor didn't just stop there: his course on *good kid, m.A.A.d city* led to themed classes involving Kendrick's work for the next five years. In 2016, he taught a class on leadership based on *To Pimp a Butterfly*; in 2017, he taught a class about emotions centered on Kendrick's *DAMN*. "Everything synthesized around the concept of *good kid, m.A.A.d city*," Diehl tells me. "I used it as a way to look at the things that happen to kids. It's a rap album that sinks into literature. He's a master storyteller, and it's such an engaging album to play through."

Whether you were a teenager in Compton or a young adult from Landover, Maryland, *good kid* forced you to think about your own upbringing, of hot summer days riding shotgun in your friend's car, going nowhere in particular. The album felt like basketball at the park on rusty goals with chains dangling from the rim, the spiritual richness of your grandma's old hymnals, the humidity so thick you can almost see it. It evoked barbershop convos, the feel of shabby concrete beneath your fresh Nike sneakers, and the taste of fried chicken wings fresh out of the grease. It was a record for the hood, for black and brown kids with big dreams and little resources, who loved their environment but knew they couldn't thrive there. It was about the unconditional love between Kendrick and his friends, Kendrick and his neighborhood, Kendrick and his parents, and how—ultimately—he'd have to leave the city but it would never leave him. It celebrated home and all the angels who didn't know they were angels, the ones who shielded Kendrick from harm, although they didn't have the same cover. Time has been kind to *good kid, m.A.A.d city*; it's now considered one of the best albums of the 2010s, and one of the best hip-hop albums of all time.

5

The Fight for Black Life

Even as Kendrick thrived, race relations continued to erode in the United States. On February 26, 2012, a seventeen-year-old boy named Trayvon Martin was in Sanford, Florida, visiting family, not thinking this trip would be his last. He'd traveled there with his father, Tracy, to stay with Tracy's fiancée, Brandy Green, in the townhome she rented in the gated Retreat at Twin Lakes community. Once there, Trayvon figured he'd walk down the street, pick up some Skittles and a can of AriZona brand juice from the 7-Eleven, then head back without any problems. But being black in the United States means you have to move differently; you don't have the freedom to just *be*. You can't wear bad days on your face. You have to look nonthreatening and make others feel comfortable, not realizing that your brown skin will never be fully accepted in a country built on white supremacy. Such supremacy is the foundation of America, right there with hate crimes, apple pie, and mass shootings. This creates someone like George Zimmerman, a neighborhood-watch coordinator, and gives him the power to trek a gated community with a handgun and the perceived right to kill. White supremacy also creates the perception that Trayvon—a tall, scrawny kid from Miami Gardens—is somehow a threat simply because he's black. White supremacy breeds the idea that blacks are monolithic, that because a young kid wears a dark hooded sweatshirt, he's up to no good and doesn't belong in certain neighborhoods. Then he's not allowed to ask why he's being followed; he was supposed to ingest the harassment and move on like it didn't happen. In a land that proclaims freedom for all, it doesn't extend those same liberties to black people. None of this is new, but on that night in 2012, the centuries-old racism that blacks endure came to a head in a very public way.

Around 7:00 p.m., Zimmerman called the Sanford Police Department to report a so-called "suspicious person" in the gated community. "This guy looks like he's up to no good, or he's on drugs or something," Zimmerman claimed in the 911 call. "It's raining and he's just walking around looking about. . . . These assholes, they always get away." Zimmerman can be heard saying "fucking coons" (a racial slur against black people) in relation to Trayvon, who's running away from his pursuit. The police told Zimmerman not to follow Trayvon, but he did anyway. According to reports, Trayvon was on the phone with his girlfriend as Zimmerman followed him in a car, openly wondering why he was being followed in the first place. An altercation ensued, and—according to Zimmerman—as he reached into his pocket for his cell phone, Trayvon threw a punch and knocked him to the ground. Trayvon got on top of Zimmerman and kept punching. That's when Zimmerman pulled a gun from his holster and fired a shot, which struck Trayvon in the chest. He was pronounced dead at 7:30 p.m. Trayvon was unarmed; he perished with just twenty-two dollars, a cell phone, a bag of candy, and some juice.

Trayvon's father didn't find out until the next morning that his son had been murdered. He was out having dinner with his fiancée and figured that Trayvon had simply gone to a movie and turned off his phone. But Tracy's greatest fear was realized when a police cruiser, an unmarked sedan, and a chaplain pulled up to the house, and he was greeted by a detective asking him to describe what clothes his son had worn the night before. Eventually, the detective came back with a photo of Trayvon at the scene, "his eyes rolled back, a tear on his cheek, saliva coming from his mouth," according to a Reuters report.

Zimmerman claimed self-defense in the killing. The police department, citing Florida's "stand your ground" law, accepted Zimmerman's claim and let him go without evidence to disprove his story. This left Tracy and Trayvon's mother, Sybrina Fulton, to wonder if justice would be served for their son. Or would he be just another black boy cut down before his prime, mourned in hashtags and candlelit vigils while his killer walked freely? In a world of fifteen-second social media clips, celebrity gossip news, and cat videos, would we care enough to mourn? Would we stop to lament this injustice, or were we that desensitized to black trauma?

It took the national media almost two weeks to care about Trayvon at all. Aside from a couple of segments on Orlando news and limited coverage in the *Orlando Sentinel* newspaper, Trayvon's death was just a blip on the radar. If it weren't for the persistence of Tracy and Sybrina, coupled with the hiring of a high-powered publicist and attorney, this story wouldn't have gotten any traction at all. Trayvon's parents launched a petition on Change.org to force Sanford police to arrest Zimmerman and for state prosecutors to fully investigate their son's death. "Trayvon was our hero," they wrote in the petition. "At the age of 9, [he] pulled his father from a burning kitchen, saving his life. He loved sports and horseback riding. At only 17 he had a bright future ahead of him with dreams of attending college and becoming an aviation mechanic. Now that's all gone." The Trayvon news coverage was a slow burn—from local, to regional, then national—due in part to the petition and online activism, with prominent civil rights leaders taking to outlets like Twitter and Facebook to denounce the teen's death. In most instances, they linked to the petition, which created a groundswell of support for the family's cause, and forced the national media to cover the story.

Still on tour with Drake and A$AP Rocky, Kendrick was watching TV on his bus when he came across the news of Trayvon's murder. He was seething, and as he told *Rolling Stone* in 2015, the incident "put a whole new anger inside me," to the point where he picked up a pen and started jotting down lyrics. An hour later, he had the first draft of a new song called "The Blacker the Berry." Trayvon's death "made me remember how I felt. Being harassed, my partners being killed," Kendrick told the publication. To him, Trayvon wasn't just some kid in the wrong place at the wrong time. *He* could've been Trayvon, shot down in cold blood as the public looked elsewhere. Not only did the news distress Kendrick, it disturbed the highest-ranking politician in the world, U.S. president Barack Obama, the country's first black president. "When Trayvon Martin was first shot, I said that this could have been my son," he told reporters at the White House. "Trayvon Martin could have been me, 35 years ago. . . . There's a lot of pain around what happened here, I think it's important to recognize that the African-American community is looking at this issue through a set of experiences and a history that doesn't go away." Central Florida, South Side Chicago, or Compton, it didn't matter: Kendrick had made similar runs to the convenience store without thinking twice about it, not worried if some glorified security guard would try to earn stripes at his expense. Trayvon was all of us, every black person in America. The bullet that pierced his skin could've punctured ours just the same.

Though the track appeared in finished form on 2015's *To Pimp a Butterfly*, Kendrick was already thinking two steps ahead, letting the anger fuel the most venomous rhymes he'd ever written. He was tapping into Compton, scrolling through the gang culture and near-death instances, funneling the angst into an unprocessed stream of intense fury. In its finished form, Kendrick spews his rage through clenched teeth, tight fists, and a furrowed brow, his tone so raspy you'd think he swallowed nails before the beat started. "You hate me, don't you?" he growls. "You hate my people, your plan is to terminate my culture." Stylistically, Kendrick had to summon a persona he hadn't tapped into for at least three years: K-Dot, the rancorous alter ego that he left behind in 2009. But this Dot was a little older and more enlightened, less interested in touting how dope he was; for "The Blacker the Berry," Kendrick seemed to tap into K-Dot's fearlessness, blending that aggression with his new-found insight to let America know just how racist it was.

Though Trayvon's murder awakened Kendrick and Black America at large, it was just the latest in a long line of savagery against unarmed people of color. In 1999, New York City police officers Kenneth Boss, Richard Murphy, Edward McMellon, and Sean Carroll fired forty-one shots at a twenty-two-year-old West African immigrant named Amadou Diallo in the Soundview section of the Bronx. Diallo had been in the U.S. for two years from his native Guinea, and when he died at the scene—from sixteen bullet wounds—there was no gun near him, just a pager and his wallet. The officers had mistaken Diallo for a serial rape suspect they'd been looking for. When Diallo had reached into his jacket to pull out his wallet, Carroll thought it was a gun and started firing; the other three officers followed suit. A year later, the four officers were acquitted of second-degree murder charges.

Then, in 2009, Bay Area Rapid Transit officer Johannes Mehserle shot Oscar Grant III, a twenty-two-year-old black man, on the platform of BART's Fruitvale station in Oakland. Grant was pinned to the ground with his hands restrained behind his back when Mehserle stood up in a panic and fired his weapon. The bullet entered Grant's back, exited his front side, ricocheted off the platform, and punctured his lung. "You shot me," Grant lamented, looking at Mehserle in disbelief. He died at Highland Hospital in Oakland seven hours later. In 2010, Mehserle was convicted of involuntary manslaughter, but wasn't found guilty of second-degree murder. He was sentenced to two years in prison;

BART reached a number of multimillion-dollar settlements with Grant's family.

The same words arise in cases like these: *fear, intimidation, suspicion, panic.* The police somehow felt afraid of Amadou's wallet, panicked by what Oscar could do facedown with his hands restrained. George Zimmerman claimed Trayvon looked suspicious, and that was enough reason to follow him through the rain and pull the trigger at point-blank range. Regardless, Trayvon's parents sought a peaceful resolution to that incident, and if they *did* demonstrate, it was at an event like the Million Hoodie March, where hundreds of supporters donned hooded sweatshirts at Union Square in New York City and asked a Florida jury to convict Zimmerman. Sadly, though, there's another word that often arises in cases like these: *acquitted.* In July 2013, Zimmerman was found not guilty of second-degree murder and manslaughter, and as of this writing, he was still free to walk the streets of Florida. It was as if—despite all the news coverage and activism—Trayvon's life still didn't matter. "Even though I am broken-hearted," Tracy Martin tweeted, "my faith is unshattered." George Zimmerman's brother, Robert, tweeted that he was "proud to be an American."

After the verdict, on the same day, three black women—Patrisse Khan-Cullors, Alicia Garza, and Opal Tometi—founded a new civil rights group called Black Lives Matter (BLM) as a direct response to Zimmerman's acquittal. Garza wrote a post on Facebook called "A Love Letter to Black People" that sought to allay fellow people of color who felt dejected by the state of race relations in America. Brimming with anger, despondence, and real talk, Garza urged readers to keep fighting injustice. "Stop saying we are not surprised," she declared in the post. "I continue to be surprised at how little Black lives matter. . . . Black people. I love you. I love us. Our lives matter." Cullors saw Garza's post and put it on Twitter with the hashtag #BlackLivesMatter; Tometi constructed the websites on which they and the public could see what was next about the Trayvon incident and others. A movement was born. But this wasn't your grandfather's activist group; while Khan-Cullors, Garza, and Tometi took their fight to the street, they also took advantage of Twitter's growing popularity, where users reacted to Zimmerman's acquittal in real time.

Social media changed the way news was consumed; no longer did viewers need to wait for the evening headlines, or for the newspaper to plop on their doorstep the next morning. The news was in their pockets; all they had to do was scroll and watch the outrage unfold.

The early days of Black Lives Matter were fairly quiet; its online presence lay dormant until 2014, when another two black men died during encounters with the police over a two-month span, which sent Black America—still raw from the death of Trayvon Martin— into a heightened state of unrest, the likes of which hadn't been seen since the civil rights era of the 1950s and '60s.

In mid-July of 2014, Eric Garner was standing outside a storefront in Staten Island, New York, when police officers accused him of selling loose, untaxed cigarettes on the street. It wasn't the first time the cops had harassed Garner; just a few weeks prior, plainclothes officers in an unmarked car had pulled up on the forty-three-year-old as he walked down Bay Street near Tompkinsville Park, where locals sell cheap wares and try to avoid police pursuits.

But according to the *New York Times*, which cited two witnesses, Garner refused to be frisked or detained, which might have raised the ire of police officers. He "shouted at them to back off," they reported. "He flailed his arms." Perhaps seeking retribution, the police encountered Garner later that month—on July 17—and questioned him after he broke up a fight on the block. Again, Garner was incredulous, pleading with the police to simply leave him alone. "I didn't do nothin'!" he can be heard saying outside the storefront. "What did I do?! I'm standing here minding my business." The encounter was videotaped via cell phone and, little did anyone know, the footage from that device would be seen by millions of people around the world. Officer Daniel Pantaleo moved in and put his forearm around Garner's neck as his colleagues helped wrestle the six-foot-two-inch, three-hundred-ninety-five-pound man to the ground. Then, as they pinned him to the sidewalk, with his head pressed against the grubby concrete, Garner whimpered a phrase eleven times, "I can't breathe," hoping that Pantaleo would release the choke hold—a move that'd been banned by the New York Police Department—and that his fellow officers would stop putting so much pressure on his chest as they handcuffed him. Video shows that, along with the choke hold, officers knelt on Garner's back, which pressed his torso against the ground and further restricted his breathing. As the life slowly drained from Garner's body, police officers ignored his pleas and proceeded with the arrest. They thought he was faking the despair as a way to avoid detainment.

Around 3:30 p.m., officers called for an ambulance to assist Garner, and emergency personnel arrived five minutes later. As he lay motionless on the ground, emergency workers were slow to give him oxygen or place him on a stretcher. The video shows emergency workers and police officers still trying to communicate with Garner although he was unconscious, and there appears to be no urgency to save his life. It wasn't until twelve minutes later that medical workers upgraded the situation to Segment 1, the highest possible level. Garner was in cardiac arrest and needed to be rushed to the hospital right away. It was too late; he was declared dead at 4:34 p.m. at Richmond University Medical Center. Two weeks later, the chief medical examiner's office ruled Garner's death a homicide caused by neck compressions from a choke hold. "Racist-ass cops on Staten Island," one woman says in the cell phone video, "this is what the fuck they do."

The circumstances surrounding Garner's death were eerily similar to a 1994 incident on Staten Island, where a twenty-two-year-old man named Ernest Sayon suffocated and died at the hands of a New York City police officer named Donald Brown. Sayon was standing outside a housing complex at Park Hill Avenue and Sobol Court when officers said they heard what they thought was a firecracker or a gunshot during drug sweeps in the neighborhood. There had been thick tension between the police and young black twentysomethings who felt they were being harassed and picked up on false charges of loitering. In some cases, according to the *New York Times*, the cops would pull down the young men's pants in a vigorous search for drugs. Sayon, described as gentle by friends and residents, had a criminal record, so he garnered extra attention in a community where some residents were already feeling unsafe. He reportedly sold crack and cocaine, but he wasn't some blood-thirsty kingpin terrorizing the block. "He never bothered nobody," his friend Corey Washington told the *Times*. "It wasn't like he was a menace to society." Still, in 1992, Sayon was arrested for drug possession and resisting arrest, in which, according to police, he "flailed his arms and rolled on the ground," causing injury to an officer's thumb. On the night Sayon died, Brown tried to detain Sayon and a struggle ensued.

The two knew each other and had an adversarial relationship. A witness, who had just parked her car along Park Hill Avenue, claimed she saw Brown beat Sayon. "I saw Officer Brown," said the woman, according to the *Times*. "He had his head in a choke-hold. He hit his head on the ground." Reports the following day said Sayon might have died from a head injury, but the chief medical examiner ruled it a homicide caused by pressure on his back, chest, and neck while handcuffed on the ground. So for Staten Island residents, Garner's death was more of the same. "It's not new to us in Staten Island, which is sad," Clifford "Method Man" Smith Jr., a Staten Island native and member of the Wu-Tang Clan, told the *Huffington Post* in 2015. "If we can just get a human level, and police can stay on a human level with the community . . . If we can just bridge that gap and get those two together . . . If we can be treated as human beings in our communities, we wouldn't have any problem with being policed."

On the morning of August 9, 2014, some 960 miles from Staten Island, Michael Brown Jr. walked into a convenience store in Ferguson, Missouri, a mostly black community roughly twelve miles outside St. Louis. The teenager could be seen on surveillance video retrieving a box of Swisher Sweets cigars, then shoving a clerk into a display case on his way out. But according to other surveillance footage, the young man had visited the store earlier that morning, shortly after 1:00 a.m., trading a brown bag for the cigarillos he'd pick up later that day.

At 11:53 a.m., a police dispatcher reported "stealing in progress" at the Ferguson Market, and Brown, wearing a white T-shirt and a red St. Louis Cardinals hat, was the prime suspect. Brown and his friend, Dorian Johnson, left the store in the direction of a Quik-Trip convenience store nearby. Then, at noon, police officer Darren Wilson arrived in an SUV and saw Brown and his friend walking down the middle of Canfield Drive. He asked them to walk on the sidewalk; Johnson said they were almost at their destination, but Brown had stronger language. "Fuck what you have to say," he reportedly told the officer. A tussle ensued between Brown and Wilson at the vehicle. Wilson pulled a handgun and threatened to shoot. "I'm standing so close to Big Mike and the officer, I look in his window and I see that he has his gun pointed at both of us," Johnson once said. "And when he fired his weapon, I moved seconds before he pulled the trigger. I saw the fire come out the barrel and I . . . knew it was a gun. I looked at my friend Big Mike and saw he was struck in the chest or upper region because I saw blood spatter down his side."

From there, Brown and Johnson take off running down the street. Wilson gets out of his car with his gun drawn and fires a second shot at Brown, striking him. Then the teenager turns around with his hands up, saying that he's unarmed and to stop shooting. Wilson fires several more shots at Brown, striking him four times. The teenager falls to the ground and dies, his body left in the street for four and a half hours.

The Butterfly Effect

In places like Staten Island and Ferguson, the deaths of Garner and Brown exacerbated long-standing strife between law enforcement and the black community. In both cities, there was a feeling that the police weren't there to protect them. And because the officers assigned to their neighborhoods weren't really *from* there, they didn't have a connection with the city or understand its dynamics. Most cities deploy white cops to patrol black neighborhoods, and it's largely white cops who claim fear after they shoot and kill an unarmed black person. This is the essence of white privilege: when you're used to having your way, it's easy to feel threatened when you're devoid of power. Because white supremacy dictates reverence to white skin, and because the police thrive on terror, they can't fathom those who won't genuflect. They can't deal when you don't act scared, so they fire handguns to reclaim authority over the people they look down upon. Garner had the audacity to say no. Brown had the gall to fight back. Those actions disrupt the systemic racism and classism that keeps America running. If people of color realized they weren't beholden to police, they'd upset the ecosystem of state-sanctioned violence that's been in place since slavery. In Ferguson, some black residents make it a point to stay home after a certain hour, knowing that they could be stopped by the police for no reason at all. Like in 2009, when Ferguson police arrested Henry Davis by mistake, and instead of letting him go, they assaulted Davis in a jail cell and charged him with property damage for bleeding on an officer's uniform. Five years later, Darren Wilson said he feared for his life when asked why he killed Brown. "It was like a five-year-old holding on to Hulk Hogan," the officer said about the size difference between him and Brown. Pantaleo never claimed he was afraid of Garner; in his incident, he and his colleagues assaulted a man who'd clearly had enough aggravation from the cops.

The wounds are still fresh for Mike Brown's father, Michael Brown Sr. He's incredibly measured when talking about his son's death, but he cuts the anecdote short to dull the pain of that day. "I got a call that he was dead in the middle of the street," Brown Sr. tells me. "I get in the car and I can't even tell you about the ride." Once he got to the scene, he saw his son's flip-flops in the road, his red baseball hat resting on its crown. "By the time I got there, Mike was covered up" with a white sheet, he recalls. "He was on the ground for four and a half hours, deteriorating." The image was unsettling, to say the least. For a while, Brown's body was not covered up, which allowed neighbors to take pictures with their cell phones for social media. That Brown's corpse was left to rot in the summer heat only amplified local tensions.

With each hour, Ferguson residents seethed. "The delay helped fuel the outrage," Patricia Bynes, a former committeewoman in Ferguson, told the *New York Times* in 2014. "It was very disrespect-ful to the community and the people who live there. It also sent the message from law enforcement that 'we can do this to you any day, any time, in broad daylight, and there's nothing you can do about it.'" Riots ensued following a candlelight vigil near the shooting scene two days after Brown was killed. Stores were broken into or set on fire. Police cruisers had windows smashed with bricks. It was akin to the riots in Kendrick's backyard—in 1965 Watts and 1992 South Central. Americans didn't know about Ferguson prior to Mike Brown's death, but they would very soon; it would be the epicenter of unrest in the United States. The black people of Ferguson had had enough; the years of unprocessed fury finally bubbled to the surface and exploded over the next two weeks. Coupled with the still-potent pain of Trayvon Martin's death in 2012 and Eric Garner's demise in July 2014, Ferguson, and Black America, was in the midst of a cultural revolution. Protesters marched down the street with their hands raised, chanting, "Hands up! Don't shoot!" referring to the way Brown was gunned down despite having his arms raised.

Meanwhile, in New York City, there was a similar fight underway. In late August, an estimated 2,500 people—led by the Reverend Al Sharpton and Eric Garner's widow, Esaw—marched through Staten Island to peacefully protest Eric Garner's homicide. Unlike the Ferguson protesters, some of whom expressed their frustration through looting stores and vandalizing property, Sharpton and Esaw preached nonviolence. "We are not against police," Sharpton reportedly told the crowd. "Most police do their jobs. But those that break the law must be held accountable just like anybody else." As they marched across the Verrazzano-Narrows Bridge into Brooklyn, they carried signs that read "RIP Eric Garner" and "Police the NYPD." And they had a chant of their own—"I can't breathe!"— echoing Garner's last words. It later became a slogan for the movement, not only for protesters in New York City, but for a world of black people who demonstrated in their own cities. It made its way into sports and pop culture later that year, emblazoned on T-shirts worn by professional basketball superstars like LeBron James, Derrick Rose, and Kobe Bryant. In their respective ways, the protesters on Staten Island and in Ferguson were forcing us to think about how we were being treated by police in our own communities, and to no longer accept the status quo as second-class citizens in the country that we built with our own hands.

Two days before the Ferguson grand jury released its decision, a young black male named Tamir Rice was gunned down in a gazebo in Cleveland, Ohio. This time it was by a rookie police officer named Timothy Loehmann, who mistook Rice's toy gun for a real one and shot him twice in the torso. Officers said they asked the young boy to raise his hands, but instead he reached for the toy gun in his waistband, which prompted Loehmann to fire. Once again, yet another officer—this time Loehmann—claimed he feared for his life, even though he shot Tamir within two seconds of arriving on the scene. Tamir's fourteen-year-old sister couldn't even help; when she ran to his aid, an officer tackled her, put her in handcuffs, and stuffed her into the back of a police car.

Their mother, Samaria, had just gotten home from the grocery store when two boys knocked on her door and told her that Tamir had been shot. She ran across the street to see what had happened, like any well-intentioned parent would do. But when she got there, she was stopped by police and threatened with arrest. "They told me to calm down or I was gonna be in the back of that police car," Ms. Rice tells me. She went with her son to MetroHealth Medical Center, where doctors worked to save his life. But after she was shadowed by police officers and given little information, Ms. Rice called the local news and told them what went down between Tamir and Cleveland police. "It was a whirlwind of a disaster," Ms. Rice recalls. "They had no answers about why he was shot." Tamir would never make it out of the hospital. He died from his injuries the next morning. He was just twelve years old.

The Butterfly Effect

This tragedy shouldn't have happened at all. Before he was a member of the Cleveland Police Department, Officer Loehmann quit the Independence Police Department after he was deemed emotionally unfit to serve. The department's deputy chief, Jim Polak, questioned Loehmann's ability to make the right decisions in stressful situations and said he shouldn't be trusted to handle firearms. According to the report, the officer showed up "weepy" and "distracted" for firearms training and couldn't "communicate clear thoughts." Loehmann's handgun performance was called "dismal," and that during training he had an emotional breakdown due to issues with a girlfriend. "Maybe I should quit," the officer reportedly said. "I have no friends." Polak said Loehmann displayed a "dangerous loss of composure" during live range training and that neither time nor training would correct his behavior.

Loehmann joined the Cleveland Police Department in early 2014 under false pretenses. He claimed he left Independence because he wanted more action. In turn, the Cleveland force failed to investigate his background and let Loehmann roam the streets with a gun. So Tamir's blood wasn't just on Loehmann's hands, it was on the hands of the entire department, which didn't do enough to make sure the officer was ready for the job. Their shortcomings took Tamir's life. Loehmann wasn't charged with a crime.

At the age of twelve, with the whole world in front of him, there's no telling what Tamir could've been—an athlete, an artist, who knows. Ms. Rice remembers Tamir as a fun, affectionate kid who was very attached to her and his older sister. He liked to draw and loved to play soccer, basketball, and football. "He was a busy little boy, a hyper child," his mother remembers today. And he loved PBS—*Sesame Street* and *The Big Comfy Couch* were his favorite shows. Tamir had big dreams, even as a young kid. "He always wanted to do more," his mother says. "He wanted to play even more basketball and soccer." She remembers the little things about Tamir, the fact that he picked up potty training very young, was a talented swimmer, and never needed training wheels on his bicycle: "No one showed him how to do anything, he did it on his own." Even at five years old, Tamir was outspoken and liked to make his family laugh. He was gonna be tall, so much so that in the first grade, teachers used to call on Tamir in class because he stood head and shoulders above his classmates. He was also a character who loved to lighten the mood.

Michael Brown Sr. can't help but think what could've been if the convenience store employee hadn't called the police to claim his son was stealing ("He was picking up what he was owed," he says), if the police hadn't been looking for him, if Wilson hadn't stopped to talk to him. "Big Mike" would likely still be alive, still writing rhymes and uploading music to SoundCloud, still making his family laugh, still listening to Kendrick Lamar on his computer. "He just graduated and wanted to be a rapper," Brown Sr. recalls. "He had his own dreams, things he wanted to figure out on his own." Rapping under the name Big Mike, the teenager used to spit bars about becoming a star and making it out of his neighborhood. He was clearly a novice, but was planning to attend vocational school while learning more about sound engineering.

Racial tensions escalated even further after that, but the nation still had its eyes trained on Ferguson and the grand jury decision. Then it happened: on November 24, 2014, the grand jury decided not to bring criminal charges against Officer Darren Wilson in the death of Mike Brown. Rage consumed the protesters. New York fumed and Ferguson exploded. "Burn this bitch down," Mike Brown's stepfather, Louis Head, yelled to the crowd following the grand jury decision. That's just what they did: police cruisers and businesses along West Florissant Avenue were set on fire. The riots went against the wishes of Michael Brown Sr., who said that destroying property wasn't the way. He wanted a peaceful protest, just like the one on Staten Island, New York. "Let's not just make some noise," went a line from a family statement, "let's make a difference." It was too late, though; the people had suffered enough. The years of police harassment, the questionable traffic tickets that led to arrest warrants, the feeling that they didn't belong in their own community. The people demanded answers. The pain, anger, and resentment finally bubbled over, and most musicians responded in kind. Before his show in St. Louis as one-half of Run the Jewels (with rapper-producer El-P), rapper Killer Mike tore into Ferguson officials, lamenting Mike Brown's death and the grand jury decision. "Tonight, I got kicked on my ass when I listened to that prosecutor," he told the crowd through tears. "I *knew* it was coming. . . . I have a twenty-year-old son and a twelve-year-old son and I'm so afraid for them." In Seattle, Macklemore took to the streets to protest the Ferguson decision. Q-Tip, of the legendary rap group A Tribe Called Quest, joined protesters in New York City to demonstrate there. J. Cole released a song called "Be Free" that mourned Mike Brown's death. "Can you tell me why," the rapper lamented, "every time I step outside I see my niggas die?!"

In the middle of all this, Kendrick released a song called "i," an upbeat ode to self-love that didn't fit the social climate. Ferguson and New York City were raging, and some wondered why the rapper dropped such a happy-go-lucky track at that time. Black people were incensed and some wanted to lean into that anger: *Our brothers and sisters are being murdered without consequence and someone needs to pay.* As a community, black people are forgiving—perhaps too forgiving—and with the high-profile killings of Trayvon Martin, Eric Garner, Mike Brown, and Tamir Rice, it seemed the black community had run out of fucks to give. Kendrick's "i" wasn't protest music, at least not in the way we're used to hearing it. It wasn't Sly and the Family Stone pushing you to "Stand!" or Gil Scott-Heron forecasting the revolution. It wasn't even the music from Kendrick's own backyard: Dr. Dre's "The Day the Niggaz Took Over," from his classic 1992 album, *The Chronic*, captured the mood of pissed-off black people who'd had enough of the Los Angeles Police Department and were ready to fight back. Ice Cube's "We Had to Tear This Mothafucka Up" could've been a sequel to N.W.A's "Fuck tha Police," a song that he cowrote. "I can't trust a cracker in a blue uniform," Cube proclaimed on the track. In fairness, Dre's and Cube's protest songs addressed an issue that hit very close to home: brutality from their own LAPD. And while Kendrick wasn't directly affected by the issues in Ferguson, Cleveland, and Staten Island, and of course there's nothing wrong with expressing love of self, "i" felt like a tone-deaf softball from one of the world's most gifted lyricists. Whether Kendrick saw it or not, he was an artist whom people looked up to, with the kind of critical voice that was needed as racism escalated in 2014. To drop "i" at that time felt like a misfire. There was concern that Kendrick was going pop and started to feel himself a little. "i" perplexed those used to Kendrick's navel-gazing introspection, and his jovial side would take some getting used to.

Kendrick heard the criticism. "I would hate to stay stagnant," Kendrick told *Fader*. "I would hate for you to say there's no growth. You're supposed to innovate and not only challenge yourself but challenge your listeners and wow your listeners, and let them catch on. 'Cause when you're an artist, nobody should dictate what you should do, you should just do it." Indeed, there's an unfair expectation on musicians to retread their best work, so when listeners heard "i," some worried that Kendrick's forthcoming album would stray too far from the brilliance of *good kid, m.A.A.d city*. In fans' eyes, he had to top that record, or at least come close to it. We found out later that "i" was more than a re-created Isley Brothers song; Kendrick was emerging from a dark place that we didn't even know about. If *good kid* addressed the trauma he endured as a teenager, "i" let us into the survivor's guilt he suffered through as an adult. "I done been through a whole lot / Trial, tribulation, but I know God," Kendrick rapped. "As I look around me / So many motherfuckers wanna down me." We learn that he'd contemplated suicide in recent years, and that the now-famous musician was dealing with perceived mistrust in his circle. With his success came heightened expectations and new friends with their hands out.

As a result, the already-reluctant star recoiled even further. On the song, he mentioned his life as a story for younger kids to study (a direct request from his mom via voicemail on *good kid, m.A.A.d city*). It seemed Kendrick was thinking of his own mortality and took steps to think about a future he or others might not see. In an interview with Hot 97, Kendrick said he wrote "i" "for the homies that's in the penitentiary right now . . . for these kids that come up to my shows with these slashes on they wrists, saying they don't want to live no more." Kendrick had been under this kind of pressure since the ascendance of *good kid, m.A.A.d city*: he was no longer just the voice of Compton, he was now the voice of his generation, just like his idol Tupac Shakur before him.

So yes, "i" was noble in that regard, but it simply wasn't the right time for it. The families of Trayvon, Eric, Mike, and Tamir needed our love first. A major blow came on December 3, 2014, when a Staten Island grand jury decided not to indict Officer Daniel Pantaleo in the choking death of Eric Garner. By then, after a year of letdowns and injustice, the decision wasn't surprising, it was just the latest reminder that the American justice system doesn't value black life. Then, in 2019, five years after the incident, federal prosecutors determined that Pantaleo would not face civil charges in Eric Garner's death. He was fired soon after. Meanwhile, Esaw Garner vowed to keep seeking justice for her husband. "As long as I have a breath in my body," she said, "I will fight the fight until the end." Then, in what many perceived to be retaliation for filming Garner's murder, New York police officers harassed Ramsey Orta for capturing the viral video. Orta, Garner's friend, had been arrested before the 2014 incident, and ever since that day, he was targeted by law enforcement for holding them accountable. "The cops had been following me every day since Eric died, shining lights in my house every night." In 2016, Orta pleaded guilty to various drug and gun possession charges and was sentenced to four years in prison. At the time of this writing, he is still awaiting release.

In 2017, the police officer who shot Tamir Rice was fired by the city of Cleveland—not for his conduct in Tamir's killing, but for allegedly putting false information on his job application. A year later, this same officer was hired by a police department in the small Ohio village of Bellaire.

By 2019, Samaria Rice said race relations in Cleveland hadn't improved at all. The police officer who shot her son lobbied to get his job back. And in Ferguson, Mike Brown Sr. opened a museum to honor his son's memory. In the five years since Brown Jr.'s death, six men tied to the Ferguson protests have died under mysterious circumstances, each one either shot and his remains found in a torched car, or—in the case of Bassem Masri, reportedly found unresponsive on a bus following a fentanyl overdose. Others supposedly took their own lives, though the mother of Danye Jones believes he was lynched. On August 9, 2019, Mike Brown Sr. asked the state to reopen the case and find justice for Mike Jr. But because of the city's history with police and the incident with his son, he is still having a tough time trusting the cops. "It's the uniform that makes us cringe," Mike Brown Sr. tells me. "I still tense up. I'm trying to stay positive, but the system needs to be torn up, burned, and started again with new policies."

In December 2014, singer D'Angelo set the bar for what black protest music was supposed to sound like in the modern era. *Black Messiah*, his long-awaited and often-delayed third studio album, was released on the evening of the fifteenth, and through it came the anger, helplessness, and misery of being a black person in 2014, and watching your brothers and sisters be gunned down in the streets. Just like Kendrick, D'Angelo had been dubbed the savior of his genre (in this case R&B) after his 2000 album, *Voodoo*, was released to widespread acclaim. With its grainy black-and-white cover—a crowd of uplifted black hands—*Black Messiah* responded directly to the uprising in Ferguson and the grand jury decision in Staten Island. Also like Kendrick, D'Angelo spoke only through his music; you were unlikely to hear from him if he didn't have music to promote. *Black Messiah* wasn't entirely protest music; the songs "Really Love" and "Another Life" were sugary soul ballads akin to what he'd performed in the mid-1990s as a laid-back crooner with a leathery voice and cornrowed hair.

Elsewhere on the album, though, D'Angelo spoke to the pain that black people felt everywhere. On "The Charade," he sings: "All we wanted was a chance to talk / 'Stead we only got outlined in chalk." Then there was "1000 Deaths," a murky, psychedelic rock track about being sent to, and being prepared for, war. The battle itself was up for interpretation; it could refer to a fight in a foreign land or one closer to home. And with lyrics like "I won't nut up when we up thick in the crunch / Because a coward dies a thousand times / But a soldier only dies just once," it was perhaps the most revolutionary track in the singer's discography. At that point, musicians were releasing Ferguson-influenced songs here and there, though not a full-scale record that addressed the wide-ranging despair within the black community. "When was the last time someone of [D'Angelo's] stature came out with a political record?" Russell Elevado, a recording engineer and frequent

D'Angelo collaborator, once asked Red Bull Music Academy. "No one is talking about any social issues. Let's bring that back, too." *Black Messiah* harkened back to records like Sly and the Family Stone's *There's a Riot Goin' On* and Curtis Mayfield's *Curtis*, as meticulous funk and soul with black plight at the center. Musicians like Sly, Curtis, and D'Angelo spoke to us and *for* us. They created music in which we could see our full, beautiful selves, and they helped us remember that we weren't second-class citizens, even when the world tried to render us invisible. America can beat you down if you let it, but through Sly's howl, Curtis's falsetto, and D'Angelo's hum, you felt the beauty and bleakness of black culture. Sometimes that's what protest is. It isn't solely about picket signs and clever chants, it's about the full breadth of the experience, about wading through the misery and finding light through it all. *Black Messiah* would be the first in a trio of albums, released between winter 2014 and spring 2015, that were shaded by the deaths of unarmed black people at the hands or guns of police. Kamasi Washington's sprawling opus, *The Epic*, was the third record of that set. Through its mix of gospel, jazz, and soul, Washington's album emitted the spiritual essence that Black America needed. Songs like "The Rhythm Changes," "Askim," and "The Message" were meant to heal a community of people and help us move forward from the pain and outrage we felt on a daily basis. "There's a deeper level of healing that needs to happen for the world in general," Washington once told me for a *Washington Post* profile. "There's a mass of people who are broken." While *Black Messiah* and *The Epic* were critical darlings, Kendrick released an album around that time that was going to shake the musical landscape and have a profound effect on Black America for several years. It would be even more audacious than *good kid, m.A.A.d city* and push projects like *Overly Dedicated* and *Section.80* even further to the background. For his next act, Kendrick had a word for his entire race.

6

King Kendrick

As Kendrick toured the U.S. with Kanye West in 2014, he started opening his mind to new forms of music. "You would have thought it was a tour bus for someone over the age of 55," producer Sounwave once told *Spin*. Kendrick had grown up listening mostly to West Coast hip-hop, and by his own admission, he had missed out on transcendent rappers like Nas and the Notorious B.I.G. at the height of their respective powers. To find new inspiration, he went further into the pantheon of revolutionary black music, to iconic jazz trumpeters like Miles Davis and Donald Byrd, and funk legends like Sly Stone and George Clinton. Kendrick was exploring freedom in his life and in his music, and these creators personified that. Miles had changed the direction of jazz at least three times, first in 1959 with his breakthrough album, *Kind of Blue*, then in 1969 with *In a Silent Way* and in 1970 with *Bitches Brew*. *Blue* is lauded for ushering a more modal sound into jazz; *Silent Way* and *Brew* marked the beginning of Miles's electric period, where he broadened his music to include traces of funk and rock into the mix. Sly and George were outlandish at a time when America wasn't open to such black artists. In the late 1960s, when mainstream music took a psychedelic, acid-fueled turn, they crafted sounds that were equally uplifting, acerbic, and iconoclastic.

Miles, Donald, Sly, and George were all free black men, creatively and spiritually, who indirectly showed Kendrick that he could be the same type of musician. But such freedom is challenging to obtain in rap music, a genre indebted to bravado and street cred. Sure, he was more visible now, but he was still his own man, and TDE was more inclined to do their own thing, not what fans expected them to do. Kendrick wanted to innovate, but he had to do it within a genre among stars who'd rather rap about flashy cars and bedazzled jewelry instead of depression, Christianity, and the trappings of fame. Kendrick played this music so much that he started to become one with it. That, combined with the South Africa trip, made his soul even older and wiser.

For his next album, Kendrick wanted to discuss these topics by using jazz, funk, and spoken word as the backdrop. Jazz and funk were forgotten genres that hadn't been blended into mainstream hip-hop for at least fifteen years, when the rapper Common did so for his 2000 masterpiece, *Like Water for Chocolate*. Yet while Com's blend felt brighter and more tethered to the jazz-rap hybrids of early nineties luminaries A Tribe Called Quest and Gang Starr, Kendrick envisioned something a little darker and more esoteric. "Tribe was the beginning of it, and they also changed the temperament of rap at the time. Rap was pretty aggressive and they took it back a little bit, and they created a wave of artists who were headed in that direction," says Hank Shocklee, a Hall of Fame record producer who, in the 1980s and '90s, was the main architect of Public Enemy's bombastic sound. "I've always thought jazz was the next evolution for hip-hop. Before, it was more funk." Shocklee had seen the blending of hip-hop and jazz firsthand. In the late eighties, the producer took A Tribe Called Quest's first six-song demo to Def Jam Records creator Russell Simmons: "He didn't get into it because it wasn't aggressive and they weren't yelling. The beats weren't hard. There were those groups of people who didn't understand it because it was a divergence from what they were listening to. That's where music is always gonna go. It's about moving things forward and not looking backwards, and those are the artists who tend to last throughout time. Those who are not afraid to push the envelope in areas where no one was willing to go."

Kendrick wanted an ambitious mix of bebop and psychedelic jazz, James Brown–centric funk, atmospheric soul, and off-centered beats. And most important, it had to be *black*—real black—from the music to the topics it addressed. Kendrick started brainstorming ideas for his next album right after he finished *good kid*, and knew immediately that it needed to address the black community as a whole. Our people needed healing; the rapper wanted "to help put a Band-Aid on the things that's been going on in our communities," collaborator Terrace Martin once told Revolt, "and just to do something legendary." Kendrick wanted the album to be for all of us, though with his own personal awakening at the center. He was going to call it *Tu Pimp a Caterpillar*, or Tupac for short, as yet another way to honor a rapper who had such a profound effect on him. But he soon renamed it *To Pimp a Butterfly* to reflect the challenges of his newfound celebrity and the music industry's stronghold on its artists. "The word 'pimp' has so much aggression, and that represents several things," he told MTV News in 2015. "For me, [the album title] represents using my celebrity for good. Another reason is not being pimped by the industry through my celebrity." In many ways, Kendrick was rejecting the very notion of fame, that because he had a little more money and greater recognition, he was supposed to submit to an industry—and a country—that would never have his best interest at heart. While he'd been grinding for twelve years to reach this moment, Kendrick still had challenges dealing with it.

Though, if *To Pimp a Butterfly* was going to be Kendrick's most ambitious work, the path to completion would be the most challenging. He wanted a fresh live sound with real instrumentation, so the musicians being brought in had to be experts. Kendrick had one rule for himself and the players: Don't limit yourself conceptually. "Just create," he said, "[and] not let no type of boundary stop me from doing what I was doing." Where he had the concept of *good kid, m.A.A.d city* several years before its release, it took two years of writing, revising, traveling, and scrapping ideas for *To Pimp a Butterfly* to materialize.

It had to be an L.A. record, with local players that captured the full breadth of the city's jazz and funk scenes. That meant Terrace Martin, a producer and multi-instrumentalist with a deep affinity for those genres, had to be the go-to guy for this project. Terrace had been close to TDE's orbit; he'd produced songs for *Section.80* and *good kid, m.A.A.d city*, so the collective trusted him to bring the best musicians into the sessions. Terrace had graduated from Locke High School in South Los Angeles, a top-tier institution known for its world-class jazz program, helmed by Reggie Andrews, who in the 1960s and '70s had been the bandleader of Reggie Andrews and the Fellowship, and a keyboardist for Karma, a soul, jazz, and funk group. Andrews was a legend, and he mentored some of the best jazz and funk musicians this world has ever seen: Terrace, bass virtuoso Stephen "Thundercat" Bruner, funk and soul vocalist Patrice Rushen, and tenor saxophonist Kamasi Washington. Terrace was a Cali guy who embodied the ethos of L.A. jazz: he was cool, unhurried, and incessantly creative. Like Kendrick, the art was paramount to Terrace; with each saxophone wail, modulated vocal and piano chord, the producer paid homage to the rich history of jazz in South Los Angeles. In the 1940s, Central Avenue became the epicenter of jazz in L.A., where local musicians Eric Dolphy and Charles Mingus cut their teeth in venues like the Downbeat, Club Alabam, and the Dunbar Hotel.

South L.A. has a rich, ancestral spirit that you feel as soon as you touch down. The souls of drummer Billy Higgins, tenor saxophonist Harold Land, pianist Horace Tapscott, and beatmaker Ras G loom heavily in the air, guiding your voyage through tiled concrete and black-owned businesses. The essence emanates from the World Stage, a performance art space co-owned by Higgins and Kamau Daáood, that once allowed up-and-coming musicians like Terrace and Kamasi to play. "Billy Higgins pretty much gave us a key," says trombonist Ryan Porter, an L.A. native who was featured on *To Pimp a Butterfly*. "Me, Terrace, the Bruner brothers. I'm pretty sure that was everyone's first gig. They put your name in the window, made you feel good. We were all teenagers, but as jazz musicians, it gave you a place to go." Between riots, systemic racism, and police brutality, the city of L.A. had endured many cultural shifts over the years, but the Leimert Park neighborhood was a respite from all that. "It was kind of a cultural place where you just felt that harmony," Porter says. "There's people walking in dashikis. There's brothers wanting to talk to you about books. There's coffee shops where you can go, and barbershops where you can go and hear people talking about things in the conscious community and what's happening in your area. These were jazz musicians doing that."

Tapscott might have been the foremost purveyor of this: As leader of the Pan Afrikan People's Arkestra in the 1960s and '70s, the pianist, teacher, and activist made it his mission to bring jazz and other forms of black music to children in Los Angeles. He put students in his band and gave them their first chance to play in a professional group. Indirectly, a new generation of L.A. jazz musicians came from that movement in the seventies, which created artists like Ryan Porter, Terrace, Kamasi, and Thundercat. Some of their parents studied with icons like Tapscott and Higgins, and passed what they learned down to their children. Those same children brought that energy to their respective music and *To Pimp a Butterfly* as a whole.

Also in Leimert Park was an open mic called Project Blowed, where the city's abstract lyricists convened every week to meet with like-minded wordsmiths to test new material or exude steam. It was a safe haven for esoteric poets like Aceyalone, Busdriver, and Myka 9; this wasn't an open mic in the traditional sense, as the poets were somewhat left of center and eschewed the same ol' gun-toting narratives deployed by street rappers. If you were performing at Project Blowed, you had to come with something lyrically dexterous. Whether directly or indirectly, Kendrick was a student of Project Blowed and its abstract lyricism; his creative aesthetic was more attuned to it than any other subset of L.A. underground rap. "Even if he wasn't around that, Kendrick likely knew someone who was connected with it," Porter says. "It was almost like a hip-hop support group. There was no way you could be in L.A. and not be affected by that vibe."

From all this history came *To Pimp a Butterfly*: the unapologetic blackness of a Tapscott record, the hard bop of a Mingus classic, the frenetic swing of a Higgins track, the offbeat flow of Aceyalone and Myka 9. Rappers tend to make music to sound good in the car: the bass has to rattle the trunk and shake the windows to the point of near breakage. But Kendrick had done all that before: his early mixtapes, along with *Section.80* and *good kid, m.A.A.d city*, were hip-hop records for die-hard rap heads to drive to. For *To Pimp a Butterfly*, he wasn't focused on making radio singles or festive songs for nightclubs. Hell, his listeners might not like or understand this album—because it was gonna be *different*. Kendrick's work required patience and thoughtful ears, and *To Pimp a Butterfly* was no exception. He wanted listeners to be slowly drawn into the record, even if it took a few plays or even a few years for it to lock in.

Behind those intentions, however, *To Pimp a Butterfly* was shaping up to be stellar or messy, grand or disappointing. Though Kendrick had a lot to say about his new life, about black pain, and what he had seen in South Africa, it was not entirely certain that the album would be a classic. In the months leading up to its release,

Kendrick gave an interview to *Billboard* that didn't do him any favors. The interviewer asked the rapper's thoughts on the killings of unarmed black men by police—in Ferguson, specifically. And instead of showing sympathy for what had happened to Mike Brown, Kendrick's answer made him sound like an "All Lives Matter" proponent who blamed the victim and not the aggressor. "I wish somebody would look in our neighborhood knowing that it's already a situation, mentally, where it's fucked up," he said. "What happened to [Michael Brown] should've never happened. Never. But when we don't have respect for ourselves, how do we expect them to respect us? It starts from within. Don't start with just a rally, don't start from looting—it starts from within." The response spoke more to Kendrick's own childhood as a traumatized black boy than the struggles happening in Ferguson. That he wasn't far removed from his own upbringing in Compton and still grappling with trauma was the essence of his comment.

The response ignited a small firestorm on social media, and triggered harsh criticism from fellow artists who wondered why, as a black man, Kendrick would say such a thing. On Twitter, rapper Azealia Banks said Kendrick's comments were the "dumbest shit I've ever heard a black man say." Then Kid Cudi, who'd been credited with ushering in a hazier, emo style of rap, criticized Kendrick indirectly with a subtweet asking black artists not to "talk down on the black community like you are Gods gift to niggaz everywhere." Then there was the third verse of "The Blacker the Berry." Now finished and released as the second single off *To Pimp a Butterfly*, it appeared to blame black people for their own mistreatment—the notion, on the surface, was that we couldn't be upset with police shootings when black people in gangs shot and killed each other all the time. At the end of the song, Kendrick raps: "So why did I weep when Trayvon Martin was in the street / When gang banging make me kill a nigga blacker than me? / Hypocrite!" That, too, set off a firestorm of emotions from listeners online who lambasted the rapper for respectability politics.

In an interview with journalist Rob Markman for MTV News, Kendrick said that he wasn't trying to put down the black community. "These are *my* experiences," Kendrick said. "This is *my* life that I'm talking 'bout. I'm not speaking *to* the community. I'm not speaking *of* the community. I am the community. It's therapeutic for myself because I still feel that urge, and I still feel that anger and hatred for this man next door . . . that ill will to want to do something." He had a history of such ambiguity, like these lines on "m.A.A.d city": "If I told you I killed a nigga at sixteen, would you believe me? / Perceive me to be innocent Kendrick that you seen in the street." And this one from "Hol' Up": "As a kid I killed two adults, I'm too advanced." Then, on "Institutionalized," from *To Pimp a Butterfly*: "I'm trapped inside the ghetto and I ain't proud to admit it / Institutionalized, I could still kill me a nigga, so what?" There'd also been the question of whether or not he'd ever been in a gang. Kendrick grew up on the west side of Compton—Piru territory. Over the years, he'd denied being affiliated on songs and in interviews, but lyrics like "Step on my neck and get blood on your Nike checks"—which appeared on "good kid"—left the door open for such inquiry. The line could mean that he was indeed in a gang, or that the crew had his back because he was cool with them.

"I've only been in this industry three or four years," Kendrick told MTV News. "I can't forget twenty years of me being in the city of Compton. When I say these things, [it's reminding me] that I need to respect this man, because he's a black man, not because of the color that he's wearing. I did a lot to tear down my own community."

Kendrick had never been a leader before, at least not on this level. It was one thing to be revered in Compton, but to be admired throughout the country and the world was something else entirely. Nothing in the celebrity handbook can prepare you for the day when a teenage kid says that your music legit saved his life, and shows you the slits on his wrist to prove it. Then the parasites come, the newfound friends and hangers-on who simply want to be around someone famous, and they need "just a couple dollars" to get through. And you can't mask the guilt of not being there physically for your family. Homesickness kicks in, and living out of a suitcase quickly loses luster. Before you know it, the home and the people you once knew have changed forever. Kendrick was torn between his new and old lives, and he wanted *To Pimp a Butterfly* to reflect this dichotomy. "It was me tackling my own insecurities, but also making it to where you can relate as well," he once said. "The whole body of the story is me basically accepting my role as a leader, learning how to accept it, and appreciating it and not running away from it. . . . The main thing that we're scared of as people is change—from a social standpoint [to] a day-to-day standpoint. I wanted to embody that in this record." Indeed, Kendrick was becoming a new person, and so were the people around him.

One day, producer Steven "Flying Lotus" Ellison was on the

tour bus with Kendrick, running through instrumentals he'd been working on for his own project. Lotus was considered a pioneer in the famed L.A. beat scene, where like-minded producers like Toki-monsta, the Gaslamp Killer, Samiyam, and Ras G whipped funk, jazz, hip-hop, and electronica into a cosmic blend of dance music. Lotus was a disciple of his great-aunt, Alice Coltrane, whose mix of spiritual jazz was meant to elevate the mind beyond the trappings of this planet. Lotus had been known to embody the same ethos. On albums like *Los Angeles*, *Cosmogramma*, *Until the Quiet Comes*, and *You're Dead!* the producer piled all sorts of genres into one pot, leading to a kaleidoscopic blend still rooted in the astral jazz that Coltrane used to create. There was one track in particular that caught Kendrick's attention, a driving funk loop with quick drums and a thick, wobbly bass line. It was a weird hybrid with the oversized knock of a Dr. Dre beat and the kind of spacey electronics you'd hear on an early seventies Funkadelic track. It was squarely within Lotus's wheelhouse; Kendrick's, not so much. "I asked him, 'What is that?'" the rapper once told the Recording Academy. "He said, 'You don't know nothing about that. That's real funk. . . . You're not going to rap on that.' It was like a dare."

The music was conceptualized by Lotus and frequent collaborator Thundercat, whose frenetic style of bass playing made him a go-to musician for rapper Mac Miller and singer Erykah Badu. Lotus and Thundercat were at the computer studying George Clinton. "He became the fuel for creating," the bassist once recalled. "I was really blown away that Kendrick was so into that song." Lotus and Thundercat were Clinton disciples, and in 2008, Lotus launched his own record label, called Brainfeeder. With artists like

Thundercat on his roster, Lotus's imprint became a go-to source for the same sort of esoteric funk that Clinton used to create. It also screamed L.A., just like Kendrick's music, but it captured a side of the city with which many outside it were not familiar. Largely because of the gangsta rap movement of the eighties and nineties, and due to newer rappers like Kendrick, many outsiders viewed L.A. as a rap town, but Lotus's and Thundercat's style was tailored to urban alternative kids who listened to artists like Clinton but also metal, punk, and indie rock. So, on the surface, Lotus and Kendrick was an odd pairing, but that showed just how deep the rapper wanted to dig on his new work. In fact, Kendrick asked Lotus who he envisioned on the track he played on the tour bus. "I laughed and said George Clinton," the producer said. "I never thought it would actually happen."

In its finished form, "Wesley's Theory" opens *To Pimp a Butterfly*—with Clinton as a feature—as a cautionary tale about the perils of success and the recklessness it could bring. The "Wesley" here is actor Wesley Snipes, who in 2010 was convicted of tax evasion and sent to federal prison for three years. Yet Kendrick wasn't evoking Snipes's name as a diss, but as a symbol of what can happen to black men in the United States without proper financial education. Kendrick suddenly had more money than he'd ever had before, and with that came the impulse to spend it, especially if you had grown up where he did. If you came up broke, on and off food stamps, you felt like you'd arrived once you earned thousands, let alone millions, of dollars. But public schools never taught you how to manage money—at least not in black neighborhoods—so Kendrick had had to figure it out on his own, and *fast*. Because he'd always kept to himself, and because his rampant tour schedule led to even deeper insulation, "Wesley's Theory" made Kendrick sound paranoid, like Uncle Sam was coming any minute to wash away his good fortune. Though if making it big scared Kendrick as a black man, at least he had one major ally who'd been through something similar. "Remember the first time you came out to the house? You said you wanted a spot like mine," Dr. Dre recalled via voicemail on the song. "But remember, anybody can get it, the hard part is keeping it, motherfucker."

"Wesley's Theory" inspired *To Pimp a Butterfly*'s album art, which made a powerful statement on its own. Against foreboding shades of gray, Kendrick and his friends—most of them shirtless— flash stacks of cash with their faces beaming. They're expressing the utmost joy and reassurance, as if they'd endured hell and achieved their own version of the American dream. They're in front of a photoshopped White House; on the ground before them is a dead, white judge with his eyes blacked out. In the middle is Kendrick, smiling wide and holding an infant child. He looks relaxed, comforted, free. For him, *this* was real life and what fame was all about: sharing it with the Day Ones who still called him Dot.

The song and cover represent the very moment Kendrick signed his major-label deal, right when the sense of achievement sets in and he felt he needed to spread the wealth. "It's going back to the neighborhood and taking the folks that haven't seen nothing and taking them around the world," Kendrick told MTV News of his mind-set. "Whether you want to call them ignorant or not, they need to see these things—whether it's the White House, whether it's Africa, whether it's London."

It seemed Kendrick's heart was in the right place; that he couldn't save everyone was eating him alive. That explains a song like "u," a moody, two-part saga near the album's middle that walks listeners right into the hotel room where Kendrick almost lost himself. It's easily the rapper's most vulnerable track, with raw lyrics delving into the suicide he contemplated, and the younger sister he couldn't guide. She got pregnant with her first child as a teenager, and Kendrick blamed himself for letting it happen: "Where was your antennas? / Where was the influence you speak of? / You preached in front of one hundred thousand but never reached her." On the song, Kendrick rhymes from the perspective of a naysayer, possibly a close friend or family member, or even the negative voices in his own head. Kendrick simply couldn't quell the doubt that laid heavily on his heart, and "u" depicted the mood swings he battled, and the frayed relationships that he had trouble restoring. The session for that song was disturbing. "He just walked in, turned all the lights off, and he walked into the booth," engineer Ali told Revolt TV. "And he didn't come out for three hours." Said Sounwave, "Everyone who walked in that session had tears in their eyes."

The tracks were just about done for *To Pimp a Butterfly* when Terrace Martin called in his friends to add live instrumentation to the beats. One time in particular, the musician was in the studio playing the music of Willie Bobo, a legendary Latin and jazz percussionist, when the sound caught Kendrick's ear. "He walks in one day like, 'What is that?'" Martin recalls. "He's like, 'That shit dope!'" Then the two started talking about jazz when Martin asked Kendrick if he'd seen *Mo' Better Blues*, the 1990 Spike Lee film in which actor Denzel Washington plays a fictional New York jazz trumpeter named Bleek Gilliam. Kendrick hadn't seen the movie, so they watched it. There's a scene near the end where Spike Lee's character, Giant, is assaulted in the alley behind the nightclub as the band plays a frenetic jazz breakdown onstage, all drum fills, undulating bass, and surging trumpet wails. "Our eyes opened up because the power of that music got the point across real quick. Because of that music, that scene was so intense," Martin says. "Kendrick was like, 'Man, we need to do some shit like that.'"

That night, the producer drove to his home in Porter Ranch and wrote a song similar to what they'd heard in the pivotal *Mo' Better Blues* scene. But he didn't want to use a drum machine or anything synthetic. He played a demo on his baby grand piano and texted the file to Kendrick: "I wanted to give him a melody that felt like some type of alarm clock, like tension was building." Over the next couple of days, Martin got the musicians together: Robert "Sput" Searight on drums, Brandon Owens on bass, Craig Brockman on organ, Marlon Williams on guitar, and Robert Glasper on piano. "Kendrick walked into the session and we started *playing* that motherfucker," Martin recalls. "Everyone's eyes lit up in the whole room. Everybody there was like, 'What the fuck is this?!' I felt good about the music, but when I saw him happy, I said, 'I'm 'bout to really go *in* on this motherfucker.' It was recorded in one take. That's how we made 'For Free?'" Martin left and came back to the studio an hour later; by then, Kendrick had started putting words to it. "This. dick. ain't. *freeee*," Martin recalled in his best Kendrick voice. "And I said, [gasp] 'Oh my *God*.' We 'bout to piss these motherfuckers off. I said, 'Thank God, it's about to get uncomfortable for people.' And I *loved* that."

Though Martin resists taking credit for *To Pimp a Butterfly*'s jazz-leaning sound, he was responsible for bringing in some of the genre's biggest names. Before that record, a name like Robert Glasper's wasn't well known in the mainstream, even if his 2012 LP, *Black Radio*, won the Grammy Award for Best R&B Album. He was hip-hop's best-kept secret, and only one of two guys—trumpeter Roy Hargrove being the other—who blurred the lines between rap, jazz, and soul, and made it cool for younger people to embrace older genres of music. In the mid-2000s, Glasper worked with famed rappers like Mos Def and Q-Tip, and alongside soul mavens like Erykah Badu, Maxwell, and Bilal. He could perform it all: at the helm of the Robert Glasper Trio, he skewed closer to hard bop and traditional covers; as leader of the Robert Glasper Experiment, he became more electronic and abstract, blurring the lines among jazz, rock, and electronica. But while Glasper's name rang bells with niche audiences, he wasn't considered a mainstream star at first. "I was known as the 'crossover dude,'" he says today. "I'm the first non-singing R&B artist to win the Grammy for Best R&B Album. When I won, it gave everyone a different kind of hope, like, 'Oh, we can do outside-of-the-box stuff.' But when *To Pimp a Butterfly* came, it was perfect timing for everyone involved." Working with Kendrick gave him the chance to ascend in his own career. "When *good kid, m.A.A.d city* came out, I was obsessed with that record. I told Terrace, 'Bro, for the next record you gotta get me on something,'" Glasper recalls. At the time, Glasper was working on his *Black Radio* follow-up, *Black Radio 2*, and asked Martin to introduce him to Kendrick because he wanted to get the rapper on a track.

The Butterfly Effect

The pianist soon traveled to L.A. to record a live album called *Covered* at Capitol Studios. Once there, he got a call from Martin. "He was like, 'Yo, you still here in L.A.? I'm at Dr. Dre's studio with Kendrick right now. We need you for this song. Can you come through after you finish recording?' I got in an Uber or a Lyft and headed over. When I got there, they were doing the song 'For Free?'" Kendrick had never seen Glasper play live, but the rapper liked what he saw, and once "For Free?" was finished, he asked the pianist to play on other album tracks. "He told the engineer, 'Yo, pull up so and so. Pull up 'Mortal Man.' Then he'd tell me to play what I heard. So I'd listen once, then I'd play. I did that for eight songs in a row." In the liner notes for *To Pimp a Butterfly*, Glasper's name is listed as a contributor to five tracks, the last of which was "Complexion (A Zulu Love)." "At this point, Thundercat was there. He showed up in a raccoon suit with a tail and everything, but he acted like nothing was wrong," Glasper remembers with a laugh. "Like, 'Are you a mascot or . . . ?'" In a separate phone conversation, the producer Mono/Poly—who contributed to the 2016 follow-up, *untitled unmastered* EP—remembers the same exact story about Thundercat: "Terrace was like, 'Oh, he's *serious* right now,' kind of joking about it, and for some reason, I was there and I said, 'Watch, whatever they make today? It's gonna be a hit. Whatever Thundercat does this day in this studio.' Even though it was so silly, I just knew everything was gonna work out. *That's* when they started adding more to 'These Walls.'" ("These Walls" won a Grammy for Best Rap/Sung Performance.)

Glasper was in the zone for "Complexion (A Zulu Love)": "They hit record and I played it down. When the tape stopped,

I kept going. That was the vibe. I changed the chords a little bit. When I looked up, Kendrick was looking at me through the glass like, 'Keep going.' When I walked out of there, he was like, 'Man, that was dope! On that part I'mma bring a whole new beat onto it and I'mma rap in a different voice.' That became the Rapsody part. That part happened because I just kept playing. I literally kept playing, which made him say, 'Oh shit! I'mma add a different bass line and different drums.' Everything happened so fast—'Play on this, play on that.'" To get Rapsody on the song, Kendrick's manager, Dave Free, called producer 9th Wonder, who owns Jamla Records with Rapsody as his featured artist. The idea for Kendrick and Rapsody to work together had been brewing since 2013, a day after the "Control" verse. "9th hit me like, 'Dave just hit me, and Kendrick wants to send something.' I was like, 'Wow,'" Rapsody told MTV News. Then in January 2014, 9th and Rapsody met at House Studio in Hyattsville, Maryland, and recorded the verse for *To Pimp a Butterfly*. In keeping with the song's concept, she decided to fasten the idea of "Complexion" to her own upbringing as a brown-skinned woman in a country preoccupied with hue. "I'm not like the redbones, ya know?" Rapsody told Vevo. "Light skin . . . I thought [was] more beautiful when I was growing up. That's what I saw in the videos. I might be outside playing all day, or my sisters would come in and be like, 'Ooh, you done got *black*'. . . in your head you think something's wrong with being dark."

There was so much music being recorded during the *Butterfly* sessions. And if you were around, even if you played an instrument, Kendrick might snag you to add to the album in other ways. The first voice you hear—after a crackling sample of singer Boris

The Butterfly Effect

Gardiner's "Every Nigger Is a Star"—is that of Josef Leimberg, a trumpeter who played on the majority of *Butterfly*. On "Wesley's Theory," he orates the album's mission statement; on "For Sale? (Interlude)," he's the antagonist who chastises Kendrick: "What's *wrooong*, nigga? / I thought you was keeping it *gangsta* / I thought this what you *wanted*." In an interview, Leimberg says his vocal inclusion was pure happenstance. "He had heard my deep voice, I was talking to Terrace in the studio, and he said, 'Man, I gotta get that voice on my album,'" he recalls. "It wasn't until weeks later that Terrace called me and said that Kendrick remembered that. He had me come in to do some vocals, some spoken-word shit. He coached me the whole time I was recording those vocals. He knew exactly how he wanted certain inflections here and there."

Inside the studio, there was a feeling that Kendrick was making a classic, but because he and the guys were so focused on work, they ultimately eschewed any such notions and simply wanted to put out a long-lasting record. Aesthetically, the vibe was different; the studio space was superb, and as Anna Wise remembers, even the food and beverages were scaled up. Gone was the fast food; in were specialty salads and customized menus. The musicians all applaud Kendrick's genius, saying that he's a guy who doesn't rest on his laurels. Yes, he's talented, but he's always trying to improve, or at least give the public something it hadn't heard before. And he didn't settle for one or two takes on songs. "There are the people who it just comes easy to and there are people who work at it. Kendrick is both," Kamasi Washington told Pitchfork in 2017. "He can instantly write a song that's dope as hell, but then spend the time to meticulously work it out and make it perfect. You usually get only one or the other. He'd be sitting there watching me write string parts. Not a lot of people would care. . . . But he's always in the studio giving you ideas, and his instincts are incredible." Upright bassist Miles Mosley agrees. Washington called him to the studio near the end of the recording process to play on "How Much a Dollar Cost" and "Mortal Man." "He asked me to grab Big Momma, my upright bass," Mosley recalls. "I threw it in the car and went right over." Once there, he didn't know what the songs were; Washington and Martin would cue up certain parts of the track and ask Mosley to add bass to that specific section. "It was very open-ended. There weren't any preconceived notions," he says. "You didn't know what was happening, but you could tell *something* was happening. You could tell that they were in there working super intensely, and it was attached to a bigger purpose."

To Pimp a Butterfly was revolutionary in the way it included jazz and other traditional forms of black music. Jazz was thought to be for older people, performed by gray-haired veterans in smaller clubs to particular audiences. Kendrick's album took the lid off that: these musicians were the new cool, more likely to show up in L.A. Dodgers baseball hats, knitted beanies, African dashikis, and, well, raccoon suits. This wasn't the 1950s and they weren't John Coltrane, Herbie Hancock, or Charlie "Bird" Parker. "They didn't use jazz samples, and they didn't need old jazz musicians," Glasper said of the *To Pimp a Butterfly* sessions. "That's the 'real hip-hop meets jazz' right there. That was something I was already doing in my world, but for Kendrick to do it, it changed everything. It had everybody."

Ryan Porter saw the *Butterfly* sessions as a way to give new life to what were already great instrumentals from the likes of Taz Arnold, Sounwave, Rahki, and Whoarei. They had a song like "King Kunta" to work with, which was created by Sounwave and Thundercat as they watched the Japanese anime *Fist of the North Star* and ate from Yoshinoya, a Japanese fast-food chain. Because Sounwave was such a jazz head, and because that was the sound he and Kendrick were using for *To Pimp a Butterfly*, the original beat to "King Kunta" was incredibly jazz-centric, "with pretty flutes," Sounwave once told the Recording Academy. Kendrick said he liked it but to "make it nasty," he recalled. "I added different drums to it, simplified it, got Thundercat on the bass, and it was a wrap." Kendrick didn't want it to sound like hip-hop; it had to be rough and straight-up funk. He asked Sounwave to start peeling away all the jazz elements, and in its finished form, "King Kunta" is a dusty loop that sounds like Rosecrans Avenue in summertime Compton. The beat itself pays homage to a Compton rapper named Mausberg, who in 2000 released a song called "Get Nekkid." Kendrick's song has the same hard drums, synth chords, and deep bass line, and was meant to salute a talented musician who never made it big. The title nods to a slave named Kunta Kinte, the protagonist in Alex Haley's novel 1970s *Roots*. In the novel, Kunta gets his foot cut off for trying to run free; Kendrick used that as a metaphor to combat hate. "No matter what type of acts or sword you're bringing my way," he told *NME*, "you'll never cut down the legs that's running by the forces of God."

Lyrically, Kendrick took cues from another black music legend—one Mr. James Brown, the Godfather of Soul, the Hardest Working Man in Show Business. Brown was an architect of modern black music, and in a way, a pioneer of hip-hop music. The poet Gil Scott-Heron is credited with bridging the gap between rap and poetry, but Brown—with his restless funk grooves and call-and-response style, is one of black music's foremost icons. Kendrick channeled Brown on "King Kunta" and employed the same cadence, flipping a line from "The Payback" into a diss of other rappers who use ghostwriters instead of writing their own bars, a cardinal sin in hip-hop. "I can dig rappin'," he spit, "but a rapper with a ghost writer? / What the fuck happened?"

Then there are certain points in the song that seem to refer to the new crowd beginning to form around Kendrick: the song depicts the rapper's triumphant return to Compton after years of being on the road and seeing new things. Upon his reentry, the same people who doubted his ascendance are the first ones shouting his name throughout the city. That goes back to what Matt Jeezy says about the nonbelievers who criticized Kendrick in 2009 for eschewing gangsta rap for other forms of music. They shunned him and questioned his newfound direction. So, on the hook, when he asks, "Bitch where you when I was walkin'? / Now I run the game, got the whole world talkin'," he's pointing his finger squarely in the faces of those people, proclaiming himself as the king—of West Coast rap, of Compton, of hip-hop as a whole. At that point, who could deny it—Drake, maybe, but while he crafted viral pop hits, he wasn't digging deep like Kendrick. He kept us at arm's length and chose surface-level topics that didn't resonate beyond Spotify streams. Kendrick and TDE were trying to make music that would last forever in history books and school syllabi. For the song, Terrace Martin blended eras, genres, and geography. "You could take the energy of Quincy [Jones] with Michael [Jackson], the harmony of Stevie [Wonder]," Martin once told Revolt. In that way, he continued, "These Walls" felt like "Human Nature," a hit Michael Jackson song from his 1982 album, *Thriller*.

For *To Pimp a Butterfly*, Porter tells me, one of the main objectives was to get the 808 drums—bass-heavy percussion—out of the mix. "What made *To Pimp a Butterfly* so special is that we kinda walked away from that," the trombonist remembers. "Once Terrace got into the studio and started hearing what they wanted to do, and how they wanted to piece it together with the live music, we got to bring what we do into it. Some of the music, we would play these tracks and get involved with them, and then, us being accustomed to playing with each other, we'd slip off and make a whole new song right then and there. There's a whole orchestra in there for some cuts." Porter, Martin, and Glasper describe frenzied scenes full of nonstop creativity. They'd be off playing somewhere, and in another part of the studio, Washington was writing out string arrangements and letting the producers hear what he'd drafted. There were nights where Kendrick would pop up to see how the live instrumentation was beginning to sound. "Once it got to the point where it was almost done and sounding good, that's when Kendrick started coming in like, 'I wanna hear how this track came out. Because I know it was hot before I left and I want to hear what these people did,'" Porter says. "He'd come in later and the energy would change. These instruments started giving these tracks a different spirit, a different energy, so he'd have to write according to that now. He started coming in and checking out the vibe of these songs, like, 'Oh, he got Thundercat on this one!' All these different things were adding all these different colors."

While *To Pimp a Butterfly* was as much about the musicians as it was about Kendrick, everyone agrees that he deserves more credit as a producer. He had a very clear vision of what his music was supposed to sound like, and how to let air into his verses so the compositions could breathe on their own. Where some rappers tend to suffocate the beats with rapid-fire flows to demonstrate their vocal prowess, Kendrick has been called a jazz musician himself, or a spoken-word poet who approaches words with the same vigor as Martin and company did with their instruments.

For the musicians, it was never about playing *all* the notes; they were careful and measured, and played the *best* notes. Same thing with Kendrick. "He was just like one of us," Porter says. "Everything doesn't have to be written down and formatted. If we had to go with the unknown, and make something out of what's happening right here, then we were all gonna be together and make something out of this situation. He wasn't like, 'Stop it, let me write something for this.' Kendrick was going to talk about how he was feeling right now, and he's such a good poet and storyteller that it worked." By all accounts, Kendrick was very much involved with the beat construction of *To Pimp a Butterfly* and treated the music with the same vigor that he'd treat his rhymes. He's very much a jazz musician who employs the same intricate technique to his vocal delivery that Miles Davis would to releasing notes from his trumpet. Kendrick was a scientist or a grand painter, and *To Pimp a Butterfly* was to be his masterpiece. The album had heavy themes within its bright, prismatic soundtrack, which wasn't surprising for a Kendrick record. Much like "Swimming Pools" from *good kid, m.A.A.d city*, Kendrick peppered his third album with personal narratives about coming home to tell his friends what he'd learned overseas. That explains the song "Momma," a heartfelt tribute to the journey of going to South Africa and bringing lessons back to Compton for his friends and the younger generation. People from Kendrick's side of town don't often get to see the world outside of their immediate surroundings. But because he had seen how the world moves, and had actually set foot inside Nelson Mandela's jail cell, his perspective broadened and he wanted to share the knowledge. He was thinking beyond the confines of Compton and bringing a new way of thinking back to the community. "The album means so much, not only to Compton, but to Los Angeles as a whole," Lalah Hathaway tells me. Hathaway is a noted soul singer and daughter of soul music legend Donny Hathaway, whose voice is sampled on "Momma," and was called in by Martin to add backup vocals to several songs on *To Pimp a Butterfly*. "Speaking as a person who lives in this community, it means so much for him to reach back and give these kids their dreams in the palms of their hands. It's amazing that he's still so in touch with his community because a lot of people are not. The fact that he's so brilliant at making kids listen to what's important, while also making it so they're not even paying attention to what they're listening to. It's hard to get kids to listen to smart shit."

But change is difficult—Kendrick said that a few times himself during *To Pimp a Butterfly*'s press run—and one man can't change an entire gang culture with one album. Red and blue is ingrained through the city, and it's tough to convey the wonders of the Motherland to people who can't see beyond their own blocks, and can't fathom life in Africa beyond what they've seen on the news. American media likes to portray Africa as poor and downtrodden, the so-called "Dark Continent," a place that's scary and where you couldn't possibly live. Of course, race has a lot to do with that, but Africa is full of beautiful black people on the cutting edge of literature, art, business, and technology. They are proud, and whether it's Lagos, Nigeria; Johannesburg, South Africa; or Nairobi, Kenya, Africa is a bustling continent with people just as ambitious and creative as Kendrick. "Momma," with its silky bass line and woozy, off-kilter drums (courtesy of J Dilla disciple Knxwledge), is an ode to blackness and a celebration of his own ascendance. On this track and others throughout *Butterfly*, Kendrick toes the line between reality and surrealism, wrestling with his own disbelief at just how far he's come in such a short period of time. For years, Kendrick toiled away in the TDE studio—working, grinding out mixtape after mixtape, album after album—sharpening his writing ability to the point of near mastery. Now suddenly he was there, far removed from the high school cyphers in 2003 and the sidewalk freestyles with Matt Jeezy. Now he could pack basketball arenas, though he had a much different struggle to conquer: the battle to stay true and to keep his sanity intact. And while the journey to South Africa helped Kendrick realign his spirit, he still had to come home to old problems that plagued him, his friends, and Compton as a whole. On "Momma," Kendrick sees himself in the face of a young boy in South Africa, and tries to reconcile his own challenges as a youth with the ones faced by his reflection. It was time for Kendrick to unlearn all the bullshit about Africa that was taught to him in school, and to implore his friends to come home.

The Butterfly Effect

Living in Africa as a Black American is something entirely different; you don't realize just how traumatized you are until you move to the continent. The idea of even visiting Africa is presented as a vague notion that would be cool to realize one day, but to actually go is incomprehensible. Through public schooling and propaganda, the United States teaches you that it's the land of opportunity and everything else is inferior. They tell you, indirectly, that black is lesser than, while ignoring the brutal history of slavery that brought our ancestors to these shores in the first place. But once you're in Africa, you instantly feel connected with your heritage. There's an innate sense that this is where you belong, followed by the anger of not knowing your true lineage, and realizing that the public school system doesn't care to teach the full scope of black history. Sure, we're taught the usual names—Dr. Martin Luther King Jr., Malcolm X, Marcus Garvey—but there's no comprehending the full beauty of Africa until you set foot on the soil. As a Black American, and as an American in general, you're trained to be on guard at all times, to duck when you hear loud popping noises, and to always assume the worst in people. You're trained to believe that the man walking toward you is going to ask for something, that there's no way he merely wants to wish you a prosperous day, to ease the worry on your face. We're trained to look for the catch, and to be surprised when it isn't there. We shouldn't be so shocked by acts of goodwill, but we are. "Momma" perfectly encapsulates the moment when Kendrick—through a chance encounter with a little boy in town—realized he wasn't so far removed from the Motherland, at least not as much as he thought. You also don't realize the economic disparities within Africa until you've lived with them for a while. It's one thing to live in, or walk past, public housing in places like New York City, but nothing can prepare you for the so-called "slums," where millions of people live without regular access to food and clean water. It makes you realize that our problems are insignificant in the bigger picture. Kendrick realized this, too, during his time in Africa. He realized that his views of the continent were skewed, and that his being there was a dream he didn't know needed to be realized.

The song "How Much a Dollar Cost," a deep cut featuring celebrated soul singer Ronald Isley, was conceived after a chance encounter with a homeless man at a Cape Town gas station. Kendrick assumed the man wanted money and nothing else. According to the song, Kendrick reacted like many people would, by saying he didn't have the cash while quickly brushing the man off. Kendrick thought the man was addicted to drugs; he asked for ten rand—or roughly sixty-seven U.S. cents—for what the rapper assumed would be used to achieve some sort of high. After staring at each other for what seemed like forever, it turned out the man simply wanted to put Kendrick on game. This song, like others on *To Pimp a Butterfly*, has dual themes working at the same time. On one end, you have Kendrick fighting against his own ego; he's *Kendrick Lamar* now, and with burgeoning fame comes the tendency to recoil. "I know when niggas hustlin'," he raps at one point in the song. Turns out the man is actually a reflection of God, and his appearance saves the rapper from descending toward a life of despair. In that way, "How Much a Dollar Cost" draws a direct line to "Sing About Me, I'm Dying of Thirst" on *good kid, m.A.A.d city*. Also situated near the end of the album, "How Much a Dollar Cost" is almost the exact same story: Kendrick is near the end of his rope and headed for a spiritual demise when he meets a divine being right at the time he needs it most. In this instance, the man warns him to not be so consumed with money, that it could make him hollow, and that the life he fought so hard to achieve isn't everything. Sensing Kendrick's fatigue, he puts a word on the rapper's heart, encouraging him to reconnect with the higher power he discovered as a teenager.

On "I'm Dying of Thirst," the enlightenment arrived in the form of a religious woman who stopped Kendrick and his friends from killing the guys who killed their friend. At this point, a decade removed from the incident that changed his life as a teen, Kendrick recenters his divinity, which led to the unclouded reflection of "i," which found new life on the LP as a makeshift live performance that's interrupted by a physical altercation in the crowd. Once again channeling James Brown, the track's scene is eerily similar to a show on April 5, 1968, the day after Martin Luther King Jr. was killed, in which the soul icon had to calm down an audience in the Boston Garden that openly grieved the assassination of its beloved civil rights leader. Brown famously waved off security and calmed down the crowd himself. "We are black!" he declared at the show. "Don't make us all look bad. You're not being fair to yourself or me or your race. Now, I asked the police to step back because I felt I could get some respect from my own people."

In Kendrick's scene, he'd just returned from a world tour and was performing a small show in Compton. As he performs "i" onstage, this time with live drums and backup singers, a fight breaks out in the audience, causing Kendrick to halt the song halfway through. Where Brown was trying to soothe the loss of a global leader, Kendrick kept it local, tempering a crowd presumably divided over gang colors and city blocks. He was also concerned with loss—the loss of his friends in the community. "How many niggas we done lost, bro?" Kendrick asks off mic. "This year alone! We ain't got time to waste, my nigga!" If the rapper wanted *Butterfly* to heal his community and black people throughout the world, the speech and spoken-word freestyle given here crystallizes that theme. As he unpacks the speech, the fight slowly dissipates and the patrons hang on Kendrick's every word: "N-E-G-U-S description: black emperor, king, ruler, now let me finish / The history books overlook the word and hide it / America tried to make it to a house divided."

Kendrick was trying to flip the narrative surrounding the N-word while refuting the notion that people in the inner city are destined to fail. Though Kendrick's friends hadn't yet seen the world, *To Pimp a Butterfly* allowed the rapper to bring the world back to them. He was letting them know it wasn't too late to change the tale, but he was also telling the public that his people weren't just "thugs" and "gangsters" with no redeeming qualities. They were not trash; they simply hadn't been given the same chances to succeed that their white counterparts had. So the fact that they gangbanged was a direct result of their living in a country where blacks were seen as inferior. By and large, they were not afforded the best education and told of their true royal lineage. They were not N-words (with the hard *-er*), they were Negus—supreme rulers, black kings and queens, who were simply far away from home, their true home, Africa. Kendrick discovered this during his journey and, ultimately, *To Pimp a Butterfly* was a therapeutic release.

That was most evident at the end of the album. After the notes fade on "Mortal Man" and Kendrick finishes the poem he'd been unpacking the entire LP, he starts talking to someone off mic. It's his hero Tupac Shakur, not the actual Tupac, of course—he'd been dead almost nineteen years—but a repurposed version of him. The music journalist Mats Nileskär had conducted a chat with Tupac in 1994 and shared the audio with TDE for their own usage. Here, the conversation is edited to make it seem like Kendrick and Pac are in the same room. For those who'd listened to the full album, the inclusion of an unheard Tupac interview was a shock. Listeners weren't expecting to hear his voice, and to hear it come out of nowhere—at the end of such a transcendent record—was truly a jaw-dropping moment. Yet this wasn't just a chat for shock value; Kendrick had finally come back home—back to L.A., back to the one person who could understand his emotional plight. Tupac was also a Gemini, so he could too fathom the struggle of feeling like two different people, and struggling through growing pains in the public eye. Kendrick sought advice on how to deal with being rich, and how to stay prudent as a famous person. How did Tupac do it? "By my faith in God, by my faith in the game," he told Kendrick, "and by my faith in 'all good things come to those who stay true.'"

7

"We Gon' Be Alright"

Midway through *To Pimp a Butterfly* is a song that would become the anthem for protests throughout the country, although Kendrick and Sounwave had no idea the track would hit in such a manner. It was called "Alright," the beat for it composed by Pharrell Williams, the revered Grammy Award–winning producer whose credits include everyone from Justin Timberlake to Beyoncé. He had made the beat as his own version of "trap music," the popular blend of trunk-thumping bass drums and street raps that became the most popular subgenre of hip-hop in the 2010s. Pharrell said he wanted something that sounded like trap, yet more "colorful," like the music he'd been known to create as one-third of N.E.R.D. in the late nineties and as a solo artist. He wanted the beat for "Alright" to have the hard knock of a trap song, but with live instruments to give it a soulful essence. "I kind of had my Tribe Called Quest hat on that day," Pharrell once said in 2015. He'd already worked with Kendrick, producing and singing backup on "good kid" from *good kid, m.A.A.d city*. Before then, Pharrell and his assistant played one of Kendrick's mixtapes during a drive through Tokyo. That's when he knew that Kendrick was a singular talent and wanted to work with him one day.

"Alright" as we know it almost didn't happen. "That beat . . . I don't think Pharrell was even going to play it for us, but one of his close friends, [who is also one] of our close friends who set up the session, was like, 'Pharrell, you gotta play them that beat,'" Sounwave once told *Spin*. "And he played it for Kendrick, and it was there, but it was not *all* there, vibe-wise, so that was my job to layer in the drums, get Terrace [Martin] to throw some sax riffs on it, and make it *us*. It's a completely different song than the original. . . . You'd understand if you were able to compare them, but that's probably never gonna happen. You just have to have your ears open for every little sound that has potential." The instrumental was infectious, from the stuttering vocal loop announcing its arrival, to the light synth chords bathing the track in bright shades. Pharrell had been known for his stammering intros, but unlike songs of his like "Frontin'" or "Happy," where ticking drums intensified the pending beat drop, the opening vocal loop made "Alright" feel exultant—like a psalm for street corners, or aliens coming down to Earth.

Kendrick sat on the instrumental for six months before he knew what to say on it. The track sounds joyous, like it should be a party record. But because the album's theme was so serious, the rapper saw something dark within the track, something that called for unifying words. "I knew it was a great record—I just was trying to find the space to approach it," Kendrick told producer Rick Rubin for a *GQ* feature in 2015. "I mean, the beat sounds fun, but there's something else inside of them chords that Pharrell put down that feels like—it can be more of a statement rather than a tune. Eventually, I found the right words. . . . And I wanted to approach it as more uplifting—but aggressive. Not playing the victim, but still having that *We strong*, you know?" Kendrick said he faced pressure from Pharrell and Sam Taylor, a professional dot-connector in the music industry, to write something monumental, or at least *finish* the damn thing. "I didn't have any words," Kendrick continued. "P knew that that record was special. Sam knew that the record was special. They probably knew it before I even had a clue. So I'm glad that they put that pressure on me to challenge myself. 'Cause sometimes, as a writer, you can have that writer's block. And when you like a sound or an instrumental, you want to approach it the right way. So you sit on it." Six months later, the rapper started toying with different cadences.

Meanwhile, Pharrell already had a hook in mind: "We gon' be alright, we gon' be alright." "That chorus I had for a while, the feeling of that chorus," he's quoted as saying on AMC's *Hip Hop: The Songs That Shook America*. "Kendrick recontextualized it. The chorus I had was about guys in a hood environment who maybe sell dope as . . . their only means of getting out, but then you have to flush it because the cops run in. And them thinking to themselves that they just lost everything, but we gon' be alright. But Kendrick smartly looked at it and thought about it from a broader perspective, and thought about the culture, and thought about what the culture was going through at the time." The rapper framed his lyrics around the intensity of what was happening in America. "I remember hitting P on a text like, *Man, I got the lyrics*," he told Rubin for *GQ*. "And typing the lyrics to him. He's like, *That's it*." The lyrics were influenced by the severe poverty he saw in South Africa. "They struggle maybe ten times harder and was raised crazier than what I was," he told MTV News. "That was the moment I knew, 'OK, I can either pimp this situation or I can fall victim to it.' That was a turning point." But look at the lyrics closely: they also extend the album's theme of diving deeper into Kendrick's personal torment. "Alright" continued the theme of Lucy—or Lucifer the devil—as an evil spirit that dogged him as he became famous. In his world, Lucy rests in his psyche, telling him to buy expensive cars, big houses, and lots of clothes because he deserves it. Go live at the mall, Lucy says, you're a big-time celebrity now. On "Wesley's Theory" and "For Sale? (Interlude)," Kendrick introduces the character, but here he's trying to stave it off. "I didn't wanna self-destruct," he declares in a spoken-word poem near the end of the track. "The evils of Lucy was all around me."

Once completed, "Alright" became the most pop-centered song on *To Pimp a Butterfly*, an abrasive protest track made specifically for people of color who were tired of seeing their brothers and sisters killed by police. But this wasn't meant to be "We Shall Overcome" or anything *nice*. "Alright" was a fierce middle finger to the establishment and the same law enforcement that killed Eric Garner, Oscar Grant, Mike Brown, Tamir Rice, Trayvon Martin, and so many before them. The song had to be bold; it had to ruffle feathers. The lyrics had to cut straight and make listeners feel uncomfortable. And they did, especially if you weren't of the community to whom he was speaking. "And we hate popo," Kendrick declared. "Wanna kill us dead in the street fo sho'."

Released in March 2015, at the height of the Black Lives Matter movement, "Alright" took direct aim at racist cops and tapped into the pain of disgruntled black people throughout the world. It had the hostility of N.W.A's "Fuck tha Police" and the soulful grit of early seventies Stevie Wonder tracks like "Living for the City" and "You Haven't Done Nothin'." Finally, the new generation had a protest anthem that spoke truth to power. This wasn't a time for popping bottles or any other stereotype; we were under attack and needed something to release the steam. Kendrick sounded irate, but when paired with Pharrell's lush backing track and Terrace Martin's light saxophone wails, "Alright" paved a way forward for the black community, that—yes—things are messed up right now, but throughout history, we've endured the worst of humanity and still come out on top. We're in a bad way at the moment, but as long as we have each other, we'll find some form of nirvana.

Then there was the video—a dense, cinematic marvel shot in foreboding black and white. The imagery is dramatic, just like the song: a black boy facedown on the concrete, blood splattered on the face of another hoodie-clad youth. A police officer slams a man to the ground and handcuffs him. He gets up and runs, and the officer fires a shot from his service weapon. The bullet ejects in slow motion, whether or not it strikes its target is unclear. Two frames later, TDE's lead rappers bounce around in a car: Kendrick is behind the wheel as ScHoolboy Q rides shotgun; Ab-Soul and Jay Rock share a beer in the backseat. They're in a celebratory mood, pouring what looks like malt liquor out the side of the vehicle, toasting to their vitality. "I'mma be the greatest to ever do this shit!" Kendrick proclaims in the clip. "On the dead homies!" Musically and visually, the scene evokes Busta Rhymes's 1996 video for "Woo-Hah!! Got You All in Check." As he and his friends glide down the road, a soul-inflected beat kicks in and Kendrick puffs out his chest even further: "*To Pimp a Butterfly* another classic *ceedee*-ah / Ghetto lullaby for everyone that *emcee*-ah." Kendrick seemed to borrow the cadence and vocal tone of "Woo-Hah!!," the lead single off Busta's debut album, *The Coming*. Visually, the four guys in the car conjure the opening scene of "Woo-Hah!!" when Busta and friends ride through Times Square as the rapper spits the opening lines of the album cut "Everything Remains Raw." In Kendrick's video, the camera zooms out to reveal its most rewarding aspect: the TDE rappers aren't actually driving down the street; they're being carried by four police officers, a striking visual given the year of its release. Based on looks alone, the TDE rappers resembled the men the cops would likely target in the streets. "Once you get an image that strong, everything builds from there," director Colin Tilley once told MTV News. "It's not in your face like, 'Fuck this. Fuck that.' It's more like, this is what's real and what's going on in the world right now."

From there, Kendrick floats throughout Los Angeles, almost like a superhero or a spirit overlooking the city. That was done on purpose. "The whole world we created is like a fantasy, a dream world," Tilley said. The hero aspect was "him being something these kids can aspire towards. So, when they look up, it's almost like it's Superman." In doing this, Kendrick showed Compton in a positive light, a journey he started on *good kid, m.A.A.d city*. In the final frame, he raps from atop a streetlight as a cop looks on beneath him. With his fingers twisted into a makeshift gun, he fires a shot, striking the rapper, who falls to the ground—both literally and figuratively. Kendrick had been on top of the world at that point in his life. But he was human, not some savior for hip-hop or humanity. It showed that even a transcendent talent like Kendrick could be cut down in an instant. "At the end of the day, we're all human and that nobody's untouchable," Tilley told MTV News.

"Alright" drew a line back to 1989 and another rap protest song—Public Enemy's "Fight the Power"—which gave listeners a jolt they didn't know they needed. The musical theme of Spike Lee's *Do the Right Thing*, "Fight the Power" was a boastful track in which the rappers Chuck D and Flavor Flav nudged listeners to rise above oppression. "We needed an anthem," Lee once told *Rolling Stone*. "When I wrote the script . . . every time when the Radio Raheem character showed up, he had music blasting. I wanted Public Enemy." The year prior, the group had released *It Takes a Nation of Millions to Hold Us Back*, a bombastic collage of social consciousness that passed muster with the rap community, though they hadn't become mainstream stars just yet. "Fight the Power" helped them break through; their no-nonsense flows and forceful beats somehow clicked with bigger audiences. "When Public Enemy first started," Hank Shocklee recalls, "people were listening to the rhythms and the rhymes and weren't paying attention to the content. Most people just wanted ['Fight the Power'] because they thought it was noisy and aggressive and all that other stuff." Because the song was tied to a big film like *Do the Right Thing*, "it was embraced by the intellectuals of music, the writers, the scholars who were still into hip-hop. It also spawned a whole group of artists who implemented that same vibration. It was the beginning of conscious rap. We found out that all over the United States, everyone was feeling the same vibration, but no one was talking about it, no one was actually voicing that." The same went for Kendrick; the song "Alright" and *To Pimp a Butterfly* changed the vibration; it took hold as another two names became hashtags on social media: Freddie Gray and Sandra Bland.

On April 12, 2015, twenty-five-year-old Freddie Gray was arrested by six police officers in Baltimore for possessing what they thought was a switchblade, which had been deemed illegal under Maryland law. Gray was thought to be a troubled man who had grown up in the neighborhood of Sandtown-Winchester on Baltimore's west side. According to reports, he'd been arrested multiple times and served time for various drug charges. The circumstances surrounding Gray's arrest were murky: for whatever reason, he ran from the police when he saw them, and after he was handcuffed, he was seen on video saying that he had asthma and asked for an inhaler. Then he was arrested and dragged into a police van, where officers folded his body into an awkward position while putting him in custody. With his hands and feet shackled, he was said to be slammed head-first onto the van floor, even though it's Baltimore police policy to buckle prisoners into van seats during transportation. Not only did he struggle to breathe, Gray was suffering from a spinal injury but was never given medical attention. Police kept driving toward the police station, eventually reaching their destination shortly before 9:30 a.m.

On April 18, hundreds of Baltimore residents gathered in front of the Western District police station to protest his arrest and injury, and because emotions still ran high between black people and the police, the Gray incident had the potential of running hot before peace intervened. Gray died the next day, on April 19. Yet another young black man had perished under suspicious circumstances, leaving the community enraged. They wanted answers, and they wanted them right now. The Gray incident exacerbated long-simmering tensions between the police and community in West Baltimore, and on April 25—two days before Gray's funeral—an organized protest spiraled into chaos outside the Baltimore Orioles baseball stadium in the city's downtown area. Some businesses were looted. Police cruisers were pelted with rocks. There was a sense that trouble was on the way, that the small spat of violence during the April 25 protest could escalate into something much bigger if city officials didn't pay attention. A mysterious flyer on Instagram encouraged residents to "purge" (a reference to a movie of the same name, in which crime is legal for a period of twelve hours).

On April 27 and over the next five days, riots raged through-out the city. Vehicles and businesses were set ablaze. It was easily the most tenuous time in Baltimore's history, and with Black America on alert, then-mayor Stephanie Rawlings-Blake awarded $6.4 million to the Gray family as the result of a civil suit following a mistrial in his death. City officials had seen what happened in Ferguson and Cleveland, and now with its town in crisis, the mayor wanted to heal a community that'd been hurting for so long. But there was no putting a Band-Aid on *this*; no amount of money could make up for Gray's death. And just like in Ferguson and Staten Island, at least one protester's life came to an early end. Juan Grant, who was a close friend of Gray's and led a protest at the Western District police station following the incident, was shot and killed on the fourth anniversary of Gray's funeral. According to police and media reports, Grant had been driving to his grandmother's home when his car collided with a dirt bike. The person on the bike shot and killed him. Grant was a father and devoted community activist who demanded justice for his slain friend. Now Grant's family was left to wonder why he had been taken away so senselessly.

On July 13, 2015, the body of Sandra Bland was found hanged in a jail cell in Waller County, Texas, where she was detained after a minor traffic stop. In a self-recorded cell phone video made public four years later, Bland and State Trooper Brian Encinia were seen having a tense exchange on the side of the road, as the officer—holding a stun gun—threatened to tag her if she didn't get out of her vehicle. Bland's death was ruled a suicide, which raised immediate questions from activists, who already distrusted law enforcement and figured they were lying about the circumstances of her passing. Though Encinia was indicted on a charge of perjury, the charge was dismissed after he agreed to never again work in law enforcement. Bland had been outspoken about police brutality and racial injustice, and up until 2019, the public was made to believe that the officer feared for his life, and that's why he threatened her with a Taser. Yet the video said otherwise; Encinia grew increasingly frustrated with a person who knew her rights. "My sister died because a police officer saw her as a threatening black woman rather than human," Bland's sister, Sharon Cooper, once wrote in an op-ed for *USA Today*. "Our mere existence is perceived as such a threat to police officers that we're consistently asked to pay for our freedom with our bodies and sometimes even with our blood. . . . My sister was unafraid. Her strength gives us the power to continue to fight for her and say her name."

In late July 2015, amid incredibly high tensions, a crowd of protesters gathered on the campus of Cleveland State University to lament the killing of Tamir Rice. Demonstrators throughout the United States still seethed from similar deaths in other states, and almost daily, new groups of people took to the streets to rally against injustice. Following the Movement for Black Lives conference, where local demonstrators and members of Black Lives Matter met to discuss the rampant police brutality that swept the country, the group left the conference en route to the buses slated to take them to their respective homes. Standing outside, the group noticed police officers harassing a young boy for carrying what they thought was an open container of alcohol onto the bus. The boy was fourteen years old, and because the city had just mourned the death of Tamir, the strain reached a boiling point. Incredulous, the crowd questioned the transit police officer about why the child was being detained. They were pepper-sprayed. Someone in the crowd asked for the phone number of the boy's mother. She was called and was soon there talking to police. According to news accounts, the boy was released from police custody and went home with his mother. The crowd of two hundred was elated; for the first time in almost a year, they had a win against law enforcement. Soon, a chant started to billow throughout the mass:

We gon' be alright!
We gon' be alright!

It was a heroic scene, a sea of triumphant black people walking through the streets, passing police cruisers like they weren't even there. No way could this make up for the loss of life that permeated the past two years, but for a brief time, all the agony led to this moment, right there in Cleveland. In months past, the movement had escalated beyond peace and became violent at different points. But the Cleveland demonstration was a flash point for the movement overall, and now it had an anthem tying it together. Along with the strides activists made in cities like New York and Cleveland, the movement had its own "Lift Ev'ry Voice and Sing," albeit with a few cusswords. But that was the temperature of the time. We were tired of trying to overcome and wanted equal treatment *right now*.

The action was captured on video and instantly went viral. Just that quick, Kendrick's music was at the center of a political movement, and the rapper—whether he knew it or not—was suddenly the country's foremost purveyor of protest music. Kendrick and the team hadn't created the art for a viral moment, but maybe that was why it resonated so strongly. It came from an honest place, from a hole of darkness and personal torment. It just happened to connect with the masses. But because he was so forthright about his strife, and because the song used straightforward language to denounce police brutality, "Alright" hit listeners in a very real way. Alicia Garza, cofounder of Black Lives Matter, first heard the song on her way home from Ferguson, Missouri, where BLM and local demonstrators were gathered following the acquittal of Officer Darren Wilson in the shooting death of Mike Brown. "I remember seeing the ways in which these issues were being touched on," Garza tells me. "The main message underneath it was morality, like, 'What are we teaching our kids?' It was a dose of reality for lots of people, and that rarely gets into the mainstream." In 2016, as a businessman turned reality TV star named Donald Trump was running for U.S. president, protesters at the University of Illinois at Chicago chanted the hook of "Alright" after his rally was canceled for security reasons. By the end of the decade, music publications considered it one of the very best songs—if not the best song—of the 2010s. And unlike other commercial hits, which can be quantified through sales and streams, "Alright" touched people in ways that can't be measured. "You might not have heard it on the radio all day," Kendrick told *Variety*, "but you're seeing it in the streets, you're seeing it on the news, and you're seeing it in communities, and people felt it."

"Alright," and *To Pimp a Butterfly* as a whole, wasn't just of the moment; the song and album were instant classics that lobbed Kendrick into the pantheon of rap's all-time greats. Critics openly wondered if he was now the greatest rapper the world had ever seen, and whether his body of work was the best catalog ever compiled. That's lofty praise for someone who hadn't been in the game that long, who by his own admission hadn't made his best work yet. He was still working, still keeping his head down in search of the perfect project. But when *To Pimp a Butterfly* was released—by surprise on March 15, 2015, a week before it was supposed to come out—it rocked the foundation of hip-hop and music overall, from its cover art, and the flurry of unabashed black music that tumbled from the speakers. It sounded far different from *good kid, m.A.A.d city*—a fact that angered some fans who craved that record's opulent, wide-open soundscapes and tightly woven story line. *To Pimp a Butterfly* was more sprawling and more ambitious, a complicated patchwork of themes and ideas. It was angrier, denser, and made for headphone listening. More than anything, it was the sound of Kendrick battling his demons in front of his biggest audience, which not only alleviated the pressure he faced, but also somehow enabled him to connect it with all sorts of listeners. "Kendrick had so much respect from everybody," Robert Glasper tells me. "He spoke to the jazz cats, to the music nerds, to the backpack rappers, the gangsters. That album touched everybody."

That included New Jersey teacher Brian Mooney, who in 2015 dropped everything to teach a course on *To Pimp a Butterfly*. He had been teaching an English course based on Toni Morrison's 1970 novel *The Bluest Eye*, but when he heard Kendrick's opus, he thought the rapper's work could connect with more students. "There was a lot going on in the world," Mooney says. "And to think what that meant for teachers in the classroom with urban youth, how we were unpacking that with a lot of kids who are living through very real traumas. The things that they have to deal with—whether it's violence in their communities, or poverty, or an addicted parent, or gun violence. Kendrick is addressing a lot of that stuff, through talking about mental illness and his own battles with his own demons." In class, Mooney and his students analyzed many of the album's songs and spent an entire class period looking at the cover. "I remember how incredible *that* was," Mooney exclaims. "The kids were so engaged. We had a whole conversation about, well, 'Why is it in black and white?' The kids went home, they wrote commentary responses on the class blog page, and responded to songs like 'King Kunta.'" Mooney wrote a post on his personal blog about his decision to teach classes based on *To Pimp a Butterfly*. That caught the attention of TDE, and soon after, Mooney got an email from the collective that said Kendrick had read the post and wanted to connect with him. Two weeks later, he's on the phone with Dave Free to coordinate Kendrick's visit to the school in June 2015. "I had this mind-set like, 'He should *want* to come see this work in action. He should *want* to see the brilliance of our kids.'" To make Kendrick feel comfortable at the school, Mooney instituted a cipher in which the students and teachers rapped. They all rhymed over a beat once used by the rapper Ghostface Killah; that caught Kendrick's attention. "It broke the ice," Mooney says. Still, he remembers some teachers not wanting to come to the welcoming assembly for Kendrick's arrival because they felt it wasn't worth it. They had misperceptions about him and his art, and "there were definitely some racist attitudes going on," he says. In the end, Mooney drew comparisons between *The Bluest Eye* and *To Pimp a Butterfly*, calling Morrison's work a parent to Kendrick's album.

Upon its release, it was somewhat tough to describe *Butterfly*'s impact; it simply had that thing, that certain gravitas that you couldn't describe. It had an *it* factor, and as it played, there was this feeling that you were hearing something familiar and fresh happening at the same time. Artists of his ilk don't usually create sonically challenging art like this; for the most part, once they find a working formula for their music, and sell a bunch of records as a result, they tend to stay in that lane to ensure their financial security. There's rarely an impetus for going beyond the scope of what's expected. So for Kendrick to create such a record was incredibly brave, and it set the course for others to do the same. It gave greater name recognition to the musicians in its liner notes, and because of its dense jazz textures, Kendrick and the jazz experts on *To Pimp a Butterfly* have been credited with bringing the genre back from obscurity. *To Pimp a Butterfly* harkened back to the jazz of its heyday—the hard bop of the fifties, and the funk fusion of the late sixties and early seventies—and brought the music to a younger audience. Because of *Butterfly*'s adventurous nature, and perhaps due to the newfound interest in jazz, Kamasi Washington released *The Epic* soon after. *To Pimp a Butterfly* made it okay for Washington to put out such an ambitious project at a time when attention spans were shorter; a three-hour record, of any kind, likely wouldn't exist before Kendrick's project. "That record changed music, and we're still seeing the effects of it," Washington told Pitchfork. "It went beyond jazz; it meant that intellectually stimulating music doesn't have to be underground. It can be mainstream. It went beyond everything else, too: harmonically, instrumentation-wise, structurally, lyrically. I feel like people's expectations of themselves changed, too. It just didn't change the music. It changed the audience."

So not only was he changing the world for black people nationwide; he was changing the musical landscape as well. That's not to ignore the trendsetting black music that came before *To Pimp a Butterfly*, though: in 2007, long before this album was ever thought of, vocalist Janelle Monáe released an EP called *Metropolis: Suite I (The Chase)*, which blended R&B, orchestral jazz, and science fiction, resulting in a capacious mix of performance art that defined Monáe's musical career moving forward. Then, in 2014, Flying Lotus released *You're Dead!*, essentially a free-jazz album; on it, he and Thundercat explored the spirit's journey from life to death when the human frame passes away. On a smaller scale, the success of *To Pimp a Butterfly* opened the door for esoteric black music to get coverage from large rock publications. In the years prior to *Butterfly*'s release, it was almost impossible to get editors to care about the new generation of jazz artists, but in the months after, everything was a jazz record, and it was easier to get pieces commissioned on Glasper, Terrace Martin, Thundercat, Kamasi Washington, and the like. They carried with them a level of intrigue, and from the *To Pimp a Butterfly* sessions, the publications wanted to know just *what* they did to create such a vibrant blend of soul, funk, hip-hop, and jazz. The *Butterfly* cohort became stars, and with their fame came greater opportunities to push their music even further into the world. Kendrick was being hailed as a jazz savior, and as Glasper points out, the rapper began to appear in the pages of the genre's top publications. He was casting his net even further, touching bigger audiences and spreading his message. That's how Kendrick became a leader. "I feel like he's a rebel," Lalah Hathaway says. "He could come out and do and say anything. What he's talking about is what's happening in the street. His art mirrors his life."

8

The Night Kendrick Ascended

Around 2016, a harsh reality started settling in. In less than a year, the country's first black president, Barack Obama—term-limited—would be leaving the White House. And not only were we losing President Obama, we were losing his family, too: First Lady Michelle Obama, and their daughters, Sasha and Malia. The most dynamic first family ever would soon be gone, and all we would have would be memories of the previous seven years. The Obamas had swept into Washington, D.C., in 2008 on a tidal wave of hope and change, and in the black community, there were feelings of euphoria, that the country—which for so long had reminded us that we didn't belong—was suddenly liberal enough to elect a black man to the highest seat in the land. There was this notion that we had won something: we'd endured the worst of the United States and were somehow moving beyond our horrific past. Just look at the joyful tears the night Barack Obama was elected—the look of pure delight, shock, and bewilderment. *Was* this *the same America?*

In hindsight, the notion that we'd moved into some sort of post-racial America was a foolish thought, but we hadn't seen anything like this—or like Barack Obama—before. He had to be something special to navigate the American political system: equally affable, charismatic, and unflinching, he talked the talk and walked it, doing his best to bridge the gap between Republicans and Democrats while keeping his own transcendent voice. But even that raised this issue: for a black man to be elected U.S. president, he had to damn near walk on water. He had to have the perfect family, the perfect record, the coolest stride, and a smile that could light Times Square. Not surprisingly, Obama faced resistance, but he remained cool in public. Perhaps he knew that he couldn't show rage, that if he did, he'd come off as the "angry black man" typically decried in public discourse. His cool made the rest of us relax, even if the first years of his presidency weren't seamless: In 2009, the first year of his first term, Obama inherited an economy on the verge of financial collapse. The stock markets crashed, unemployment was rampant, and homeowners saw their housing values dwindle. It was the country's worst economic disaster since the Great Depression in the 1930s. To solve the 2009 crisis, dubbed the Great Recession, the president implemented a plan called the American Recovery and Reinvestment Act, an ambitious $787 billion package that provided immediate relief for businesses, families, and sectors in immediate need. Meanwhile, in what is now a curious move, Donald Trump fashioned himself as an early supporter of Obama's, especially around the topic of climate change. When he wasn't taking part in pro wrestling story lines with his friend, World Wrestling Entertainment chairman and CEO Vince McMahon, Trump was part of a contingent of business owners who favored Obama's desired shift to clean energy. In an ad published in the *New York Times*, the collective said that the shift would spur economic growth and create new energy jobs. But a year later, Trump disputed the idea of climate change altogether. Then in 2012, he tweeted that climate change "was created by and for the Chinese." This is a minor example when compared with what he'd pull in subsequent years, but it demonstrates the sort of double-talk he'd use to slowly wade into politics.

Trump once again floated the idea of running for U.S. president, just as he'd done in 1988 and 1999. But this time he seemed serious, even if liberal voters didn't see him as a threat. There was no way that *this* guy—the reality show host with a notable catchphrase ("You're fired")—had what it took to be the leader of the free world. Sure, he'd proved his mettle as a real estate mogul, but aside from a few casinos and other tall buildings bearing his last name, Trump wasn't a man most envisioned in the Oval Office one day—not even by a little bit. But slowly and surely, he started inching toward the White House, peeling off one act after another to create a new normal, a new *ridiculous* normal. In the spring of 2011, Trump had pressed Obama to release his official birth certificate to prove that he was born in the United States, and not Kenya, as some conspiracy theorists had claimed. For a while, President Obama ignored Trump's calls for his birth certificate to be released. It was "silliness," he once said, imploring the American public to stick with the issues at hand: the country was still climbing out of a financial hole, and to acknowledge Trump's noise would be counter-productive. Yet Trump went on shows like *The View* and Fox News to denounce Obama with wild claims that catered to his voting base in battleground states. Trump claimed that Obama's grandmother had witnessed Obama's birth in Kenya, and that she was on tape confirming this notion. To the world outside of New York, this was the beginning of Donald Trump the caricature, and for the next five years, he'd use tactics like these—threats and baseless rhetoric—to rile up a section of America that didn't like the country's rapidly changing demographics and political structure.

At least Obama gave a damn, which couldn't be said about his successor. When Trayvon died, Obama spoke on it through a personal lens. When twenty young pupils died as a result of a mass shooting at Sandy Hook Elementary School in Newtown, Connecticut, he wept openly, and wiped away not only his tears, but the nation's. By mid-2015, we were somewhat removed from the well-publicized police shootings of 2012 and 2014, but the pain was still raw as more unarmed blacks died at the hands of law enforcement. In fact, the carnage ramped up: though black men made up 2 percent of the U.S. population, they were nine times more likely to be killed by police officers that year, an alarming stat on its own, yet even more so given public attention on the issue. Racial tensions were high, despite having Obama in office. To be black at that time was to live in constant fear or anger over what was happening to people who looked like us. If you watched the news or scrolled through social media, it was easy to feel like your life didn't matter, that even though the president tried to instill tranquility, there was a fifty-fifty chance that you could be the next hashtag, the next news segment on CNN, the next talking point in an Al Sharpton speech.

As Kendrick gained more popularity around this time, he started to recede further from the public eye. He backed away from social media and interviews weren't as frequent. Although he made grand professional strides, Kendrick Lamar was the same Kendrick Lamar Duckworth from a tough city, the quiet and shy kid looking for peace and tranquility. Now he couldn't just *go out*, not unless he wanted to cause a scene. He had to protect himself and his feelings, and for him that meant simply staying out of sight until he had to perform. He'd always been behind the scenes, and to be a star made him draw back. Such a move only heightened the mystery surrounding him and made his light shine brighter. He released music into an industry and to fans who demanded around-the-clock access to the rapper. Because his work was so resonant and so real, listeners felt like they knew him and wanted to feel a deeper connection. Conspiracy theories started swirling around the real meaning of his lyrics. Fans, critics, bloggers, and industry insiders loved to discuss Kendrick Lamar albums like current events on the news. He became barber shop talk: *Which album is the best? Who do you think he was talking to on "These Walls"? Is he really a gospel rapper? What do you think Kendrick is working on now?* Questions like these dot a typical Kendrick convo, and for any artist making an impact, this is essentially the dream they envision. They want listeners to dive into the music and form their own narratives about it. That's the surest way to stay relevant in the short term, and that's also how they live forever.

With two classic albums under his belt, Kendrick didn't have anything else to prove to the public. He achieved in two albums what it might take others four or five albums to accomplish: Kendrick wasn't only being compared with his peers, he was now being lumped in with the greats: Jay-Z, Nas, the Notorious B.I.G., Tupac Shakur. He could only dream of these comparisons four years earlier, but now his records hit on that level, even if he couldn't fully believe it himself. He was simply saying what was on his mind as a form of release; that rap fans received it so passionately was both surprising and gratifying.

Behind the scenes, though, he was already thinking ahead to the next project, steadfast as always. "That's Kendrick," Sounwave told Red Bull Music Academy in 2019. "He was on his fourth album, skip the third album. His brain is . . . I can't explain it, but we literally just finished mastering *To Pimp a Butterfly* and he was like, 'Alright, that's cool. So for this next album.' I'm like, 'Bro, no, it's not even out yet. Let it get out first and then we'll start talking about it.' And he was like, 'No, no, don't worry about it. They gonna get that. For this next album . . . we gonna do this, we gonna do that. I want to bring this back.' You just gotta go with it because he's a genius." Kendrick still had to promote *To Pimp a Butterfly*, and he was thinking beyond the conventional setup of him and a live band, or him and Ali with nothing else. He was way past that; it was time to level up even further. He was a crossover star now, and his collaborations began to reflect his new self. Kendrick was rapping on Taylor Swift songs (on "Bad Blood"), flowing on the remix of singer Jidenna's wildly popular track "Classic Man." Surely he could flex a little bit, but he was still Kendrick, and *To Pimp a Butterfly* was still the record to beat that year. His next performance had to be the boldest act he'd ever pulled off—at least to that point.

The Butterfly Effect

On June 28, 2015, Kendrick ventured to the Microsoft Theater in Los Angeles for the fifteenth annual BET Awards. It was a star-studded affair, just like the Grammys that the rapper attended the prior year, but this show was black—beautifully black. Janelle Monáe was there. As were actors Tracee Ellis Ross and Anthony Anderson (himself a Compton native). Producer and label mogul Sean "Diddy" Combs organized an onstage reunion of 1990s stalwart Bad Boy Records. Motown legend Smokey Robinson sang "Cruisin'" and other hallmarks from his catalog. It felt like a reunion, a strong celebration of blackness. At the beginning of the show was Kendrick, standing on top of a hollowed-out police cruiser with graffiti covering its frame. In the background was a massive American flag, its ends frayed and swaying in the breeze. That alone was symbolic: at a time when the country was divided along racial and political lines, the flag represented the tattered unity in which the nation prided itself, the fabric being pulled apart and torn so gently. Standing around Kendrick were dancers, scores of them, all choreographed to move in lockstep with each other beneath a makeshift streetlight. From the outside, the scene felt chaotic, dangerous, one step away from falling apart. It represented America in 2015, with all its rhetoric and empty apologies to people of color. With each bullet came prayers for the fallen and the plea for unity from others who didn't look like us. So there was something about Kendrick standing on *that* car, his shoes grinding into its roof with a wry smile on his face. He looked powerful, like a leader, like a free black man. In this moment he became a symbol, no longer a rapper or anything mortal. You had to look up at him on that deconstructed cop car, and what a throne that was.

Kendrick was there to perform "Alright," the movement's new anthem, with all its anti-police lyrics and strong pro-black stance. The live performance, much like *To Pimp a Butterfly*, was designed to shake up the system and speak the harshest honesty. It went back to what Terrace Martin had said about Kendrick's mind-set going into the record: he was saying what needed to be said, boldly and without fear. It was about making people uncomfortable, to change the discourse surrounding black trauma, depression, and racism. "We were excited when those brothers were protesting, and the police were there, and all you heard in the background was 'We gon' be alright!'" Martin tells me. "We were excited by things that really mattered to our people. We're from L.A. and dealing with a whole line of issues. The feeling was like, 'Man, I know somebody's gonna get the message,' and I was so happy it was done because I felt like our people needed *something*. They needed something to look at, something to feel, something to listen to. I felt like our people needed and wanted something real and honest, something that was a fine display of challenge, breakthrough, and courage."

The police cruiser was designed by a painter named Blue, an acquaintance of Kendrick and TDE. The label approached him with the idea of having Kendrick perform on top of the cop car, and because the artist had sketched a live painting a month prior for the rapper's gig on *Ellen*, he was a natural fit to tag the police cruiser for Kendrick's BET Awards performance. At the BET Awards, in a room full of black people, "Alright" hit harder. There was something poignant about it, and not since N.W.A, Ice-T's "Cop Killer," or J Dilla's "Fuck the Police" had an artist been so direct about how he and his community felt about abusive law enforcement. To see it interpreted that way—atop a symbol of such mistreatment—crystallized the song and the moment. Think of the irony: a young black man, with twisted hair and ripped denim, who looked like the others being targeted by police, was publicly taking back the idea of freedom and prosperity. Then consider the shock of seeing it live for the first time, the delight in seeing someone like Kendrick take that kind of stance. The imagery was striking: we already knew him as a supreme lyricist, but with gigs like these—along with his Grammy turn with Imagine Dragons in 2014—the rapper was becoming one of the world's greatest entertainers and a full-on artiste.

But there was at least one person who did not like Kendrick's statement: talk show host and pundit Geraldo Rivera, who went on Fox News to condemn the "Alright" performance. On a segment of *The Five*, Rivera lambasted the track, saying that the song wasn't helpful. "This is why I say that hip-hop has done more damage to young African Americans than racism in recent years," he said. "This is exactly the wrong message." Kendrick, in response to the TV pundit, asked, "How can you take a song that's about hope, and turn it into hatred? The problem isn't me standing on a cop car, his attempt [dilutes] the real problem . . . the senseless acts of killing these young boys out here. For the most part, it's avoiding the truth. Hip-hop is not the problem, our reality is the problem." Geraldo's narrative was the same type of "All Lives Matter" rhetoric that some right-wing conservatives used to minimize the long-standing abuse that people of color have been exposed to for generations. To say "All Lives Matter" was to say "Let's get back to how things used to be, back when we could look away from the abuse and not have to address it." It was to ignore the privilege that created this chasm, hoping that this fad would go away. Now, due to the prevalence of social media and smartphones, there was no way to avoid the issue. You couldn't act like police brutality wasn't a problem, or that blacks in the inner city didn't have viable concerns with how they were being treated in their own neighborhoods. They were handled like they didn't belong, like they were somehow hindering police officers who were there to protect and serve. To say "All Lives Matter" was to insinuate that "we're all in this together," but U.S. history had shown that simply wasn't true. "All" meant "white," and with the rise of Black Lives Matter, a new generation of black people were saying they'd no longer be silent, that the fight of our ancestors had not gone in vain.

Geraldo's stance echoed the same argument used after each mass shooting in the States. When a young man grabs an assault rifle and shoots up a school or a mall, conservatives blame violent video games, or heavy metal music, or anything that skirts the real problem: that citizens shouldn't be able to buy an assault rifle at a department store. We pray for the fallen, we mourn for the families, but then our leaders don't do anything to regulate gun purchases. So to claim that hip-hop has done more than racism to damage the black community is a flat-out lie: hip-hop saves the community; it's the voice of the voiceless, the sound of oppressed people spinning negativity into vibrant art. Genres like soul and jazz also carry healing powers, and they, too, can get political, but not like hip-hop. When done correctly, rap knows how to cut directly to it. Jazz is mostly about tone; it's largely instrumental, so listeners have to surmise what musicians like Kamasi Washington are trying to say with their instruments. Rappers use very direct language, and Kendrick was no exception, at least on "Alright." Though he was known to shield his message behind dense layers of poetry and dual meanings, the words here don't leave anything to the imagination. This wouldn't be the last run-in between Kendrick and Fox News.

As people began to digest *To Pimp a Butterfly*, Kendrick took subtle steps toward blending his community back home. The rapper had signed a deal with Reebok to release his own sneaker with the words *BLUE* on the left shoe and *RED* on the right one. While this was Kendrick's way of trying to push for a resolution between Pirus and Crips in Compton, it was also a savvy business move. This was Kendrick trying to create the world that he rapped about. He had aspirations of the two groups getting along, or at least coming together to fight common enemies who threatened the livelihood of red and blue alike. In his view, as gang culture eradicated black men in Compton—whether by death or incarceration—there were still trigger-happy cops and shady politicians with whom to contend, and those battles were more important than fighting for city blocks they didn't even own. Kendrick's plan was ambitious; to combat a long-standing gang culture took incredible fortitude. Yet this signaled a major breakthrough for him personally: in years past, the shy kid from Compton would've never gotten involved in the battle, but now, as the hottest rapper in the world, Kendrick was using his celebrity to bring awareness to a range of issues. Finally, after twelve years of honing his craft, the rapper was on top. All that he'd seen, all those poems in Mr. Inge's class, those sidewalk freestyles with Matt Jeezy, the pressure-packed audition for Anthony "Top Dawg" Tiffith, the days of dreaming with Dave Free, being shot at, traveling up and down the road in a bus and performing to half-empty arenas, all those things led to this point—to the day where he'd have Compton on his back and the public's full attention. At last, Kendrick's father, Kenny, could see him on the BET Awards. He was dreaming big like his mother had told him to. He kept going and kept God first, just like his friends asked, and like Tupac indirectly urged him to do. The days of food stamps and Section 8 rentals were gone. The years of pain were no more.

But although Kendrick's professional dreams were coming through, an intriguing consequence began taking shape: He was becoming a political figure—however reluctantly. *To Pimp a Butterfly* was being hailed as a different kind of breakthrough, mostly because of songs like "Alright," "The Blacker the Berry," and "Hood Politics," the last of which thumbed its nose at the U.S. political system. Kendrick's new perch unsettled him; he was still coming to grips with his *own* political views—in rap music, and otherwise. In 2012, Kendrick admitted that he didn't vote, that he was disillusioned with the country's political leaders and the direction the U.S. was headed. He put his faith in God, not man. "I don't believe in none of the shit that's going on in the world," he once said. "So basically, do what you do, do good with your people and live your life because what's going on isn't really in our hands. If it's not in the president's hands, then it's definitely not in our hands." The song "Hood Politics" doubled down on this notion; Kendrick compared Congress to gang members fighting over territory, just like his friends whom the public sought to vilify. "From Compton to Congress, it's set trippin' all around," Kendrick rhymed. "Ain't nothin' new but a flew of new Demo-Crips and Re-Blood-licans / Red state versus a blue state, which one you governin'?"

In his heart of hearts, Kendrick didn't want to be the catalyst of any sort of political fodder. He was still a loner, still the isolated soul who'd rather sit in the corner and watch from afar. He preferred self-reflection; America was headed down the wrong path and he was trying to comprehend it like everyone else. He didn't have all the answers, but his music proved that he was willing to work through it with the rest of us. With his newfound stardom, Kendrick was finding out that he couldn't have it both ways, that he couldn't create that kind of music and say those kinds of things without touching nerves. He was the voice of the people now, and to sit on the sidelines was no longer an option. It was a compelling contradiction and an unintended side effect. Kendrick had high hopes for *good kid, m.A.A.d city* and *To Pimp a Butterfly*, but he didn't anticipate this level of reaction or dissection of his art so soon. Changing the course of hip-hop is one thing, but raising the ire of right-wingers was something entirely different. That's partially why Kendrick's message echoed so deeply in the black community: he wasn't *trying* to become a legislator, and that he couldn't be bullied only riled up the right even further.

Kendrick's worlds were beginning to collide. That December, President Barack Obama spoke to *People* magazine about his favorite songs, albums, and moments of 2015, and revealed that Kendrick's "How Much a Dollar Cost" was his favorite track of the year. Within the scope of pop culture, this news proved once again that Obama was a man of the people, that even though he was the commander in chief, he tapped the pulse of what was in vogue. It also showed that he was open to differing opinions and respected the free speech that Kendrick epitomized throughout *To Pimp a Butterfly*. The record wasn't at all flattering to politicians or the societal constructs that divide the country. But the president heard the art in it, and he respected Kendrick's viewpoint, even if it didn't paint him or the system in the best light. President Obama even got an explicit shoutout on "Hood Politics": "They give us guns and drugs, call us thugs / Make it they promise to fuck with you / No condom, they fuck with you, Obama say, 'What it do?'"

The president took it a step further when asked in a YouTube chat whom he'd pick in a rap battle between Kendrick and Drake. "I think Drake is an outstanding entertainer," Obama said in 2016. "But, Kendrick, his lyrics . . . his last album [*To Pimp a Butterfly*] was outstanding. Best album I think last year." Obama had been elected to the White House when Kendrick was just twenty years old, back when the rapper was still in Compton and hadn't seen the world. In those days, Kendrick could only *imagine* a way out, and no politician could solve his friends being killed in cold blood. President Obama wasn't *there* in the city; Kendrick couldn't touch or see his impact. So it was tough to fathom that some man in an office 2,700 miles away could solve the struggle in his backyard. Obama wasn't there to negotiate peace between Pirus and Crips, and he wasn't there when Kendrick's uncle got popped at Louis Burgers.

But to see Obama was something completely different; you didn't realize his magnitude until you were in the same room with him, or at least in the same vicinity. For those of us in Washington, D.C., and its suburbs, the Obama presidency hit us differently. We were on constant Obama Watch; you never knew when he'd pop up in the restaurant you were in, or if he was at the same concert you were attending. Not only was he the country's celebrity, but he was our celebrity. To see him and Michelle was the ultimate thrill, and with each passing motorcade, there was this question: "Was that . . . *him?!*"

In January 2016, Kendrick traveled to Washington, D.C., and to the White House, to meet President Obama in person. Not even a year earlier, Kendrick had photoshopped himself and his friends mobbing in front of this very building, flashing stacks of money on its lawn. But now he was there, speaking directly to the man. According to reports, they were there to discuss community building, to talk about cities like Compton and South Side Chicago and the challenges they were facing. In photos from the meeting, Kendrick looked reverent, almost intimidated by Obama's presence, like a child meeting his hero for the first time. Obama was no longer an idea; he was a living, breathing human who was just as excited to meet the rapper. "The way people look at me these days—that's the same way I looked at President Obama before I met him," Kendrick told *Billboard*. "We tend to forget that people who've attained a certain position are human. When [the president] said to my face what his favorite record was—I understood that, no matter how high-ranking you get in this world, you're human." That's what drew the two together in the first place: the two men arose from unlikely places to the pinnacles of their respective professions, and in that quiet moment in the Oval Office, Kendrick and President Obama openly wondered how they arrived *here*.

Kendrick's road hadn't gotten any easier; with great success came the pressure to top it, and to always be on. The TDE team had spoken openly about this notion of "hustling like you broke," of never ever resting on your laurels and to keep working in silence. And while Kendrick was already thinking about his next record, he had let his guard down just a little to receive praise. If President Obama liked his music, he must've been doing *something* right. As he told *Billboard*, "Even the president has got to hear that snare drum." That Kendrick became acquainted with the nation's first black president was a dream that he wished his grandmother had been there to see.

The accolades were beginning to roll in for *To Pimp a Butterfly*. Pretty much every major publication lionized it, even if they were still trying to unpack all its density. By early 2016, it'd been almost a year since the album's release, but the record just sort of stuck around, even with the lightning-fast speed of the web-driven music industry, where albums are considered old just a few months after their release. That was because musicians were largely focused on singles, not full albums as a body of work. We were in the streaming era, and there was a notion that fans didn't listen to albums as art anymore. So some musicians put their full attention into *one* song that could secure millions of plays and land on someone's playlist. Kendrick harkened back to the likes of Marvin Gaye and Stevie Wonder, both of whom saw the album medium as a listening experience meant to transport souls from one point to another. They created full suites of music, bending the culture toward them and not the other way around. At the time of this writing, Marvin's 1971 opus, *What's Going On*, was forty-nine years old and still incredibly relevant; its denouncement of war, poverty, and child neglect applied equally to the wars in Vietnam and Afghanistan. Stevie's 1976 double album, *Songs in the Key of Life*, is still volleyed as perhaps the greatest record of all time (though one could argue that any of Stevie's albums from 1972 to 1976 are in the conversation). These albums didn't conform to the arbitrary notion that mainstream records should cater to what was popular on the radio; in fact, those albums showed that they weren't overly preoccupied with mainstream acceptance. *To Pimp a Butterfly* was very much of that ilk, and Kendrick's music should be held in the same canon as Marvin and Stevie, as artists who shifted the culture, and made everything before them feel obsolete.

Post-*Butterfly*, it seemed every record had some elements of jazz or creative freedom, which led to the most fertile period of socially conscious black music since Marvin and Stevie ruled the terrain. You had records like *Freetown Sound* by the New York musician Blood Orange, which unpacked the fragility of black life over a wide-ranging soundtrack of eighties-centric funk and pop. The Barbados-born, British-based saxophonist Shabaka Hutchings traveled to Johannesburg, linked with a group of local jazz musicians, and released an album called *Wisdom of Elders*, which, much like Kamasi Washington's *The Epic*, reflected the tenor of black people through murky sonic textures and chants. The Knowles sisters had the most powerful records of the 2016 set—Beyoncé with *Lemonade* (Kendrick was a guest on album cut "Freedom") and its theme of empowerment for black women, and Solange's *A Seat at the Table*, a sprawling soul opus that helped calm the black rage burning outside. In part, Kendrick's album made it okay for his peers to *go in*, to create and release whatever their vision desired regardless of what the public and critics expected.

Through artists like these, a heightened black awareness began to emerge in pop culture, and thus a new class of protest music began taking shape. They were the new vanguard.

The scene was a familiar one: Kendrick Lamar was at the Grammy Awards, back at the Staples Center in downtown Los Angeles. This time it was 2016, two years removed from the 56th annual awards, which had now become a legendary tale. Kendrick wasn't the baby-faced newcomer who'd barely entered the industry. He was a little older, a little wiser, and walked into this year's ceremony with eleven nominations. He had been nominated for seven awards two years prior and hadn't won any. This year, *To Pimp a Butterfly* was nominated for Best Rap Album, Album of the Year, Best Rap/Sung Performance for "These Walls," and Best Rap Song, Best Music Video, Song of the Year, and Best Rap Performance for "Alright." This wasn't like 2014; because Kendrick had seen a lot more of the business, the rapper—at least professionally—was no longer the demure creator who just seemed happy to be there. He was coming to take everything. Simply put, "I want to win them all," Kendrick told *Billboard* before the awards show.

He was up against history, though: only two rap albums before his—Lauryn Hill's *The Miseducation of Lauryn Hill* in 1999, and OutKast's *Speakerboxxx/The Love Below* in 2004—had won Grammys for Album of the Year. Though *good kid, m.A.A.d city* had also been nominated for Album of the Year in 2014, Kendrick's follow-up album had touched way more people. *good kid* was stellar work, and in the years following its release, there was a large contingent of fans who held that record in higher esteem than *To Pimp a Butterfly*. Yet given the mass critical acclaim, along with the captivating live sets to promote it, there was a feeling that *To Pimp a Butterfly* had a legitimate shot to win the Grammy for Album of the Year in 2016. Kendrick winning *that* award for *that* album would've been perfect, given the way it shifted black culture.

Early in the show, Kendrick—dressed in a black dress shirt and black dress slacks with black-rimmed glasses—won Best Rap Album for *To Pimp a Butterfly*, an award that was announced and fittingly given to him by West Coast legend Ice Cube. Taylor Swift was there again, in the front row, clapping profusely as Kendrick ascended the stage to collect his trophy. When Cube announced Kendrick as the winner, everyone from actor Don Cheadle to hip-hop legend Run (of Run-DMC fame) stood and applauded the young man for what was a monumental feat. Kendrick was the toast of the Grammys, and his peers genuinely wanted him to win. Now onstage, with industry leaders in one room and a captivated TV audience at home, Kendrick flashed a big smile, took his award, and stepped to the microphone.

"Kenneth Duckworth and Paula Duckworth," he began. "Those who gave me the responsibility of knowing and understanding, accepting the good with the bad, I will always love you for that. Whitney [Alford, his significant other], I will always love you for supporting me and keeping me motivated. . . . 'Top Dawg,' us eating you out of house and home, we'll never forget that. Taking these kids out of the projects out of Compton, and putting 'em right

here on this stage to be the best they can be. This is for hip-hop. . . .
We *will* live forever, believe that."

Kendrick was a big winner that night, taking home five Grammys. And while he didn't win the award for Album of the Year—that went to Taylor Swift for *1989*—Kendrick was easily the talk of the night. And it wasn't because of any text messages he received from a peer. He had a performance—*the* performance of the Grammys that year.

Before the show, Kendrick had a very clear vision of what he wanted to do with this production. It had to be his grand coming-out party, bigger than the set he did with Imagine Dragons two years earlier. The 2016 show had to make a strong statement and be one of the grandest shows ever in the Grammys' long history. The message needed to be bold and fearless. Much like the album that brought him to this awards show, it had to make people uneasy, if not angered by the history of slavery and the prison pipeline woven into the fabric of the United States.

Kendrick found a photo of a chain gang on an unnamed road in Miami, near the South Florida Reception Center, captured on November 21, 1995. The group was mostly black, their hands and feet bound by handcuffs and shackles. He sent the photo to his stylist, Dianne Garcia. "This is my inspiration," Kendrick told her. "I want them [the performers] to look like this." The image meant a lot to him; he'd openly spoken about the history of incarceration in his family, and as he planned this epic showing, Kendrick still had family and friends locked behind bars. So this set was for them and people like them, those stuck in the system, and those who'd just gotten home and were trying to reassemble their lives, fighting against a society that still sought to keep them shackled. It was one thing to hear it on *To Pimp a Butterfly*, but to see the history right there on that stage was something different. Never before had an artist used that platform, with mostly white faces in the foreground, to be so brazen.

There he stood the night of the show, his face damp and tattered with concern. He was in a crisp prison-blue shirt, dark blue jeans, and fresh white sneakers. His shoulders were taut and there was a dip in his step as he sauntered to center stage. He lifted his hands, his wrists and ankles bound by bright silver chains. It was quiet—deathly quiet—and when Kendrick moved, you could hear the shackles clatter in the stillness. There was a black microphone stand, and Terrace Martin wearing a matching prison-blue shirt, blowing the sax in a cell onstage to Kendrick's left. As the tension mounted, Kendrick had a bold declaration for those in attendance at the awards show. "I'm the biggest hypocrite of 2015," he asserted. He repeated himself, this time more forcefully than before, punctuating his resolve. "I'm African American / I'm African, I'm black as the moon, heritage of a small village / Pardon my residence."

The lines opened the rapper's hit track "The Blacker the Berry." The song was a relentless *Fuck you* to assailants of black culture, and with all its bleak dissonance, the track was delivered boldly to the millions tuned into the Grammys. "You hate me, don't you?" Kendrick declared. "You hate my people, your plan is to terminate my culture." The song escalated into a spirited number with backup dancers and a bonfire, and Kendrick stumbled from one side of the stage to the next as if in a dream state. He was connecting the prison pipeline to his own roots as a black man, sending the message that we didn't come from incarceration. We were more than the chain gang, deeper than the prison blues in which they trapped us. Society would have you believe that we weren't worthy of equal treatment, but Kendrick was breaking down the narrative surrounding his people on the grandest platform possible. To come out there in chains took immense bravery, and to break out of them to songs like "The Blacker the Berry" and "Alright" was equally courageous.

Kendrick had the idea to transform his chain gang into a crew of African dancers when he transitioned to the gig's second sequence, and to have them bathed in paint that was only visible in black light. In the third part of the performance, Kendrick unveiled what was then an unreleased verse, one that delved into his true feelings on the killing of Trayvon Martin and the piece of his soul he lost on that fateful night four years ago: "On February 26, I lost my life, too . . . / And for our community, do you know what this does? / Add to a trail of hatred / 2012 was taped for the world to see." As the song progressed, and the instrumental grew more furious, Kendrick matched the energy with equally fervent bars that rose almost to the point of collapsing. Right as he concluded, the lights dropped out. Behind him was a life-sized geographical picture of Africa; in the middle, in regal font, read one word: *Compton*. It was the one true capital of Kendrick's heart.

The people spoke loudly that night: when Kendrick stopped rapping and the lights clicked off to illuminate the Motherland, the audience—made up of industry types and fellow musicians—stood with a thunderous ovation that rippled through the room: Common clapped and hollered like a proud father; Rev. Run peered toward the stage with a slight look of disbelief etched across his face. Kendrick just stood there, motionless and stern, taking in the moment. He was studying the crowd, looking at the expressions and hearing the adulation. His face remained serious, focused, still in character. In that moment, in those six minutes in the Staples Center, again just a few miles from Compton, Kendrick's life changed forever. It was when he became royalty, when he rose to the pantheon of cornerstone greats, when his visage seemed destined for the Mount Rushmore of music. But this was *hip-hop* and it was black as fuck, the type of hip-hop that hasn't always been supported by the academy. This wasn't the sort of rap made to be palatable. It was Kendrick bending the culture yet again, stamping his card as a once-in-a-generation talent, the likes of which we'd never see again. It was the night that America finally caught on to what Kendrick was all about. On this night, he became the king.

No one was supposed to hear the secrets, at least not in their semi-finished forms. Leading up to *To Pimp a Butterfly*'s release, Kendrick had teased the project by performing tracks that wound up not even being on the album. Those songs felt even more casual and bathed in warmth. It was the first glimpse into his thinking for *To Pimp a Butterfly*, even if the ideas weren't fully formed as yet.

After the Grammy performance, professional basketball legend LeBron James tweeted "Top Dawg" Tiffith to release the untitled tracks that Kendrick had been performing on TV. James was easily the most influential figure in the National Basketball Association and one of the most visible celebrities on the planet. So when *he* pressed Tiffith to release the tracks, the Top Dawg CEO listened. "Dam my nigga u on my head 2. . . . " he tweeted. "The fans been killing me. . . . Give me a few days 2 think." A little more than a week later, Tiffith took to social media to announce the surprise release of *untitled unmastered.*, an eight-track EP of demos recorded during the *Butterfly* sessions. Presented in rough form, the record finds Kendrick sketching out ideas over acoustic guitars and in spoken-word form. At times playful, the EP offered a rare peek into Kendrick's creative brain and just where he was going for *To Pimp a Butterfly*. But these weren't throwaway tracks: the song he performed on *Colbert* lands here as "untitled 03 | 05.28.2013." The song "untitled 05 | 09.21.2014" sprawls into an expansive jam session, produced by Terrace Martin, with Anna Wise on vocals and Thundercat plucking the bass. Martin started hearing the whispers the Thursday before the EP was set to drop. "There was word around the camp like, 'Yo, we're about to drop the secrets,'" the producer told *Billboard*. "We're about to drop the blueprints," he recalled Sounwave telling him. That was a rare occurrence for Kendrick and for TDE as a whole: they never gave peeks behind the curtain, but *untitled unmastered.* offered the sort of fly-on-the-wall perspective that fans craved of Kendrick and the squad.

The rapper had been serious-minded in recent years, but on this project, he was toying with the idea of *head being the answer* (to what is still anyone's guess), and commanding more attention as a producer fully in charge of his artistic vision. "Who doing the drums?!" he shouts from the vocal booth near the end of "untitled 02 | 06.23.2014." "Man, put that nigga on the *drums*, man!" The songs were recorded fairly early in the *Butterfly* process, before Martin called his friends Robert Glasper and Kamasi Washington to take part in the album's creation, so he was pretty much the everything-man for the record's jazz-centric elements. The track "untitled 08 | 09.06.2014." was coproduced by Thundercat and Mono/Poly, both of whom had connections to the L.A. beat scene and have created music together for a decade as friends. Mono/Poly, who's known for otherworldly blends of psychedelic trance music, one day got a text from Kendrick to send him some music for *To Pimp a Butterfly*. Through Thundercat, the duo sent the rapper a batch of instrumentals, and the rapper jumped on a simple loop of vintage funk drums with the bassist playing chords atop it.

"That was the simplest thing I'd ever did," Mono/Poly tells me. "It wasn't anything I was super psyched to show Kendrick, but that's the thing he jumped on." Neither this song nor the other instrumentals he coproduced with Thundercat made the cut for *To Pimp a Butterfly*, but it resurfaced on "untitled 08 | 09.06.2014." as one of the EP's best tracks. "What really made me respect him more was when he got on it so quick, and made it so much better than what I thought anyone was gonna make it sound like. They were up *super* late, like early morning and shit, working on it. I was like, 'This dude's dedicated.'"

There was so much music being created during those sessions that one song just sort of melded into the other, and it was tough to keep track of who played what and when. "That's how in sync that whole crew was through *TPAB*," Terrace Martin continues "We started walking alike, talking alike, playing alike, eating alike. We were like Voltron: one thing, one force. That's one thing you hear on this record—how much of a brotherhood we did have. I had forgotten about all this shit, it was just a blur of good music with my brothers." For Kendrick, Martin, and the players, they hadn't heard these tracks in almost two years. They were evolving so quickly that once *Butterfly* came out, they were already on to the next sound, searching for something new. So to hear the songs on *untitled* was to travel back in time, to an era in which they were all in the studio at once, before they changed the world. In that way, *untitled* was a bittersweet reminder that *To Pimp a Butterfly* was a specific moment in time that couldn't be replicated. Of course there would be imitators, but those songs—on *that* album, with *those* players, and *that* cover, it was lightning captured in a bottle. They were all still friends, invested in each other's lives and their respective well-being, but for the next project—whenever it would land—they needed different personnel and a new vision.

To Pimp a Butterfly and *untitled unmastered.* helped Black America soundtrack its way to a higher state of consciousness, and, if only for a little while, it helped make sense of the country's present gloom. But as the hype of those records began to fade, a bigger, scarier threat began to emerge. And this wasn't just a threat to black people in the United States, it was a danger to humanity at large.

On June 16, 2015, Donald J. Trump announced that he was running for president of the United States, ending some twenty years of speculation. "We are going to make our country great again," he told a crowd of supporters in his native New York City. Announcing his run at the fifty-eight-story Trump Tower in Midtown, the businessman positioned himself as the anti-Obama, even taking shots at the president in his forty-five-minute address. "He's actually a negative force," Trump claimed in his announcement. "We need somebody that literally will take this country and make it great again. We can do that." The term, Make America Great Again, echoed that tone of another entertainer-turned-politician, Ronald Reagan, who in 1979 had made it the hallmark of his presidential run. They both borrowed the phrase from Adolf Hitler, who in the 1930s said he wanted to "make Germany great again" and blamed Jews, socialists, and communists for what he thought was the country's deterioration. Because some didn't know the history, the phrase seemed to be innocuous, a push to return the United States to a panacea of peace and prosperity. Much like saying "All Lives Matter," the term "Make America Great Again" felt like a push from conservatives to shun the cultural progress the country had made over the past eight years, when a black man was president and his cabinet was diverse. Trump appealed to workers in Middle America who felt their jobs were evaporating and were worried about making ends meet. He spoke in broad generalizations, offering so-called tidbits on the job market that he really couldn't prove. And when he wasn't doing that, he said things that simply weren't true.

Trump had never served in Congress, on a city council, or even a school board. He simply didn't have the gravitas to build relationships strong enough to handle being president of the United States. Trump was vulgar, far different from Obama, Bill Clinton, George W. Bush, or any of the men who served as president before. He thumbed his nose at political correctness, claimed that America had gotten too soft and needed someone in charge who knew how to talk unsympathetically. Trump was a caricature, and media outlets covered his antics, perhaps thinking he had no shot at the job he sought. The thinking went like this: Once Hillary Clinton won the U.S. presidency, in a landslide, we'd all look at Trump's candidacy with a laugh, as a blip on the radar. That was the media's mistake; in its push for content, Trump was a slam dunk for news outlets who sought clicks and ratings bumps. He just kept hanging around, and in November 2015, Trump hosted an episode of *Saturday Night Live*, the long-running NBC sketch comedy show, much to the dismay of protesters who lamented his appearance. "Trump is a Yuuuge Racist," read one sign. "NBC Repent," read another.

It's too easy to say that Trump's appearance helped him become president, but between his outlandish Twitter persona and opportunities like this, he quickly became part of the narrative, and then it became usual to see him and to hear his rhetoric. It sent the wrong message at a time when activists were protesting his candidacy and many late-night hosts were taking the threat of a Trump presidency more soberly. Online, viewers were furious with media pundits for helping humanize such a person.

Indeed, Trump was a lightning rod, and to fawn over his persona was to be guilty by association. Try as we might, it was impossible to tune him out, and his ascendance was all the more puzzling. For one, he was racist: In 1973, Trump, as head of the Trump Management Corporation in New York City, was sued for racial discrimination by the Department of Justice for not renting to black tenants. In 1989, he took out a full-page ad in the *New York Times*, asking for the return of the death penalty in the case of the so-called "Central Park Five" (now the "Exonerated Five"), a group of young teenagers who were falsely accused of beating and raping a jogger in Central Park. The boys were arrested and coerced into false confessions that landed them in prison. Even after they were exonerated in 2002, Trump remained steadfast, insisting that the boys were still guilty. He refused to apologize, and in the years following the incident, Trump used the same racist rhetoric to rally a base that finally had the platform to openly spew hatred. If elected, he vowed to build a wall along the southern border of the United States and ban Muslims from coming into the country. *This* was the kind of man we were dealing with, a complete danger to civil and foreign relations, who could unravel all the goodwill the country had attained during the Obama years. Still, no reasonable person could hear his views on women and minorities and think he should be the U.S. president, right? Despite all the protests, all the vitriol he spat, all the hollow, rambling speeches, his chances of winning were slim to none . . . right?

9

Mourning in America

I'd never heard Hyattsville that quiet—ever. On the morning of November 9, 2016, the day after Donald Trump shocked the world by becoming the forty-fifth president of the United States, the city felt remarkably still, like a close relative had died. We were trying to process the despair of the previous night; foolishly, we all assumed we would wake up to the nation's first woman president. There had been feelings of optimism and overconfidence, and as the vote counts had begun rolling in, and the night shifted to morning, the country's tenor—at least in the East, West, and certain portions of the South—slowly began to shift. As Election Day waned, we started to realize that things were quickly changing for the worse, and that our lives as we knew them would never be the same. Nonetheless, Hyattsville had never been *this* immobile; usually, even at seven o'clock in the morning, there'd be some semblance of activity in the bustling Arts District. But the air felt a little gloomier, a little colder, and the clouds seemed to hover just a bit lower.

We couldn't fathom what had just happened; the city couldn't, either. Hyattsville is a smallish area just outside the northeast border of Washington, D.C. The city, like the county it is in, is majority black and mostly Democratic. So on the voting line, there was an overwhelming feeling that Hillary Clinton *had this*: there was no way she was losing to that dude, who said those things, and grabbed women by their you-know-what. Clinton was endorsed by almost every major newspaper in the country, and she'd won the popular vote the night before by a record margin. Meanwhile, Trump was endorsed by the Ku Klux Klan and seen as a proponent of white supremacy. Clinton was thought to be a shoo-in, a battle-tested politician who'd dealt with the absurd many times over and surely could handle someone like Trump. But that's where many of us fell down on the job: we took him lightly, and as that was happening, the would-be president centered his campaign in battle-ground states whose voters felt left behind by the so-called American dream. Unlike Clinton, he made it seem like he was there for them. Working-class whites felt left behind by a globalized economy that valued college degrees over blue-collar work, and by growing diversity that reduced the power of white men. Seeing Obama in power for eight years also didn't help; they sensed that the America they once knew and controlled was slipping away. So when Trump came through, with his gruff shit talk and plainspokenness, he was thought to be a beacon of light for a class of people who'd rather it be 1936, not 2016.

Both the *Washington Post* and the *New York Times* went with a simple headline: "Trump Triumphs." The New York *Daily News* opted for a more dramatic headline ("House of Horrors: Trump

Seizes Divided States of America"). On the cover of the *L.A. Times* in big type: "STUNNING TRUMP WIN." Indeed, it was a stunning upset, and there was a feeling that Trump somehow stole the White House with the help of Russia, which reportedly spread propaganda on social media and hacked Clinton's campaign to induce mistrust in American democracy. Minorities wept openly; it seemed the country had made its decision, and that we needed to go somewhere, anywhere, else. Hysteria ensued since here was no longer an option; when Trump won, many of us said we were moving to other countries, because the place we'd known to be home finally showed it wasn't that at all. It never really was, and to live under Trump's rule didn't feel safe. If law enforcement had been a threat in recent years, what was going to happen with Trump in office and bigotry so out in the open? It felt like we didn't have any allies. We were scared, angry, shocked, and disillusioned. Overnight, we went from feeling empowered by the president to feeling despised by the president-elect. We didn't quite know how to process what had happened: What do we do with the fear? The sorrow, the anger, the frustration? How do we swallow that, pick up the pieces, and move forward? What could we tell our children, especially those who'd known only Obama as president? How could we explain the tears?

Up the street in the neighborhood coffee shop, we traded grave looks and tepid shrugs, not really addressing the elephant in the room. We wallowed in the haze, dousing it with drip coffees and chai lattes, falling into our respective work routines and soldiering on as best as we could. Yet no amount of caffeine could wash this away: this was a national nightmare with dire global implications. The joke was on us and it wasn't funny anymore.

Trump's racism emboldened other racists who had lain dormant during the Obama years. Between his talk of the border wall and his long history of bigotry against black people, suddenly you started to see more incidents of vandalism in cities that hadn't had those problems before. The Southern Poverty Law Center (SPLC) reported an immediate uptick in harassment in the first ten days following Trump's election, counting 867 hate incidents. According to the SPLC, the number of hate incidents increased in almost every state; most of the incidents took place on university campuses and in elementary, middle, and high schools. A few of these incidents were against white nationalists (the group that actively supported Trump's behavior), but the vast majority of these crimes were done to commemorate Trump's election as president. In Silver Spring, Maryland—a city just up the road from Hyattsville—a rector at the Episcopal Church of Our Saviour discovered a sign offering Spanish services had been ripped and vandalized with the words "TRUMP NATION WHITES ONLY," according to *Time*. I covered education for a local newspaper in Montgomery County for almost four years (from 2007 to 2010), and these sorts of incidents hadn't happened in Silver Spring during my time there. "Montgomery County—it's not the kind of place where racial incidents happen, but since last Tuesday they've been increasing in number," parish administrator Tracey Henley told *Time* in 2016. "A year ago," Henley continued, "it wasn't possible to be a racist bigot and get elected president. People now feel free to say racist things that they wouldn't have said before."

Like it or not, this was the new America. That, or the old America was waking up. This was the America that our elders used to tell us about, where a short walk to the grocery store meant being harassed. Our parents and grandparents had struggled with such racism, but to minorities who grew up in the 1980s and '90s, this level of discrimination was totally new. If you're not white in the United States, you're deemed "other" and treated differently, but this harassment bit harder than anything in recent years, and a walk outside meant life or death—depending on where you were. Still, in cities like Hyattsville and other left-leaning towns throughout the country, there was a glimmer of optimism, although it was tough to fully embrace at the time. Maybe the election was just a blip and somehow we'd "be alright"? Maybe that was the American dream for which our ancestors prepared us: that, when the horizon looks bleak, the only thing we can do is to hold firm to our ideals and do our best to weather the storm. But who knew? We couldn't see that far ahead; our emotions were too raw, our future too dim. One thing was clear following Trump's win: he was going to undo all of Obama's work, just because he could. The would-be president was driven by ego and a tremendous will to be recognized for—well—*everything*. Kendrick struggled to reconcile what had just happened in America. "We all are baffled," he told *i-D* back then. "It is something that completely disregards our moral compass." Obama also had a tough time reconciling what had just happened in the election. In *The World as It Is*, a book written by former Obama adviser Ben Rhodes, the author remembered the president's dejection. He wondered why the American public would vote for a "cartoon," and the results made him question if he'd miscalculated his work in office. That was the Trump effect: his victory made us question everything we thought to be true.

Trump's election made Obama's departure much more bittersweet. It's one thing to pass the baton to someone with some level of decency and political acumen, but to have a hardened white supremacist running the country is quite unusual. And over the next two months, we looked to Obama for the last time as commander in chief and wondered what was next. We struggled with the words *last* and *final*: his last White House Correspondents' Dinner, the final time he'd speak to the press corps. It's possible that we took the Obamas for granted; we were so used to grace and maturity in the White House that we assumed it would be there forever.

During this time, Kendrick was noticeably silent, occasionally popping up to do an interview here and there, but he largely stayed out of the public eye. He had been incredibly busy in 2015, and with the dust fully settled from *To Pimp a Butterfly* and *untitled unmastered.*, Kendrick went back to the lab, to his home in Los Angeles to conceptualize his next steps. But there was no telling just what that would be, or how he'd follow his first two major-label releases.

"I have ideas," Kendrick told producer Rick Rubin for the October 2016 *GQ* cover story. "I have a certain approach. But I wanna see what it manifests. I wanna put all the paint on the wall and see where that goes." Kendrick was twenty-nine years old and even further removed from the grind of trying to make it in the music industry, yet he remained focused and kept his ear attuned to what was next. So just like he'd done for *Butterfly*, he toiled away on new material that could've been something grand or nothing at all. Kendrick is a scientist in that way; he'll write, throw away, conceptualize, and tinker with ideas, and those songs either fit into some sort of coherent project or they sit in the vault to never be heard again (unless LeBron James nudges him to release the secrets). Kendrick still had childhood trauma, survivor's guilt, and isolation to work through, and the closer he got to thirty, the clearer he became about what ailed him and what he needed to do to heal. Your brain shifts to this level of atonement the closer you get to that age; right away, the pleasures you sought as a youth no longer make sense, and nights at home with your loved ones ring louder than being out at some club with nothing but trouble to get into. For Kendrick, that meant spending more time with Whitney, to whom he'd reportedly gotten engaged in 2015. For the first time in at least three years, Kendrick had a little while to actually sit down and enjoy what he'd accomplished. True to the rapper's nature, he wasn't going to rest for long.

Kendrick started talking about the idea for his next album as he created *To Pimp a Butterfly*, though at the time, it was just a series of rough concepts that didn't really gel together. While *Butterfly* was meant for the entirety of the black race, and though Kendrick thrived on such ambition, he wanted the next album to be a little closer to the ground—like a culmination of everything he'd released to that point, yet with God firmly at the center. His most notable work had referenced the divine to some degree, but he'd never delved into it for the entirety of an album. On *good kid* and *Butterfly*, God arrived at the precise moment Kendrick needed Him most, just when his life was taking a sharp turn. The rapper had hinted toward it, most notably on *good kid*'s "Sing About Me, I'm Dying of Thirst" and

Butterfly's "How Much a Dollar Cost," but he hadn't fully dissected his own spirituality. Kendrick was reverting his focus inward, back to his old neighborhood, and back to the people doing the ground-work to make it better. If his earlier albums spoke to those in his peer group, his subsequent work was to address his current stature as a community leader. He had different muses now—his little niece, who lights up when she sees him on TV, and his cousin, Carl Duck-worth, a member of the Hebrew Israelites, who encouraged him to know his merit as a spiritual being. Once again, he was trying to move beyond hue: on *To Pimp a Butterfly*, red and blue didn't matter, only black—black skin and black people. Now he was in search of something even deeper; no matter your complexion, all believers—whether black, white, or brown—must answer to God.

The albums *good kid* and *Butterfly* registered as avant-rap, and it'd been a while—probably since the old K-Dot days—that Kendrick rapped for the sake of rapping. And he wasn't in a rush, either; with *those* two records on his résumé, the lyricist bought himself more time to fall back and figure things out at his own pace. One thing was for sure, though: the new album couldn't sound like anything on *To Pimp a Butterfly*. "We needed to do the opposite of what our opposite thoughts were," Terrace Martin told the Recording Academy.

Kendrick was in a zone and simply couldn't stop working. One thought led to the next, then to something else. In years past, when he struggled publicly with his mental health, Jesus was there as a salve, a way out of the despair that gripped him and his friends who were suffering in the city. He, like other believers, called on God in his darkest moments, when life-or-death situations were on the horizon and he needed an immediate lifeline—like on "Bitch, Don't

Kill My Vibe" ("I am a sinner who's probably gonna sin again"), and on "Alright" ("If God got us then we gon' be alright"). Perhaps because he'd become a lightning rod for political pundits, and because he never wanted to be a political pundit himself, Kendrick had isolated himself. Even after he'd done so much for others and released music to lift an entire race, he seemed to think people didn't care about him. In his mind, he'd prayed for so many others, but these same people weren't praying for him. It'd just been interview after interview, tour after tour, incessant feature and appearance requests, and much of it had grown formulaic. It was easy for Kendrick to feel abandoned. In a 2015 interview with *Billboard*, he talked about the rapture: "We're in the last days, man—I truly in my heart believe that," he said. "It's written. I could go on with Biblical situations and things my grandma told me. But it's about being at peace with myself and making good with the people around me." Kendrick's parents weren't especially religious and he wasn't raised in a church. Much of what he knows about Jesus and the Bible came from his grandmother, whose mix of real talk and religious teaching helped cultivate the precocious young man. In his music, Kendrick hadn't yet discussed how God resides through everything—through the peaks and valleys, the tragedy and the triumph. God is there as a calming spirit, a guide, a spiritual conduit between this world and the afterlife. For Kendrick, God was the way to stay connected with his grandmother and with close friends who were murdered in Compton. He saw God as a protector and a way to stay centered as the world spiraled out of control. In years past, he'd presented God as his salvation *alone*, but he'd never openly questioned the higher power about why people suffer, and specifically, why he had to endure so much agony. Was it karmic retribution for all the bad things he'd done before he knew better? Bible verse Luke 12:48 says the following: *For everyone to whom much is given, from him much will be required.* Because he'd been so blessed personally and professionally, perhaps it was time to honor God by spreading his word and giving to those who didn't have the same type of access or celebrity. So in late 2016, the rapper didn't have a full picture of his next album, but he did know it would be the most spiritually inclined record he'd compiled to date. It was also Kendrick's most direct, the one that addressed the state of the world at large head-on, and stripped away some of the veneer that characterized *good kid, m.A.A.d city* and *To Pimp a Butterfly*. For the first time, he wanted to write about what was happening right here and right now. "We're in a time where we exclude one major component out of this whole thing called life: God," Kendrick once told the *New York Times*' *T* magazine. "Nobody speaks on it because it's almost in conflict with what's going on in the world when you talk about politics and government and the system."

In late August 2016, Kendrick and his creative team were in New York City looking for artistic inspiration. There, they clicked play on singer Frank Ocean's newly released studio album, *Blonde*, and were taken by the vocalist's vulnerability and the stark way in which he presented his art. *Blonde*, unlike Ocean's previous album, *channel ORANGE*, was almost entirely piano and voice; the recessive soundtrack allowed his vocals to shine through, giving us an unbridled glimpse into his life. Like Kendrick, Frank Ocean had become a star in 2012 with his major-label debut. Kendrick and the team played *Blonde* nonstop for a whole day, then they had a jam session that

Sounwave and the producer DJ Dahi—who last worked with Kendrick on *good kid, m.A.A.d city*—convened. They cut a song, a woozy, surreal number—that eventually became "YAH.," where Kendrick namechecks Geraldo Rivera and Fox News for misrepresenting the "Alright" performance and takes the temperature of a ravenous public that wishes to know more and more about the increasingly reclusive musician. Wrote Kendrick, "Fox News wanna use my name for percentage . . . / Somebody tell Geraldo this nigga got some ambition."

Not long after the election, Kendrick wrote a verse for a then-untitled song that pointed the finger at the current state of America: the war it initiated with other countries, the borders that Donald Trump was obsessed with, the murder allowed by its leaders, and the capitalism that kept us divided by class. "The great American flag is wrapped and dragged with explosives," he wrote. "Donald Trump's in office / We lost Barack and promised to never doubt him again / But is America honest, or do we bask in sin?" The verse became the last on a song called "XXX.," which would arise near the end of his next album, the directly titled *DAMN*. The LP was meant to be a victory lap of sorts, a grand coronation for the Greatest Rapper Alive who might very well be the Greatest Rapper of All Time. But it wouldn't be a Kendrick album without complicated themes to wade through, so while he wanted the LP to feel sharper than anything he'd done as a mainstream MC, he also wanted to give listeners food for thought that could be unpacked decades down the road. *DAMN.* needed to have the same intensity as *To Pimp a Butterfly*. If his previous records presented his neighborhood and race to music aficionados and crate diggers, Kendrick's next work was meant for nightclubs and street ciphers. "We wanted to make it for all arenas—car, we want you to be in the club, or just flying listening to it and just vibing to it," he once told Big Boy on his radio show. "That whole approach was from the jump. At the same time, we wanted to have something in the lyrical content where it connects, where it's not just lyrics, but it's something you can actually feel. It's stories that you can feel, emotions you can feel, and emotions you can relate to." For a while, the album was going to be titled *What Happens on Earth Stays on Earth*, but was switched to *DAMN.* to capture the record's true energy. It's probably the loudest album Kendrick had released to that point, and with all its aggressive music, the LP just screams "DAMN" when assessing it. Then, with all the contradictory feelings woven throughout the LP, the phrase "Damned if I do, damned if I don't" began to surface. The phrase spoke to how Kendrick was feeling those days. The opening song, "DNA," is where he sheds his old skin, unpacking the dichotomy of past and present lives in a hail of a never-ending flow. This was a new, meditative Kendrick, but don't get it twisted: that Zen could still snap at the drop of a dime, and the days of poverty made him more eager to dominate music. Simply put: he'd been broke before and he wasn't going back to that.

He was a student of the rappers who had come before him, and through his vocal nuances, one could hear links to Eazy-E, the fire-breathing cofounder of N.W.A, whose crass, autobiographical style of rap influenced a new generation of equally audacious lyricists. So Kendrick needed someone from that era, someone like Kid Capri, a legend who in the early nineties was the resident DJ for Russell Simmons's *Def Comedy Jam* on the cable network HBO. "He called to ask me if I'd work with him," Capri told the Recording

Academy in 2017. "He told me the direction of the album being God and spirituality, but he already knew what he had in his head and he came up with a lot of what I needed to say." Capri is the narrator of *DAMN.*, his unmistakable voice making the record feel like an old-school mixtape. "I wanted it to feel like just the raw elements of hip-hop, whether I'm using 808s or boom-bap drums," Kendrick told Beats 1 radio host Zane Lowe. "The initial thought was having [Kid Capri] on some real trap 808 shit. Something I've never heard from him." Not only did *DAMN.* feel vintage, it felt intense, as it ran through various beats and ideas at a breakneck pace. On "LUST.," the rapper once again treks through the recent election, as if to rationalize what he'd just seen: "We all woke up, tryna tune to the daily news / Lookin' for confirmation, hopin' election wasn't true." By saying that we were worried about what's next, that we were saddened by the results, he was tapping into the very lifeline of Black America. That he was the voice of the people further amplified the message.

For several months, Kendrick and Sounwave locked themselves in the studio, resting in sleeping bags until they had a fully formed album to put out. And when they thought the record was done, they'd go back in and fine-tune it some more, tweaking and bending the sound until it was perfect for them. Despite their success, or maybe *because* of their success, Kendrick and Sounwave still had the verve to literally sleep in the studio. The stakes were at their highest; the music world watched TDE closely. But this is how you become the greatest rapper ever, by putting in this kind of work when the cameras aren't rolling and no one's there to snap your picture for Instagram. Greatness is achieved in the trenches, when nothing but the will to be an icon is your creative fuel. The greats are all the same—Beyoncé, Serena Williams, LeBron, and the like: they're never satisfied with where they are now. They're always looking ahead, always looking to improve, always looking to break new ground. The will to transcend never leaves. When you're Kendrick Lamar, and you've come from the city he did, and seen the things that he's seen, there's always this innate feeling of restlessness, that even though you're a multi-time Grammy Award winner, you still have to work at being great. There's always a new message to be told, a new wrinkle in the way you disseminate thoughts.

At this point, Kendrick was a millionaire a few times over, but he still had something to say. For it to truly take shape, he and Sounwave had to become one again—just as they did for *Butterfly*. If the previous album was shepherded mostly by Terrace Martin, *DAMN.* was brought to life by Sounwave, who, along with Kendrick, was responsible for much of the album's sonic direction. While much of *To Pimp a Butterfly* was written on the road and recorded in different studios, *DAMN.* was recorded in one studio, where Kendrick's collaborating producers quite literally had to sleep in the studio as well. The requirement was intense, but Kendrick had the cachet to demand such a thing. "If you had a girlfriend, she had to come visit you at the studio. It was that environment," Sounwave told *GQ* in 2017.

Two months before the record was set to release, he and Kendrick put extra pressure on their collaborators to stay, and even forgo going to get food, so the record could get done on time. "You wanna go get something to eat? You're not serious," Sounwave told *Fader*. "You're gonna be in this studio and you're gonna starve with us until it's perfect. Luckily, it's everybody we love—it's like having a sleepover with all your cousins." They took every last second they could to finish *DAMN.*, tweaking the sound—flipping and reversing beats, switching out beats, and changing the speed of Kendrick's voice at the very last minute. Indeed, the sessions were moving quickly, and missing one meant missing a day's worth of ideas, or having your idea scrapped for something totally different. So Kendrick's collaborators almost had to be in the studio just to be seen. As they did with *To Pimp a Butterfly*, the creators communicated mainly by cell phone when they weren't in the studio, trading files via text message and fleshing them out once they were all in the same place.

As much as *DAMN.* is about Kendrick evaluating his relationship with God, he was also reconciling his relationship with himself, learning to accept his shortcomings—his fears, doubts, and pain en route to his own ultimate survival. Sans a few features—Rihanna on "LOYALTY.," U2 on "XXX.," Zacari on "LOVE."—Kendrick goes at it alone, which makes the already-reserved rapper sound even more isolated. That's what he was going for here; *DAMN.* plays like a series of diary entries. For the first time, it sounded like Kendrick was bending to the pressure of belonging to the world, and combined with the conflicts he faced at home and within his own psyche, *DAMN.* was the sound of Kendrick seeking help from a higher power. For the past few years, he belonged to and told everything for the culture, but who was praying for him? Who were the people helping him shoulder the pain? Kendrick had been living in a fishbowl; it was not like he could just go out for a walk, or even run down the street to the grocery store without causing a scene. So at home, or in the studio, Kendrick had nothing but time to think about his true allies and where the world was headed. That led to some of his most clear-eyed music ever, because it was so raw and of the moment, and at the end of *DAMN.*, he left no mistake about how he felt as a man, a U.S. citizen, a brother, and an MC. That after everything he's given to the culture—*Section.80*; *good kid, m.A.A.d city*; *To Pimp a Butterfly*—Kendrick still wrestles with his self-worth. He still wonders if he's enough, or if after all that, if he's even appreciated for what he's given Black America; does it even matter in the long run? Did the community even care, and will they remember his intention? It's the same question that Obama asked himself when leaving the White House, that despite the wave of goodwill that typified his years in office, he openly wondered if he miscalculated the entire thing. That nagging self-doubt never goes away—no matter if you're a world-famous, Grammy Award–winning poet and rapper, or the outgoing president of the United States.

On "FEAR.," Kendrick reviews the fears of his life—from childhood through adulthood. Here, he breaks down his life in ten-year increments—when he was seven, seventeen, and twenty-seven. On the early part of the song, he unpacks the fear that his mother instilled as the disciplinarian of the house; then, as a teenager, he's afraid of the cops in his neighborhood, and how back then, he thought he might've died at their hands. Then, as a grown man, around the time *To Pimp a Butterfly* was being recorded, Kendrick delves into the fear of no longer having privacy: "My newfound life made all of me magnified / How many accolades do I need to block denial? / The shock value of my success put bolts in me / All this money, is God playin' a joke on me?"

DAMN. was released on Good Friday, April 14, 2017, with a stark, no-frills cover that was in exact contrast to the rapper's previous album sleeves. Compared with the Polaroid images of *good kid*, and the White House photoshop of *To Pimp a Butterfly*, the cover of *DAMN.* centered Kendrick against a red-brick wall and white T-shirt, his head cocked to the side and his eyes in a dead gaze. On purpose, the rapper looked tired and dejected. Released after Trump had already taken office, Kendrick's face epitomized what the rest of us were feeling: we were all tired, scared, and fearful of what the world was going to look like soon. Yet when the cover was revealed, it caught a few fans off-guard. It wasn't artful, and the title was perplexing. *Perhaps DAMN. is an acronym for something? It must have some deeper meaning; it's not just* DAMN. *is it?* Kendrick's graphic designer, Vlad Sepetov, wanted the *DAMN.* cover to be loud and abrasive, to start a conversation with a simple image. "I sort of bucked a lot of what my teachers taught me," Sepetov tweeted three days before the album dropped. "It's not uber political like tpab but it has energy."

Then there was this conspiracy theory: the chatter that Kendrick was going to release a companion album that Sunday—Easter Sunday—called *NATION.*, making his 2017 record a double disc ultimately called *DAMN.NATION.* Kendrick later laughed at that theory, saying that *DAMN.* was it (though a companion album released on Easter Sunday would've been amazing). But that spoke to the ravenous nature of Kendrick's fan base and just how much they demanded of the rapper. *To Pimp a Butterfly* had made such an impact on culture that they wanted as much music as possible from him. Critics ate it up, too, pointing directly to the album's concluding song, "DUCKWORTH.," which unpacks a wild story about a chance encounter between Kendrick's father, Kenny, and a guy named Anthony from Watts, who twenty years later would give

Kenny's son a record deal and shepherd him to the top of the music industry.

This is where Kendrick flexes his storytelling ability, and over a shape-shifting four minutes, he weaves in and out of producer 9th Wonder's beats with keen precision. Long before Anthony Tiffith became "Top Dawg" the music mogul, he was in the streets. One day, he walks into a local Kentucky Fried Chicken, where he sees "a light-skinned nigga that talked a lot / With a curly top and a gap in his teeth." That was Kendrick's dad, Ducky; he was working the window at the KFC that day. Tiffith was planning to rob that KFC and stood in Ducky's line to demand cash. Ducky knew that Tiffith had robbed and shot up this same KFC before ("back in '84," Kendrick rapped; Ducky gave him free chicken and two extra biscuits to stay on his good side. As the story goes, Tiffith liked him so much that he didn't shoot him when he robbed the joint. Who knew that, years later, they'd be connected through Kendrick and laugh about the KFC incident in the studio. "My pops came to the studio after I'd been locked in with him for a minute," Kendrick told Beats 1 DJ Zane Lowe. "He heard I was dealing with Top Dawg, but my pops personally don't know him as 'Top Dawg,' so when he walked in that room and he seen that Top Dawg was this guy, he flipped. Still till this day they laugh . . . and they trip out and they tell the same story over and over to each other."

As a whole, *DAMN.* outlined the personal battle between Kendrick's id, ego, and superego, and how the real strife he'd been facing was within this entire time. It wasn't that the world wasn't praying for him or that people were out to get him, it's that he still had work to do on himself as a man. He was still fighting to stay righteous, struggling to balance the trappings of fame with an enlightened path away from the spotlight. Over its fourteen songs, Kendrick pivoted between darkness and light, wrestled with the end of the world as he saw it, and the urgency to make amends with himself and God before it was too late. In many ways, *DAMN.* was the culmination of *Section.80*, *good kid, m.A.A.d city*, and *To Pimp a Butterfly*, and was the most fully realized dissection of spirituality that he'd released. Before *DAMN.*, Kendrick was still *in the world*, still very much a rap star forging his path. With this album, he became something else, almost a mythical being or a supernova. No, he wasn't perfect and, yes, he was still very much a flawed human being. But he radiated a different energy. It was almost regal.

DAMN. marked the first time that Kendrick introduced an alter ego for his music. Kung Fu Kenny was based on actor Don Cheadle's character in the action comedy film *Rush Hour 2*; there, Cheadle's character studies martial arts and owns a Chinese restaurant. The two starred together in Kendrick's "DNA." video, and afterward, the rapper invited Cheadle to Coachella, where he was debuting a short kung fu movie starring himself. Later that night, Cheadle logged into Twitter and saw that somebody had written, "Don Cheadle, the original Kung Fu Kenny" on his timeline and posted a picture of him in *Rush Hour 2*. "I was like, 'Wait a minute.' So I texted [Kendrick]. I said, 'Is Kung Fu Kenny me?'" he told *Entertainment Weekly*. "He's like, 'That's what the surprise was. Damn.' I was like, 'Oh, I didn't get it at all.' He's like, 'Yeah that's what the surprise was, so . . . surprise.'" Not surprisingly, the Grammy nominations followed: Best Rap Album, Album of the Year, Best Music Video, Best Rap Song, Best Rap Performance and Record of the Year for "HUMBLE.," and Best Rap/Sung Performance for "LOYALTY."

This time, Kendrick was on the East Coast, in the world-famous Madison Square Garden for the 60th Annual Grammy Awards, which had now become a second home for him. This time he opened the show as a massive, digitally imposed American flag wafted swiftly on a screen behind him. Soldiers marched in formation as the guitar chords of "LUST." billowed throughout the arena. Given the time and tenor of America, the performance took not-so-subtle jabs at U.S. politics in an era still raw from Trump's election and the racism that showed itself. The set transitioned to "DNA." Three minutes in, the lights dropped out to the sound of a gunshot, and the camera cut to comedian Dave Chappelle, who could either have been the show's host or a sign that something had gone terribly wrong with Kendrick's set. As viewers, we didn't know what the hell was going on.

"Hi," Chappelle said in his usual nasal tone. "I'm Dave Chappelle, and I just wanted to remind the audience that the only thing more frightening than watching a black man be honest in America, is being an honest black man in America. Sorry for the interruption, please continue." On cue, the camera cut back to the stage. Fire erupted from it. Kendrick was in his Kung Fu Kenny garb as he spit an unheard-before rap, and a stage companion beat a drum in the middle of the platform. There was another gunshot and the lights dropped out *again*. This time Dave Chappelle looked puzzled. "Is this on cable?" he asked. "This CBS? 'Cause it looks like he's singing and dancing, but this brother is taking *enormous* chances. Rumble, young man, rumble!"

By this point, it was clear that Dave was part of the set, egging Kendrick on. For the last section of the rapper's performance, he dropped out the beat as his dancers, clad in red, fell one by one by assassins' bullets, sending yet another message to the powers that be that the United States was in peril by its own doing. Kendrick was simulating a mass shooting; with each verbal shot, his company all dropped down until he was the only one left standing. As the song ended, he paced in the middle of the stage, stone-faced and resolute. The crowd, which included Miley Cyrus, Bruno Mars, and Lorde, gave him a standing ovation.

These kinds of performances now had become commonplace for Kendrick Lamar, who went home with five Grammy awards that night—for Best Rap Performance, Best Rap/Sung Performance, Best Rap Song, Best Rap Album, and Best Music Video. Though winning awards had also become commonplace for him, he still looked like that grateful Compton kid on the stage. "Hip-hop, man," he said through a huge smile, peering gleefully at his Best Rap Album Grammy. "This the thing that got me on the stage, this the thing that got me to tour all around the world, support my family and all that. Most importantly, it showed me a true definition of what being an artist was. From the jump, I thought it was about the accolades and the cars and the clothes, but it's really about expressing yourself and putting that paint on a canvas for the world to evolve for the *next* listener and the next generation after that. This trophy for hip-hop." Kendrick was half right. Yeah, it was a win for hip-hop, but there in that moment, he was no longer just creating and winning for himself. A win for *DAMN.* felt like a win for the very culture that was still climbing out of a dark place socially. His wins became our wins, they were wins for everything right and good in hip-hop and creativity, and for people approaching their lives with the same kind of positive intention. As it turns out, those Grammy wins were just the beginning, and pretty soon he'd have a more prestigious award on his shelf: the Pulitzer Prize for Music.

Rappers don't win that award. There was still a large contingent of listeners and academics who didn't think hip-hop was a viable art form. Forget the global impact, nevermind the way it shifted fashion, speech, and music overall, some in the older guard heard only the vulgarity and wrote it off as low-scale black music that didn't deserve shine. Since the Pulitzer board first instituted an award for music in 1943, each winner has been a jazz or classical project. That all changed in 2018 when *DAMN.* broke the mold and was deemed the following by the Pulitzer board: "a virtuosic song collection unified by its vernacular authenticity and rhythmic dynamism that offers affecting vignettes capturing the complexity of modern African-American life." That Kendrick was awarded such a prize spoke to his crossover ability and the depth of his music. His life and art had evolved greatly—from in a garage with Dave Free in Compton, to the now-legendary TDE studio, to now one of the most prestigious awards in history. Kendrick was selected unanimously for the Pulitzer Prize for Music, and that was after a group of jurors openly wondered why hip-hop wasn't being considered for such a grand prize.

"At one point they said, 'Look, we're considering work that has hip-hop influences, why aren't we considering hip-hop itself?'" Pulitzer Prize administrator Dana Canedy tells me. "And one of the jurors said we should think about Kendrick Lamar. They, right there in real time, decided to download the album and listen to it, and thought that it was technically so brilliant, and that it was such an important piece of work, they decided to make that a nomination." Though *DAMN.* was a critical darling and a sonic marvel, some critics wondered why the Pulitzer board didn't give the award to *To Pimp a Butterfly*, which had strong jazz elements and had made a massive cultural splash, two years earlier. Nonetheless, Kendrick had at least three albums that could've won the Pulitzer, so this was a pronounced achievement for hip-hop either way. The rapper wrote a personal letter to Dana Canedy, thanking her for recognizing his art. "He said when he got word that he won that he thought it was a joke," she says. "He is such a kind, gracious, humble, spiritual young man. I kept saying to myself, 'I can't imagine this young man on a stage rapping, it seems like he ought to be in a choir.' He was so humble and sweet, but when he turns it on, on the stage, he takes on a completely different persona and it's completely fascinating."

Kendrick notched another first around this time: In February 2018, TDE released *Black Panther: The Album*, a soundtrack to the Ryan Coogler–directed blockbuster Marvel superhero film starring Chadwick Boseman, Lupita Nyong'o, and Michael B. Jordan. Kendrick and Top Dawg cocurated the soundtrack and handpicked each South African musician who landed on the LP. It was supposed to represent their version of Wakanda, the fictional African country where the film is set. "I've been a massive Kendrick fan ever since I first heard him, since his mixtapes, and I've been trying to track him down," Coogler told NPR. "Eventually I caught up with him a couple years ago—first with Anthony 'Top Dawg' Tiffith, who runs his label, and then later on sat down with him and Kendrick and just spoke about how much his music affected me. He talked about my movies that he had seen, and we said if the opportunity comes, we'd love to work with each other on something." Kendrick, Top Dawg, and Sounwave started compiling the soundtrack in August 2017 while touring *DAMN. Black Panther* became a massive cultural smash and the highest-grossing solo superhero film of all time, a powerful feat given its majority-black cast. It won three Oscars, and Kendrick was nominated for an Oscar for his collaborative song "All The Stars" with vocalist SZA (who by then had become a masterful songwriter and musician in her own right).

DAMN. and *Black Panther: The Album* punctuated a rise that we'd never seen before, the likes of which we'd never see again. Surely, Kendrick wasn't done—he still hadn't written his best verse or delivered the perfect album—but that's also what made him great, and that's why his art connected the way it did. He'd vanish again soon enough, popping up in occasional photos and one-off concert appearances, leaving us to ponder his next move. By early 2020, weeks after the House of Representatives voted to impeach President Donald Trump, and after Trump's approval to kill Iranian general Qasem Soleimani put us all in jeopardy, chatter began to surface about his next, well, *anything*. It had been too long since *DAMN.* lit up the industry and his art ignited the soul of Black America. But that's what Kendrick did best: he'd always left us wanting more; we'd have to wait once more as he recharged, recentered, and reconfigured his spirit. "All I can do is continue to be an actual human being," Kendrick once said. "And to show them that I go through the same emotions, and the same feelings that y'all go through. All I can do is express myself and hope you take something from it."

Notes

Chapter 1: How "You Got Robbed"

1   *He was shy*: Josh Eells, "The Trials of Kendrick Lamar," *Rolling Stone*, June 22, 2015, https://www.rollingstone.com/music/music-news/the-trials-of-kendrick-lamar-33057/.

3   *With guest appearances*: Rob Markman, "Kendrick Lamar's *good kid, m.A.A.d. city* Is Now Certified Gold," MTV News, December 2, 2012, http://www.mtv.com/news/2499851/kendrick-lamar-good-kid-maad-city-certified-gold/.

5   *Though the town wasn't*: Angel Jennings, "Compton Selected to Receive Federal Aid to Reduce Violent Crime," *Los Angeles Times,* September 28, 2015, https://www.latimes.com/local/lanow/la-me-ln-compton-selected-to-receive-federal-aid-20150928-story.html.

7   *But he did*: "2013 Grammy Winners," Grammy Awards, Recording Academy, accessed March 24, 2020, https://www.grammy.com/grammys/awards/56th-annual-grammy-awards-2013.

8   *"You got robbed"*: Tom Breihan, "Read Macklemore's Apology Text to Kendrick Lamar for Winning Best Rap Album Grammy," *Stereogum*, January 27, 2014, https://www.stereogum.com/1644301/read-macklemores-apology-text-to-kendrick-lamar-for-winning-best-rap-album-grammy/news/.

8   *"I think it was uncalled for"*: "Kendrick says Macklemore went too far + who 'i' is for & the state of HipHop," YouTube video, posted by "HOT

97," November 3, 2014, https://www.youtube.com/watch?v=tItZsM cLSRM.

9   *"It felt cheap"*: "Drake Calls Macklemore's Grammy Apology Text 'Wack as F——k,'" *Rolling Stone*, February 12, 2014, https://www .rollingstone.com/music/music-news/drake-calls-macklemores- grammy-apology-text-wack-as-f-k-81580/.

9   *"Then he came back on"*: "Kendrick says Macklemore."

9   *"Knowing how the Grammys"*: Rebecca Tucker, "Macklemore on Ken- drick Lamar's Grammy Snub: 'I Had an Unfair Advantage Due to Race,'" *National Post*, January 28, 2014, https://nationalpost.com /entertainment/music/macklemore-on-kendrick-lamars-grammy- snub-i-think-i-have-an-unfair-advantage-due-to-race.

10   *"The language that I used"*: Elias Leight, "Macklemore on Hip Hop & Cultural Appropriation: 'I Need to Know My Place, and That Comes from Me Listening,'" *Billboard*, December 30, 2014, https://www.bill board.com/articles/news/6422361/macklemore-race-hip-hop-cultural -appropriation-hot-97.

10   *25 had shot quickly*: Gil Kaufman, "Adele's '25' Hits Diamond Status in Less Than a Year," *Billboard*, September 27, 2016, https://www.bill board.com/articles/columns/pop/7525493/adele-25-hits-diamond -status-10-million-less-than-a-year.

10   *"They absolutely, positively"*: Joe Coscarelli, "'More Artists Are Going to Boycott': The Grammys Face Fallout after Fraught Grammys," *New York Times*, February 13, 2017, https://www.nytimes.com/2017/02/13 /arts/music/beyonce-adele-grammys-backlash.html.

11   *"Believe the people"*: "OK Ken and David . . .," Frank Ocean's Tumblr page, February 12, 2017, https://frankocean.tumblr.com /post/157125310721/ok-ken-and-david-as-much-as-i-hate-to-make-you.

Notes

11   *In 1989, rap duo*: Joe Coscarelli, "The Boycott Before: Rap and Resentment at the 1989 Grammys," *New York Times*, February 11, 2016, https://www.nytimes.com/2016/02/11/arts/music/the-boycott-before-rap-and-resentment-at-the-1989-grammys.html.

11   *According to the Recording Academy*: "Grammy Awards Voting Process," Grammy Awards, Recording Academy, accessed April 3, 2020, https://www.grammy.com/grammys/awards/voting-process.

12   *"human like we are"*: Melinda Newman, "Jay-Z Honored as Clive Davis' Pre-Grammy Gala Draws Performances from Alicia Keys, Migos & More," *Billboard*, January 28, 2018, https://www.billboard.com /articles/news/8096635/jay-z-honored-as-clive-davis-and-recording-academys-pre-grammy-gala-beyonce-alicia-keys.

12   *"Along with the official guidelines"*: Rob Kenner, "Hate Me Now: What It's Like to Be a Grammy Voter," Complex, January 20, 2014, https:// www.complex.com/music/2014/01/how-does-grammy-voting-work.

12   *"Richie was far"*: Kelsey McKinney, "The Grammy Voting Process Is Completely Ridiculous," Vox, February 15, 2016, https://www.vox .com/2015/2/4/7976729/grammy-voting-process.

13   *"We need a culture change"*: Melinda Newman, "Recording Academy Invites 900 New Voting Members Based on Task Force Recommendations to Increase Diversity," *Billboard*, October 4, 2018, https://www .billboard.com/articles/news/8478236/recording-academy-invites-900-new-voting-members-task-force.

15   *"I think it's mostly the music"*: Christopher R. Weingarten, "Macklemore Talks 'Gemini,' His Upcoming Career Reset without Ryan Lewis," *Rolling Stone*, September 14, 2017, https://www.rollingstone. com/music/music-features/macklemore-talks-gemini-his-upcom ing-career-reset-without-ryan-lewis-124464/.

Notes

16   *"Fight on!" Mandela once wrote*: Sahm Venter, ed., *The Prison Letters of Nelson Mandela* (New York: Liveright, 2018).

17   *"This is a place"*: Dave Chappelle, "Kendrick Lamar by Dave Chappelle," *Interview*, July 12, 2017, https://www.interviewmagazine.com/music/kendrick-lamar-cover.

17   *Chappelle had inked*: Christopher John Farley, "On the Beach with Dave Chappelle," *Time*, May 15, 2005, http://content.time.com/time/arts/article/0,8599,1061415,00.html.

19   *The shooting death of Chad Keaton*: "LA's Most Wanted: Murder Victim Chad Keaton," Fox 11 Los Angeles, September 11, 2016 (the incident occurred July 12, 2013), https://www.foxla.com/news/las-most-wanted-murder-victim-chad-keaton.

20   *"It was something that just accumulated"*: Dorian Lynskey, "Kendrick Lamar: 'I am Trayvon Martin. I'm All of These Kids,'" *The Guardian*, June 21, 2015, https://www.theguardian.com/music/2015/jun/21/kendrick-lamar-interview-to-pimp-a-butterfly-trayvon-martin.

20   *"I felt like I belonged in Africa"*: Andreas Hale, "'To Pimp a Butterfly': Kendrick Lamar shares history," Grammy.com, May 15, 2017, https://www.grammy.com/grammys/news/pimp-butterfly-kendrick-lamar-shares-history.

25   *traced back to kwaito*: Sabelo Mkhabela, "Hip-Hop & Kwaito's Long Love-Hate Relationship," *OkayAfrica*, April 20, 2017, https://www.okayafrica.com/south-african-hip-hop-kwaito-long-love-hate-relationship/.

27   *Forbes has been criticized*: Refiloe Seiboko and Simon Allison, "AKA, Burna Boy and the African Unity Concert That Wasn't," *Mail & Guardian*, November 22, 2019, https://mg.co.za/article/2019-11-22-00-aka-burna-boy-and-the-africanunity-concert-that-wasnt/.

Chapter 2: "California Love"

30   *Before World War II*: This and other statistics on Compton are taken
        from Ayala Feder-Haugabook, "Compton, California (1867–)," *Black
        Past*, August 20, 2017, https://www.blackpast.org/african-american
        -history/compton-california-1867/.

30   *in 1971, a gang called the Crips*: Celeste Fremon, "Behind the Crips
        Mythos," *Los Angeles Times*, November 20, 2007, https://www.latimes
        .com/archives/la-xpm-2007-nov-20-et-book20-story.html.

30   *In 1972, the Bloods*: "Pirus," United Gangs, accessed April 3, 2020,
        https://unitedgangs.com/bloods-2/pirus/.

34   *"It's the world before N.W.A"*: "N.W.A on Their Legacy: 'It's the World
        before N.W.A and the World after N.W.A,'" *Billboard*, online video,
        November 23, 2017, https://www.billboard.com/video/nwa-on-their-
        legacy-its-the-world-before-nwa-and-the-world-after-nwa-6663745.

36   *In August 1965*: Information on the 1965 Watts riots taken from "Watts
        Riots," Civil Rights Digital Library, March 3, 2020, http://crdl.usg.
        edu/events/watts_riots/?Welcome, and "Watts Riots," History.com,
        August 21, 2018, https://www.history.com/topics/1960s/watts-riots.

36   *In 1991, almost two weeks*: The story of Latasha Harlins and Soon Ja
        Du can be found in several places, most notably Angel Jennings, "25
        Years Later, Vigil Marks Latasha Harlins' Death, Which Fed An-
        ger during Rodney King Riots," *Los Angeles Times*, March 16, 2016,
        https://www.latimes.com/local/california/la-me-0317-latasha-harlins-
        vigil-20160317-story.html.

37   *"A guy was out there"*: "Kendrick Lamar: 'I Can't Change the World
        Until I Change Myself First,'" *Morning Edition*, National Public Ra-
        dio, December 29, 2015, https://www.npr.org/2015/12/29/461129966

Notes

/kendrick-lamar-i-cant-change-the-world-until-i-change-myself-first.

41 *"My father said"*: Jessica Hopper "Kendrick Lamar: Not Your Average Everyday Rap Savior," *Spin*, October 9, 2012, https://www.spin.com/2012/10/kendrick-lamar-not-your-average-everyday-rap-savior/2/.

43 *On YouTube, there's a video*: "Kendrick Lamar In High School Rapping," YouTube video, posted by "Entertainment Scoop," July 23, 2015, https://www.youtube.com/watch?v=un-W1qsKC1Q.

44 *Shawn "Jay-Z" Carter*: Elias Leight, "10 Things We Learned from Jay-Z's Interview with David Letterman," *Rolling Stone*, April 6, 2018, https://www.rollingstone.com/tv/tv-news/10-things-we-learned-from-jay-zs-interview-with-david-letterman-629627/.

46 *"He was telling me"*: "Life & Rhymes: Kendrick Lamar," YouTube video, posted by "Google Play," October 23, 2012, https://www.youtube.com/watch?v=Tse4hze7Au4.

48 *"Uncle Mike helped me"*: "New Juice: 8 Influential People to Watch," *Vibe*, August 26, 2013, https://www.vibe.com/photos/new-juice-8-influential-people-watch.

48 *"He was always like"*: Datwon Thomas, "Kendrick Lamar and Anthony 'Top Dawg' Tiffith on How They Built Hip-Hop's Greatest Indie Label," *Billboard*, September 14, 2017, https://www.billboard.com/articles/news/magazine-feature/7964649/kendrick-lamar-anthony-tiffith-interview-billboard-cover-story-2017.

48 *The streets still tugged*: Kris Ex, "More Levels, the Brains behind Top Dawg Entertainment," *XXL*, October 24, 2012, https://www.xxlmag.com/news/2012/10/tde-sidebar-kendrick-coverage/.

Notes

50   *The rapper grew up*: "Bounty Hunter Bloods," United Gangs, accessed April 3, 2020, https://unitedgangs.com/bounty-hunters/.

50   *Snoop Dogg was still around*: Touré, "Snoop Dogg: America's Most Lovable Pimp," *Rolling Stone*, December 14, 2006, https://www.rollingstone.com/music/music-news/snoop-dogg-americas-most-lovable-pimp-67188/.

53   *"I was chasing him"*: "Jay Rock On Meeting Kendrick, His Motorcycle Accident, & 'Redemption,'" YouTube video, posted by "HOT 97," June 20, 2018, https://www.youtube.com/watch?v=OSrn52pynsQ.

54   *In 2005 alone*: Megan Garvey, "Compton Killings Highest in Years," *Los Angeles Times*, January 2, 2006, https://www.latimes.com/archives/la-xpm-2006-jan-02-me-compton2-story.html.

56   *"He was like"*: Jeff Weiss, "Sounwave: How the Kendrick Lamar and 'Black Panther' Producer Quietly Made America's Soundtrack," *Rolling Stone*, May 29, 2018, https://www.rollingstone.com/music/music-features/sounwave-how-the-kendrick-lamar-and-black-panther-producer-quietly-made-americas-soundtrack-629632/.

57   *"They weren't coming"*: Insanul Ahmed, "Who Is Ab-Soul?," Complex, July 10, 2012, https://www.complex.com/music/2012/07/who-is-ab-soul/joining-tde.

59   *"I walked in"*: Insanul Ahmed, "Who Is SchoolboyQ?," Complex, February 3, 2012, https://www.complex.com/music/2012/02/who-is-schoolboy-q/.

59   *If you ain't one*: Jordan Darville, "Top Dawg Entertainment's Hilarious Studio Rules Should Be the New Constitution," *Fader*, June 7, 2017, https://www.thefader.com/2017/06/07/top-dawg-studio-rules-shut-up-and-look-ugly-for-the-homies.

Notes

Chapter 3: The Birth of Kendrick Lamar

71   *Jay Rock was the first*: Shawn Setaro, "Strange Days: How Kendrick Lamar Became a Star with Help from Tech N9ne," Complex, March 22, 2019, https://www.complex.com/music/2019/03/kendrick-lamar-became-star-help-from-tech-n9ne-strange-music.

68   *"K-Dot—this was"*: Nerisha Penrose, "Kendrick Lamar & Kobe Bryant Talk Career Growth & Defining 'Greatness' at Complexcon 2017," *Billboard*, November 7, 2017, https://www.billboard.com/articles/columns/hip-hop/8029975/kendrick-lamar-kobe-bryant-interview-complex-con-video.

72   *"They ain't on my level"*: Quoted in skoroma, "Ice Cube Explains Why He Refuses to Work with New Rappers," HipHopDX, March 26, 2010, https://hiphopdx.com/news/id.10902/title.ice-cube-explains-why-he-refuses-to-work-with-new-rappers.

74   *"He's the same person"*: "Flying Lotus on His New Album 'Flamagra,' Solange Changing His Studio Habits & the Beauty of Dr. Dre's Elusive 'Detox' Album," *Billboard*, May 20, 2019, https://www.billboard.com/articles/columns/hip-hop/8512211/flying-lotus-interview-flamagra-solange-mac-miller-dr-dre-kendrick-lamar.

76   *"We got a call like"*: Charles Holmes, "Kendrick Lamar Reveals That He Got His First Call from Dr. Dre in a Chili's," MTV, December 12, 2017, http://www.mtv.com/news/3052718/kendrick-lamar-dr-dre-chilis-phone-call/.

77   *"It came to a point"*: "Kendrick Lamar + The Maccabees," *Future Sounds with Annie Mac*, BBC Radio 1, https://www.bbc.co.uk/programmes/b05xqnf4.

78   *He's been called a coach*: Jayson Greene, "The Compton Sessions: How Dr. Dre Created His Comeback," *Pitchfork*, August 12, 2015, https://pitchfork.com/features/overtones/9703-the-compton-sessions-how-dr-dre-created-his-comeback/.

78   *"I was in Detroit"*: "Dr. Dre FULL INTERVIEW (Part 1) | Big-BoyTV," YouTube video, poseted by "BigBoiTV," March 26, 2015, https://www.youtube.com/watch?v=xoQy2BUdxhg.

79   *"It was a rock"*: "Kendrick Lamar – GGN News S. 2 Ep. 2," YouTube video, posted by "SnoopDoggTV," August 16, 2011, https://www.youtube.com/watch?v=wpW5dDJzBas.

83   *it peaked at number 72*: "Kendrick Lamar," uDiscoverMusic, accessed April 3, 2020, https://www.udiscovermusic.com/artists/kendrick-lamar/.

90   *"They taught me"*: Erika Ramirez, "Kendrick Lamar Talks 'Section.80,' New Album and Upcoming Videos," *Billboard*, September 2, 2011, https://www.billboard.com/articles/columns/the-juice/467608/kendrick-lamar-talks-section80-new-album-and-upcoming-videos.

91   *Then in August*: "Kendrick Lamar Gets Passed Down Torch HiiiPower Live Music Box Los Angeles, CA 8/19/11," YouTube video, posted by "hawaiiangroove," August 21, 2011, https://www.youtube.com/watch?v=KYjyVjI2-z0.

92   *"a weird kid"*: Tom Breihan, "Kendrick Lamar: *Section.80*," *Pitchfork*, July 21, 2011, https://pitchfork.com/reviews/albums/15653-section80/.

92   *Over at XXL*: Adam Fleischer "Kendrick Lamar, *Section.80*," *XXL*, July 5, 2011, https://www.xxlmag.com/rap-music/reviews/2011/07/kendrick-lamar-section-80/.

Notes

Chapter 4: A Star Is Born

95   *"This was before*: Lizzy Goodman, "Kendrick Lamar, Hip-Hop's Newest Old-School Star," *New York Times*, June 29, 2014, https://www .nytimes.com/2014/06/29/magazine/kendrick-lamar-hip-hops-new est-old-school-star.html.

97   *"I know it's fifteen thousand people out there"*: "Studio Life: Kendrick Lamar talks Club Paradise Tour & 'Cartoons & Cereal,'" YouTube vid-eo, posted by "3 Little Digs," February 27, 2012, https://www.youtube .com/watch?v=pLLznVTQI5Q

97   *"It was about"*: Steven Horowitz, "Kendrick Lamar Explains Why He Signed to Aftermath & Interscope," *HipHopDX*, August 13, 2012, https://hiphopdx.com/news/id.20777/title.kendrick-lamar-explains -why-he-signed-to-aftermath-interscope.

104   *"I wanted to do something that felt good"*: Insanul Ahmed, "The Making of Kendrick Lamar's 'good kid, m.A.A.d city,'" Complex, October 23, 2012, https://www.complex.com/music/2012/10/the-making-of-kend rick-lamars-good-kid-maad-city/before-the-album.

105   *It peaked at number 17*: "Chart History: Kendrick Lamar," *Billboard*, accessed April 6, 2020, https://www.billboard.com/music/kendrick -lamar/chart-history/HSI/song/753377.

105   *"We've done a lot, but we haven't sold any records"*: Benjamin Meadows-Ingram, "Kendrick Lamar: The Story Behind 'good kid, m.A.A.d city,'" *Billboard*, October 22, 2012, https://www.billboard.com/articles /news/474529/kendrick-lamar-the-story-behind-good-kid-maad-city.

117   *"setting spiritual yearnings"*: Jody Rosen, *"good kid, m.A.A.d city,"* Rolling Stone, October 22, 2012, https://www.rollingstone.com/music /music-album-reviews/good-kid-m-a-a-d-city-185646/.

117   *"autobiographical intensity"*: Jayson Greene, "Kendrick Lamar: *good kid, m.A.A.d city*," *Pitchfork*, October 23, 2012, https://pitchfork.com/reviews/albums/17253-good-kid-maad-city/.

117   *Upon its release*: For the Billboard chart history of *good kid, m.A.A.d city*, see "Chart History: Kendrick Lamar," *Billboard*, accessed April 6, 2020, https://www.billboard.com/music/kendrick-lamar/chart-history/TCL/song/762071, and Bryan Rolli, "With 'Good Kid, M.A.A.D City,' Kendrick Lamar Tops Eminem for Billboard 200's Longest-Charting Hip-Hop Studio Album," *Forbes*, September 18, 2019, https://www.forbes.com/sites/bryanrolli/2019/09/18/kendrick-lamars-good-kid-maad-city-surpasses-eminems-the-eminem-show-to-become-longest-charting-hip-hop-studio-album-on-billboard-200.

117   *Em was one of his biggest*: Victoria Hernandez, "Eminem Declares Kendrick Lamar's 'good kid, m.A.A.d city' A 'Masterpiece,'" *HipHop DX*, October 22, 2016, https://hiphopdx.com/news/id.40965/title.eminem-declares-kendrick-lamars-good-kid-m-a-a-d-city-a-masterpiece.

118   *"No disrespect to nobody"*: Quoted in Steven Horowitz, "Nas Begins Recording Twelfth Studio Album, Names Favorite Albums of 2012," *HipHopDX*, January 9, 2013, https://hiphopdx.com/news/id.22477/title.nas-begins-recording-twelfth-studio-album-names-favorite-albums-of-2012.

118   *Kendrick revealed that*: "Exclusive: Kendrick Lamar Reveals He Wanted Nas on 'Sing About Me,'" *Vibe*, March 22, 2013, https://www.vibe.com/2013/03/exclusive-kendrick-lamar-reveals-he-wanted-nas-sing-about-me.

119   *"I'd be lying to you"*: Kendrick Lamar, "Writer at War: Kendrick Lamar's XXL Cover Story," *XXL*, January 6, 2015, https://www.xxlmag.com/news/2015/01/writer-war-kendrick-lamar-own-words/.

120   "With Kendrick's album": Jaleesa Jones, "Georgia Students Study Kendrick Lamar for Class," *USA Today*, September 1, 2014, https://www.usatoday.com/story/college/2014/09/01/georgia-students-study-kendrick-lamar-for-class/37395771/.

Chapter 5: The Fight for Black Life

123   *boy named Trayvon Martin*: Dan Barry et al., "Race, Tragedy and Outrage Collide after a Shot in Florida," *New York Times*, April 4, 2012, https://www.nytimes.com/2012/04/02/us/trayvon-martin-shooting-prompts-a-review-of-ideals.html, and Daniel Trotta, "Trayvon Martin: Before the World Heard the Cries," Reuters, April 3, 2012, https://www.reuters.com/article/us-usa-florida-shooting-trayvon/trayvon-martin-before-the-world-heard-the-cries-idUSBRE8320UK20120403.

126   *"Trayvon was our hero"*: "Prosecute the Killer of Our Son, 17-Year-Old Trayvon Martin," Change.org, accessed April 6, 2020, https://www.change.org/p/prosecute-the-killer-of-our-son-17-year-old-trayvon-martin.

127   *"When Trayvon Martin was first shot"*: "President Obama's Remarks on Trayvon Martin (Full Transcript)," *Washington Post*, July 19, 2013, https://www.washingtonpost.com/politics/president-obamas-remarks-on-trayvon-martin-full-transcript/2013/07/19/5e33ebea-f09a-11e2-a1f9-ea873b7e0424_story.html.

128   *In 1999, New York City police*: Michael Cooper, "Officers in Bronx Fire 41 Shots, and an Unarmed Man Is Killed," *New York Times*, February 5, 1999, https://www.nytimes.com/1999/02/05/nyregion/officers-in-bronx-fire-41-shots-and-an-unarmed-man-is-killed.html.

128   *Then, in 2009, Bay Area Rapid Transit*: Jill Tucker, Kelly Zito, and

Heather Knight, "Deadly BART Brawl—Officer Shoots Rider, 22," *SFGate*, January 2, 2009, https://www.sfgate.com/bayarea/article /Deadly-BART-brawl-officer-shoots-rider-22-3178373.php.

130   *In mid-July of 2014, Eric Garner*: Joseph Goldstein and Nate Schweber, "Man's Death after Chokehold Raises Old Issue for Police," *New York Times*, July 18, 2014, https://www.nytimes.com/2014/07/19/nyregion/staten -island-man-dies-after-he-is-put-in-chokehold-during-arrest.html.

132   *eerily similar to a 1994 incident*: "A Death on Staten Island," *New York Times*, May 15, 1994, https://www.nytimes.com/1994/05/15/nyregion /one-neighborhood-two-lives-special-report-death-staten-island-2- paths-cross.html.

133   *On the morning of August 9*: "What Happened in Ferguson?," *New York Times*, August 13, 2014, https://www.nytimes.com/intera ctive/2014/08/13/us/ferguson-missouri-town-under-siege-after-po lice-shooting.html.

135   *Ferguson police arrested Henry Davis*: Joseph Shapiro, "In Ferguson, Mo., Before Michael Brown There Was Henry Davis," *All Things Considered*, National Public Radio, September 12, 2014, https://www.npr .org/2014/09/12/348010247/in-ferguson-mo-before-michael-brown- there-was-henry-davis.

136   *"The delay helped fuel"*: Julie Bosman and Joseph Goldstein, "Timeline for a Body: 4 Hours in the Middle of a Ferguson Street," *New York Times*, August 23, 2014, https://www.nytimes.com/2014/08/24/us /michael-brown-a-bodys-timeline-4-hours-on-a-ferguson-street.html.

138   *Tamir Rice was gunned down*: Ryllie Danylko, "Cleveland Police Officer Fatally Shoots 12-Year-Old Tamir Rice: The Big Story," Cleveland .com, November 24, 2014, https://www.cleveland.com/metro/2014/11 /cleveland_police_officer_fatal.html, and "Officer Who Killed Tamir

Rice Found Unfit in Previous Police Job," NBC News, November 27, 2014, https://www.nbcnews.com/news/us-news/officer-who-killed-tamir-rice-found-unfit-previous-police-job-n261111.

141 *"Tonight, I got kicked"*: "Killer Mike's pre-show Ferguson Grand Jury speech," YouTube video, posted by "Stephen Bolen," November 24, 2014, https://www.youtube.com/watch?v=MQs7CWKHM9w.

143 *"I would hate to stay stagnant"*: Maud Deitch, "Exclusive: Kendrick Lamar Sings Taylor Swift's 'Shake It Off,'" *Fader*, November 4, 2014, https://www.thefader.com/2014/11/04/kendrick-lamar-interview-halloween-taylor-swift.

144 *retaliation for filming Garner's murder*: Chloé Cooper Jones, "Fearing for His Life," *The Verge*, March 13, 2019, https://www.theverge.com/2019/3/13/18253848/eric-garner-footage-ramsey-orta-police-brutality-killing-safety.

147 *"There's a deeper level"*: Marcus J. Moore, "Kamasi Washington Says the Moment Is Right for His Three-Hour 'Epic,'" *Washington Post*, August 20, 2015, https://www.washingtonpost.com/express/wp/2015/08/20/kamasi-washington-says-the-moments-right-for-his-three-hour-epic/.

Chapter 6: King Kendrick

149 *"You would have thought"*: Patrick Bowman, "Sounwave Details the Making of Kendrick Lamar's Landmark 'To Pimp a Butterfly,'" *Spin*, April 24, 2015, https://www.spin.com/2015/04/sounwave-interview-kendrick-lamar-to-pimp-a-butterfly/.

151 *"The rapper wanted "to help put a Band-Aid on the things that's been going on in our communities""*: Peter Walsh, "Kendrick

Lamar's Producers Talk the Making of 'To Pimp a Butterfly,'" *XXL*, April 30, 2015, https://www.xxlmag.com/news/2015/04 /kendrick-lamars-producers-talk-making-pimp-butterfly/.

152 *"The word 'pimp'"*: "Kendrick Lamar Breaks Down Tracks From 'To Pimp a Butterfly' (Pt. 1) | MTV News," YouTube video, posted by "MTV," March 31, 2015, https://www.youtube.com/watch?v=AUEI_ep9iDs.

156 *"I wish somebody would look"*: Joe Lynch, "Kendrick Lamar Talks Ferguson: 'What Happened Should've Never Happened,'" *Billboard*, January 8, 2015, https://www.billboard.com/articles/news/6436333 /kendrick-lamar-on-ferguson-police-michael-brown.

166 *"9th hit me like"*: Adam Fleischer, "How Do You End Up Featured on Kendrick Lamar's Album? Rapsody Tells Her Story," MTV News, March 16, 2015, http://www.mtv.com/news/2106673/rapsody-kend rick-lamar-complexion-a-zulu-love-to-pimp-a-butterfly/.

167 *"There are the people"*: Jeff Weiss "Kamasi Washington on the Music That Made Him a Jazz Colossus," *Pitchfork*, October 3, 2017, https:// pitchfork.com/features/5-10-15-20/kamasi-washington-on-the-mu sic-that-made-him-a-jazz-colossus/.

169 *"No matter what type"*: "Kendrick Lamar on How He Wrote 'King Kunta,'" YouTube video, posted by "NME," June 5, 2015, https:// www.youtube.com/watch?v=vm_Xb9c6__Q.

Chapter 7: "We Gon' Be Alright"

181 *"I kind of had"*: Kory Grow, "See Kendrick Lamar Perform Death-De- fying Stunts in 'Alright' Video," *Rolling Stone*, June 30, 2015, https:// www.rollingstone.com/music/music-news/see-kendrick-lamar-per form-death-defying-stunts-in-alright-video-74253/.

Notes

182   *"I knew it was"*: "Kendrick Lamar Talks to Rick Rubin About 'Alright,' Eminem, and Kendrick's Next Album," *GQ*, October 20, 2016, https://www.gq.com/story/kendrick-lamar-rick-rubin-gq-style-cover-interview.

186   *"Once you get an image"*: Andres Tardio, "Exclusive: We Got All the Answers about Kendrick Lamar's 'Alright' Video," MTV News, June 30, 2015, http://www.mtv.com/news/2201127/kendrick-lamar-alright-video-colin-tilley/.

187   *"We needed an anthem"*: Kory Grow, "Riot on the Set: How Public Enemy Crafted the Anthem 'Fight the Power,'" *Rolling Stone*, June 30, 2014, https://www.rollingstone.com/movies/movie-news/riot-on-the-set-how-public-enemy-crafted-the-anthem-fight-the-power-244152/.

188   *Freddie Gray was arrested*: Natalie Sherman, Chris Kaltenbach, and Colin Campbell, "Freddie Gray Dies a Week after Being Injured during Arrest," *Baltimore Sun*, April 19, 2015, https://www.baltimoresun.com/news/crime/bs-md-freddie-gray-20150419-story.html.

190   *the body of Sandra Bland*: Katie Rogers, "The Death of Sandra Bland: Questions and Answers," *New York Times*, July 23, 2015, https://www.nytimes.com/interactive/2015/07/23/us/23blandlisty.html.

190   *"Our mere existence"*: Sharon Cooper, "Sandra Bland's Sister: She Died Because Officer Saw Her as 'Threatening Black Woman,' Not Human," *USA Today*, May 13, 2019, https://www.usatoday.com/story/opinion/policing/spotlight/2019/05/13/sandra-bland-sister-police-brutality-policing-the-usa/1169559001/.

191   *In late July 2015*: Dusty Henry and Alex Young, "Cleveland State University Conference Attendees Chant Kendrick Lamar's 'Alright' in Protest against Police," *Consequence of Sound*, July 29, 2015, https://

consequenceofsound.net/2015/07/cleveland-state-university-protest
ers-chant-kendrick-lamars-alright-in-protest-against-police/.

193   *"You might not have heard"*: Andrew Barker, "How Kendrick Lamar Became the Defining Hip-Hop Artist of His Generation," *Variety*, November 2017, https://variety.com/2017/music/features/kendrick-lamar-career-damn-to-pimp-a-butterfly-1202619725/.

Chapter 8: The Night Kendrick Ascended

200   *To solve the 2009 crisis*: Farhana Hossain et al., "The Stimulus Plan: How to Spend $787 Billion," *New York Times*, accessed April 3, 2020, https://www.nytimes.com/interactive/projects/44th_president/stimulus.

207   *"How can you take"*: Colin Stutz, "Kendrick Lamar Responds to Geraldo Rivera: 'Hip-Hop Is Not the Problem, Our Reality Is,'" *Billboard*, July 2, 2015, https://www.billboard.com/articles/columns/the-juice/6620035/kendrick-lamar-responds-geraldo-rivera-alright-bet-awards.

210   *"I don't believe in none"*: Steven Horowitz, "Kendrick Lamar Addresses Backlash over Refusal to Vote," *HipHopDX*, August 28, 2012, https://hiphopdx.com/news/id.20924/title.kendrick-lamar-addresses-backlash-over-refusal-to-vote.

211   *That December, President Barack Obama*: Tierney McAfee and Sandra Sobieraj Westfall, "Kendrick Lamar Vs. Bruno Mars: POTUS and FLOTUS' Favorite Songs, Movies and Moments of 2015," *People*, December 9, 2015, https://people.com/books/barack-obama-and-michelle-obamas-favorite-songs-movies-and-moments-of-2015/.

212   *"I think Drake"*: Keith Wagstaff, "Obama Picks Kendrick over Drake

in YouTube Interview," NBC News, January 13, 2016, https://www
.nbcnews.com/tech/internet/obama-picks-kendrick-over-drake-you
tube-interview-n497571.

213   *"The way people look"*: Adelle Platon, "Kendrick Lamar Opens Up
about Meeting President Obama: 'No Matter How High-Ranking
You Get, You're Human,'" *Billboard*, February 4, 2016, https://www
.billboard.com/articles/news/magazine-feature/6866105/kendrick-la
mar-meeting-president-obama.

216   *He had been nominated*: "Kendrick Lamar," Grammy Awards, Recording Academy, accessed April 3, 2020, https://www.grammy.com
/grammys/artists/kendrick-lamar.

216   *only two rap albums*: Mesfin Fekadu and the Associated Press, "Diddy
Calls Out Grammys for Not Respecting Black Music 'To the Point
That It Should Be,'" *Fortune*, https://fortune.com/2020/01/26/diddy
-grammys-hip-hop-black-music-clive-davis-gala/.

217   *"Kenneth Duckworth and Paula Duckworth"*: "Kendrick Lamar Wins
Best Rap Album: 'To Pimp a Butterfly,'" Grammy Awards, Recording Academy, February 15, 2016, https://www.grammy.com/gram
mys/videos/kendrick-lamar-wins-best-rap-album-pimp-butterfly.

218   *He had a performance*: Micah Singleton, "Grammys 2016: Watch
Kendrick Lamar's Stunning Performance," *The Verge*, February 15,
2016, https://www.theverge.com/2016/2/15/11004624/grammys-2016-
watch-kendrick-lamar-perform-alright-the-blacker-the-berry.

224   *"We are going to make"*: "Here's Donald Trump's Presidential Announcement Speech," *Time*, June 16, 2015, https://time.com/3923128
/donald-trump-announcement-speech/.

226   *In 1973, Trump*: Jonathan Mahler and Steve Eder, "'No Vacancies'
for Blacks: How Donald Trump Got His Start, and Was First Ac-

cused of Bias," *New York Times*, August 27, 2016, https://www.nytimes
.com/2016/08/28/us/politics/donald-trump-housing-race.html.

226   *In 1989, he took out*: Jan Ransom, "Trump Will Not Apologize for Calling for Death Penalty over Central Park Five," *New York Times*, June 18, 2019, https://www.nytimes.com/2019/06/18/nyregion/central-park-five-trump.html.

Chapter 9: Mourning in America

230   *Trump was endorsed by the Ku Klux Klan*: Scott Detrow, "KKK Paper Endorses Trump; Campaign Calls Outlet 'Repulsive,'" NPR, November 2, 2016, https://www.npr.org/2016/11/02/500352353/kkk-paper-endorses-trump-campaign-calls-outlet-repulsive.

232   *The Southern Poverty Law Center*: Mark Potok, "The Trump Effect," *Intelligence Report*, February 15, 2017, https://www.splcenter.org/fighting-hate/intelligence-report/2017/trump-effect.

232   *In Silver Spring, Maryland*: Katie Reilly, "Racist Incidents Are Up Since Donald Trump's Election. These Are Just a Few of Them," *Time*, November 13, 2016, https://time.com/4569129/racist-anti-semitic-incidents-donald-trump/.

233   *"We all are baffled"*: Touré, "An In-Depth Conversation with Kendrick Lamar," *i-D*, October 16, 2017, https://i-d.vice.com/en_us/article/j5gwk7/an-in-depth-conversation-with-kendrick-lamar.

233   *In* The World as It Is: Ben Rhodes, *The World As It Is* (New York: Penguin Random House, 2019).

236   *"We needed to do"*: Andreas Hale, "Kendrick Lamar, Pluss, Terrace Martin & More On Making 'DAMN.' | Album of the Year," Grammy Awards, Recording Academy, January 25, 2018, https://www.gram

Notes

my.com/grammys/news/kendrick-lamar-pluss-terrace-martin-more-making-damn-album-year.

238   *"We're in a time"*: Wyatt Mason, "Three Iconic Musicians on Artistic Creation," *T: The New York Times Style Magazine*, March 1, 2017, https://www.nytimes.com/2017/03/01/t-magazine/beck-tom-waits-kendrick-lamar.html.

238   *Kendrick and his creative team*: David Browne, "Kendrick Lamar's 'Damn.': Inside the Making of the Number One LP," *Rolling Stone*, May 1, 2017, https://www.rollingstone.com/music/music-features/kendrick-lamars-damn-inside-the-making-of-the-number-one-lp-128446/.

239   *"We wanted to make it"*: "Kendrick Lamar on Damn., His Sister's Car & Being The G.O.A.T.," YouTube video, posted by "BigBoyTV," June 29, 2017, https://www.youtube.com/watch?v=fYFfkBSo2mg.

241   *"I wanted it to feel"*: "Kendrick Lamar: 'DAMN' Interview | Apple Music," YouTube video, posted by "Beats 1," April 27, 2017, https://www.youtube.com/watch?v=zwNhoyDjAPg.

242   *"If you had a girlfriend"*: Dan Hyman, "Why Kendrick Lamar and Sounwave Camped Out in Sleeping Bags to Make *DAMN.*," *GQ*, April 22, 2017, https://www.gq.com/story/sounwave-kendrick-lamar-damn,.

242   *"You wanna go get"*: Ben Dandridge-Lemco, "Sounwave Explains Every Song He Helped Produce on Kendrick Lamar's *DAMN.*," *Fader*, April 24, 2017, https://www.thefader.com/2017/04/24/sounwave-interview-kendrick-lamar-damn-track-explainer.

251   *"I've been a massive"*: Daoud Tyler-Ameen and Sidney Madden, "Here's How 'Black Panther: The Album' Came Together," The Record, NPR, February 6, 2018, https://www.npr.org/sections/therecord/2018/02/06/582841574/heres-how-black-panther-the-album-came-together.

Acknowledgments

I've been asked this question a lot over the past two years: Why Kendrick Lamar? The answer is always simple: Why not? Though he isn't done creating (as of this writing), there's no denying the grand impact he's had on music and black culture over the past decade. His story is worth celebrating, so why not give him flowers now? Why can't we acknowledge their impact while they're still working? To wait until they're gone seems cold and unnecessary. We lost Kobe Bryant too soon. Pop Smoke passed when he was just becoming a star. More than anything, I hope you see the light in this work, that while it delves into the good and bad and raises some questions, it's meant to be a resounding document for today's readers and future generations.

And while he's all set on praise from strangers, I want to formally thank Kendrick Lamar for creating honest, thought-provoking art. Thank you for taking risks, for showing your generation that it's okay to go against the grain. You could've easily followed good kid, *m.A.A.d. city with good kid, m.A.A.d. city II*, or *To Pimp a Butterfly* with something equally steeped in jazz and funk, but you've always changed course, making it cool for music to say something forthright and uncomfortable. I respect the quiet you exude, the stealthy demeanor through which you and TDE operate. I appreciate you all from afar.

There's been a lot of goodwill surrounding this book, and for that, I am truly appreciative. Thanks to my literary agent, William

Acknowledgments

LoTurco, for listening to my ambitious ideas, and to Jason Reynolds and Todd Hunter for guiding me very early in the process. Big thanks to Phonte Coleman, Erik Otis, Kim Robinson, and Ashley Dior-Thomas for your immense help behind the scenes—whether you shared resources or offered words of encouragement, it really meant a lot and I'll never forget it. Much love to all the friends who made sure I remained human; you all know I'm a perfectionist, and your "just checking in" messages helped me through some tough creative days. Sincerest love to dear friends like Briana Younger, Andre Taylor, Carl "Kokayi" Walker, and Yudu Gray, Jr., who were there when this was just an idea and encouraged me every step of the way.

Of course, this book wouldn't exist without the goodwill of the people in it. Sincerest thanks to everyone who saw the positivity and made time to speak with me. There are far too many of you to name (sidenote: I'd always cringed when I read that in album liners, but now I understand), but I truly appreciate you all. I realize it's my name on the cover, but this book is a combination of *Songs In The Key of Life* (Stevie Wonder's landmark 1976 album) and *Everything's Fine* (Jean Grae and Quelle Chris' stellar 2018 album) with great voices and perspective filtered throughout the work, even if I orchestrated it. This much isn't lost on me, either: It was tough to explain the focus of this book in an email, especially when there are so many things commanding our attention. That it was the first, or one of the first, books on Kendrick likely caused some reticence. He's such a private guy and some worried that I was digging for dirt. As you can see, *The Butterfly Effect* wasn't a celebrity biography in the traditional sense; it's a testament to the

Acknowledgments

creative community, and how staying true to your vision can ultimately change the world.

It's taken a while to get to this moment, and I wouldn't be here without family, colleagues, mentors, and editors who saw something in my work and decided to give me a chance. To my mother, Delores, my first best friend, and closest supporter. You've always been the ultimate parent, and from an early age, you let me determine my path without steering me to what you wanted me to do. You let me discover and guided me with a loving hand when I faltered. To my aunt Pam, my creative twin: I discovered the world through your record collection, and you were the first to teach me that great music is great music, no matter where it originated. I've always loved your real-talk perspective; it helped me through some tough moments. I learned a lot about music, culture, and life from my cousins Ike, Tiffany, and Eric. As a kid, I'd watch MTV for hours; then we'd play cassettes that I was too young to hear: N.W.A, Boogie Down Productions, Too $hort, Public Enemy, and so on. My cousins gave me a serious education in music; they're the reason why I dig in the crates now. Love to my aunts Claudia and Claudette, my uncle Joe, and all my paternal aunts, cousins, uncles, nieces, and nephews. Big blessings to my siblings: Judy, Fella, Katina, and Angie. I love and think about you all even if we don't talk every day. Love to my in-laws: Mr. and Mrs. Koroma, my sisters-in-law, Satia and Kamilah, and my brother-in-law, Mohamed. Thanks to Suitland High School as a whole, and to the Class of 1999, especially. We had some stars graduate from that class! Blessings to Bowie State University as well; the experience was immense.

Eternal love and gratitude to the *Prince George's Sentinel* and

Acknowledgments

The Gazette newspapers. Thanks to Vanessa Harrington and Ulric Hetsberger for showing me what leadership looks like, and to my colleagues for being the best reporting team in the region. Without a doubt, the biggest mentor in my career was Michelle LeComte, a tough-minded yet loving editor who'd scream at you on deadline, then sing your praises if you submitted a great article. She taught me how to be strong and compassionate, and to tell the truth with care. Thanks to the best reporting squad in the world: Janel Davis, Sean Sedam, Doug Tallman, Clyde Ford, Alan Brody, and Margie Hyslop. It was an honor to work beside you all. You're all rock stars and I still can't believe I got to share space. Thank you, Ginny Suss, for letting me write for Okayplayer (another sidenote: go back and check the "Boards" archives: there are plenty of people who came through that site who are now steering culture). Thank you, Godallahtruth Hall, for ushering me into the DC music scene, and to Jon Fischer at the *Washington City Paper* for bringing me into the fold. Peace to all the publications that ever gave a shot: SoundSavvy, Beats Per Minute, Prefix, Potholes In My Blog, BBC Music, *Rolling Stone*, MTV Hive, *Billboard*, *Spin*, NPR, *The Atlantic*, *The Washington Post*, Pitchfork, *Entertainment Weekly*, *The Nation*, *The Fader*, and WTOP. I'd be remiss if I didn't thank J. Edward Keyes for calling me up to Brooklyn from Washington, DC in the first place. You have the most nuanced ear for music I've ever encountered, and whether you want to admit or not, you're a great friend, editor, and person who deserves all of the things. Bandcamp Daily is the squad.

To Brooke Hawkins: You've been my dear friend since high school, back when we compiled the Class of '99 yearbook and shared laughs in the hallway. You've been there through every major life event, always with a smile and words of encouragement. You've always seen things in me that I don't see in myself, and as I worked on this project, you were always there to cheer me on. I've watched you become a great writer, editor, wife, and a mother, and with each milestone, you've grown exponentially. Keep shining. Keep winning. Keep fighting the good fight.

To Brian Wallace: I still think about the first time I met you, at Suitland High School in gym class. I think about that basketball game and how you got the best of me (I paid you back, though), and how we've become brothers. I think of your family and how loving you all are. I've known you, Trecia, Felicia, Araina, and Mr. and Mrs. Wallace for twenty-plus years, and now you have your own beautiful family. You heap heavy superlatives on me, but I applaud you for being the real star. You're a shining example of quiet resilience and strength, and I pray that I'm able to possess one-tenth of your character someday. I'm working on it.

To my wife, Mabinty: You are the love of my life, my heart, and my soul. It's been an honor to witness the grace through which you navigate life. You are the living embodiment of spirituality and persistence, and your spontaneity keeps me human. I adore your ambition, the way you command every room you enter. I'm your biggest fan and cheerleader, and I'm thankful to God for having met you all those years ago. Your patience is immeasurable; you gave me space to write this book while holding me close. You were there for me every day and I'm very grateful. You're a divine light and the world is better with you in it.

And now for the customary disclaimer (though I mean what

Acknowledgments

I'm about to say): sincerest apologies to anyone I may have forgotten. The last two years have been something else; I hope you understand. If you've been an active part of my life during that time, please know that I appreciate you, and God willing, I will tell you so personally. Thanks to everyone who's shown interest in this book. May it resonate in your spirit.

About the Author

Marcus J. Moore is a music journalist, editor, curator, and pop culture commentator whose writing can be found in *The Nation*, Pitchfork, *Entertainment Weekly*, Bandcamp Daily, NPR, *The Atlantic*, BBC Music, and MTV, among others. He's created nationally syndicated playlists for Google, discussed new music live on FM radio, contributed to national shows and podcasts, and hosted live interviews and guest-hosted live shows on Red Bull Radio. In 2009, Moore launched his own site—DMV Spectrum—which covered music and entertainment in Washington, DC; Maryland; and Northern Virginia. He is originally from the Washington, DC, area, and now lives in Brooklyn, New York. *The Butterfly Effect* is his first book.

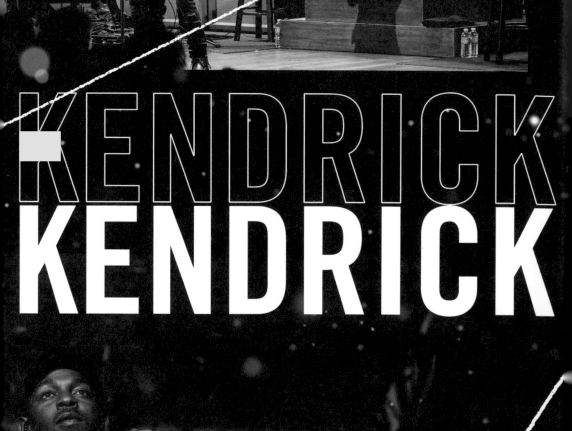